WHAT'S IT ALL ABOUT
ALFIE?

THE AUTOBIOGRAPHY OF
STOKE CITY'S MR DEPENDABLE

ERIC SKEELS
WITH SIMON LOWE

PUBLISHED BY HERO BOOKS
1 WOODVILLE GREEN
LUCAN
CO. DUBLIN
IRELAND

Hero Books is an imprint of Umbrella Publishing
First Published 2022
Copyright © Eric Skeels and Simon Lowe 2022
All rights reserved

ISBN 9781910827529

Cover design and formatting: jessica@viitaladesign.com
Photographs: Simon Lowe, *The Sentinel* and the Skeels family collection

Dedication

To my father, Thomas

And all of my teammates at Stoke City
over two amazing decades

Contents

Acknowledgements

WHEN I WAS first approached to write my autobiography, I wasn't quite sure why anyone would want to read about my story. I'm a fairly straightforward kind of feller, and, although I lived and played through the 1960s and 70s, when there were lots of shenanigans going on with drinking and the like, that wasn't the life I led. I stayed sensible and professional for as long as my body could keep me earning a living as a footballer.

I'm grateful that that proved to be until I was 37 years old, and I still turned out a bit for local non-league teams after that.

So, you won't read about too many drinking exploits or glamorous nights out with Miss World in this memoir. My life wasn't like that of George Best. I spent my time trying to tackle him, to stop him… not be like him.

I'd like to thank everyone who has helped me with this book. Firstly, and most importantly, my wife Pauline, who has encouraged me, particularly knowing that I'm quite shy and not used to talking about myself that much. Especially Simon Lowe, who has guided me through writing this book, with lots of chats on Saturday mornings before Stoke matches. He then helped shape my thoughts and ramblings into something I'm really proud of. Then there is the publisher, Liam Hayes of Hero Books, who believed in me and my story enough to produce this book which you are now reading. We have also had a lot of help from the local paper in Stoke-on-Trent, the *Sentinel*, and especially their Stoke City reporter Pete Smith and editor Rob Cotterill. Finally, Angela Smith, who believed in me and my story, and has helped ensure that Stoke fans will get a chance to step back into times past, when football was a very different game to the one we watch today.

Thanks to everyone!

They have all helped me bring my story together into something that I hope gives you a good idea of what life was like for a lad from Eccles in Manchester, who had very little in the way of life prospects when I was born right at the start of the Second World War. I had no idea at any point as a teenager, when I was playing for the Adelphi Boys Club and the Albion Football Club in the Eccles and District league, what was to unfold. There were no academies back then. The route to becoming a professional footballer was paved with twists of fortune and my story is fairly typical in that regard. I took my chance when it came along, and for that opportunity I am truly thankful.

Now, looking back on my 17-year career at Stoke City Football Club, for whom I am still, proudly, the holder of the record for most competitive appearances, I've enjoyed remembering all the events that happened (well, those I can recall) and trying to make sense of my life. While I've been living it, it has very much felt as if I've just gone with the flow, seizing on my chances when they came, fighting for every opportunity. It's only now, with hindsight, that I can see some themes that have helped me be successful and how they all came from my background.

It's been a pleasure being an honorary Stokie, and I hope you enjoy the read.

Eric Skeels
Newcastle-under-Lyme, August 2022

Prologue

MY MOTHER DISAPPEARED from my life when I was so young, at an age which means I can barely remember her at all. As I understand it, mum was a woman who liked good times and in the middle of the war effort all sorts of things went on, I'm sure. Apparently, she was a bit of a rum bugger by all accounts, although I know no details and I don't suppose the age difference helped. She was a lot younger than my father.

All I knew was that she had gone off with some other feller and moved down south somewhere. Whatever it was that took her away from us, I was too young to know or be told, and now all my siblings have passed away I will never know the truth... if they ever did. It's gone to their graves with them, I suppose.

Dad never had any photographs of her around the place, understandably, although I did see their wedding photos, so at one stage I did know what she had looked like in the summer of 1936 when they wed, but her image was never imprinted on my mind.

Strangely, though, I think I may have seen her many years later. It was when I was playing for Stoke and we got on a train to go down south to Southampton. When we arrived and disembarked, we were waiting outside the station for taxis to take us to The Dell, the Saints' ground, when I suddenly became aware of this woman on the other side of the road, staring at me.

I thought nothing of it at first, but the longer we waited, the more she kept looking at me. I didn't know what to do. I was a bit embarrassed, because she kept looking at me from a distance as I stood against the wall waiting for the taxi.

I began wondering. *Could it be her? My mum?* I don't really know why that thought came into my head, but it just sort of popped in for some reason.

Thinking about it afterwards, I reasoned that maybe she had read in the local paper about Stoke City coming to play Southampton and had seen my name in the travelling squad. It's obviously an unusual name, Skeels, and she must have known I was a footballer, I suppose, although I don't know if she had any contact at all with my father after she left, as I have no idea what happened to her.

But I still have this feeling that was her that day outside Southampton railway station. Why else would some random woman who looked about the right age to be my mother just keep looking at me?

She never approached me or said anything, and when we got into the taxis and sped off to The Dell to play, my thoughts were only on the game from that moment onwards. It was a strange incident, but it's one which I do think about every now and then.

Could that woman have been my mum?

I like to think so.

CHAPTER 1

Eccles, Few Cakes

I COME FROM Eccles, a town to the west of Manchester, in the city of Salford, although these days it's just part of the huge conurbation of Greater Manchester. Back when I was growing up it felt like its own town, in which you knew people, could say hello and leave your front door open when you went out and not be worried about being robbed, or any of that kind of thing.

I've never lost the feeling of living in a community like that and I think that's why I settled so well in Stoke-on Trent when I came to move to the Potteries because of that sense of togetherness, people having no airs and graces. North Staffordshire folk even coped with my soft Mancunian accent, although I never really picked up the Potteries twang to become a fully-fledged Stokie.

I was born on October 27, 1939, just a few weeks after the Second World War had begun, the youngest of five children, all boys. But we had a very unusual family situation as, although I was brought up by a single parent, oddly for those times it was my father who was the lone provider.

Dad's name was Thomas Skeels, a name he gave me as my middle name… Eric Thomas Skeels. Thinking about it now, he didn't really have much luck in life. His first wife Mary died and his second wife, my mother Marjorie, then left him when I was very young. I'm not exactly sure what age, but it would have been when I was about two or three, during the war.

I'm not sure what Mary, dad's first wife, died of but she was the mother of my three oldest brothers… half-brothers really, and I didn't know them that well.

When dad remarried to Marjorie, who was a little over 20 years younger than him and was only 18 when they wed, he and mum had Albert, my full brother, who was about 18 months older, and then me.

Bill was my oldest half-brother, but I didn't see a lot of him because he was so much older than me, by over 20 years or so, and he was married and lived quite a long way away. Then my other two half-brothers were Jim and Sidney. We didn't see a whole lot of them either, to be honest, so really it ended up for the whole of my childhood being dad, Albert and me, despite it seeming like we had a much bigger family.

AS FAR AS I'm aware, my dad never had another lady friend. He never seemed to have any interest in women after losing his two wives in such completely different ways. I certainly never saw him with anyone else for the rest of his days. Consequently, we never had any feminine influence at all in our house.

My wife Pauline tells me she can tell this because of the way I am now. When we met, I wasn't neat and tidy at all, but my wife has trained me up. She also says that because I don't go and talk to people much, she is sure that is another sign. I prefer to let people come and talk to me; that makes me feel more comfortable. Then if I get on with them and they are interesting, I'm happy to relax and talk. I'm not one to hold court and tell tall stories or anything like that.

We had plenty at Stoke who had the gift of the gab during my playing days. There were some right characters, like Don Ratcliffe, Jimmy McIlroy, Terry Conroy and Alan Hudson. More about them later.

Pauline says this is all because my dad was a typical northern man who barely spoke a word to me and Albert, aside from the odd gruff direction to wash my hands before eating. I think it was just his way and that he was simply dedicated to making sure we had as good a start in life as we could possibly get.

My father was one of those proper old time, salt of the earth men who worked a lot and spoke little. He was a very dedicated and loyal person. A farmer originally, he worked on a farm out near Barton airport, over towards Irlam, which was where he met and married his first wife Mary. Then, after she died, he came out of the farming business and went and worked for a brickies, which was a tough way to earn a living, although after the war there was plenty of building to reconstruct

Manchester to be done, so he didn't struggle for work at all.

While Dad went working all day, Albert and I fended for ourselves, which meant we were off the leash quite a lot, bounding around the streets of our neighbourhood. We just got on with life after my mother left and my old man would get us ready for school, then head off to work. We didn't have school meals at that time, there wasn't really such a thing at our primary school. Instead, dad would give us a few bob and we'd go to a local cafe and get a pie for lunch and take it outside to eat, so we could wolf it down and get playing. After school we'd go home at tea time and the old man would come home from work, and we'd have dinner.

He wasn't a cook though, so we lived on takeaways; in those days it was mostly fish and chips. We had two local chippies, one was open twice during the week and the other one also opened twice, but at different times on different nights, so we could have fish and chips four times a week.

We'd just buy one large portion, take it home wrapped, unwrap it on the kitchen table and all three of us would pick away at it. It wasn't put on a plate in individual portions like you probably would do nowadays, but that's how we lived then. I suppose you might call it hand to mouth.

We never did a weekly shop or anything like that. We'd just buy food on the day, or on a Saturday for the Sunday. Usually our Sunday lunch, instead of roast beef, would be meat and potato pies from the shop up the road. They would be bought on the Saturday and then kept cool, before being warmed up over the fire, with dad peeling some spuds to go with it and making a bit of gravy. It was lovely. That would be our best meal of the week.

In between times, we might have cheese on toast, which would be cooked over the fire, as we never had a stove. That's just the way we were brought up. Hardly the nutritional diet of modern athletes, but it didn't seem to do me any harm.

And yes, the famous Eccles cake, named after the town of my birth, was very occasionally part of my diet. I suppose with all those currants, it was a relatively nutritious treat, but at home we rarely had anything other than a basic savoury meal. But that flaky Eccles cake pastry was delicious, and they made them big, round and flat in those days… so you could sink your teeth into them.

I'm salivating just thinking about one now.

BEING BORN JUST as the Second World War started, I grew up amidst the bomb-damaged landscape of suburban Manchester. I only remember a few snippets from the war, as I had only reached five-and-a half years of age by the time it ended.

Within a five-minute walk of our house was Barton Bridge (officially known as the Barton Swing Aqueduct) on the Manchester Ship Canal. The bridge allowed boats in the Bridgewater canal, that came down from the direction we lived in, to cross the main canal. It's very unusual because it carries water from one canal over water from a second one. We used to go down and watch it being opened from a nearby factory walkway. It was fascinating watching it swing to the side to let the huge ships through on the Manchester Ship Canal heading towards Liverpool.

Over the other side of that, about a mile away from us, was Trafford Park, where all the steel factories and munitions factories and everything were situated. They were targets for the German bombers that flew over Manchester, often using the straight line of the Ship Canal for navigational guidance. So, planes would regularly be flying overhead at night, releasing bombs and, as soon as we'd hear the sirens, we'd vacate the house out into the canvas shelter we had in the garden.

Once you were in there, you couldn't have any light on at all. You just lay there, listening to bombs banging away as they fell on those factories; the anti-aircraft guns trying to down the Luftwaffe planes… just hoping a misdirected one wasn't going to land in our garden,.

It's how Old Trafford, Manchester United's ground, just another mile or so to the east, ended up being bombed. It wasn't targeted, at least I don't think so, but became collateral damage because of its proximity to Trafford Park. I suppose the Germans may have been aiming for Barton Bridge. Thankfully, they missed it and it's still in use now, well over 100 years after opening.

Dad often wouldn't be with us when we were cowering in the garden, as he was a community air raid warden, walking round the streets, making sure people weren't showing any lights. He was always a great servant my dad. I realise that now. Back then, we were just glad not to have him telling us off for messing around while the bombs fell.

That canvas shelter in the garden served a second purpose outside of air raids, mind. If it was a nice day, we'd put these sort of steel girders out to support it and make it into a games room outside to keep out of the old man's way. We'd have friends round and play dens. It was great fun.

I wasn't particularly aware of food being rationed, as we never really had much anyway. As I grew up knowing nothing else, we never felt any loss because of rationing. In fact, when it ceased in July 1954, I didn't really notice any change at all, despite being 14 years old. We just didn't really have any money, so could only afford the same amount of the things that had been rationed, anyway… like butter, sugar, bacon, meat, cheese and preserves.

THE HOUSE THAT I grew up in at 147 Cawdor Street, Eccles was a council house. It was semi-detached and the 'semi' next door had a couple living in it who kept themselves to themselves. Obviously, we rented it, but it was a nice house with a small back garden, but then a decent-sized front garden. Across the way was a massive wall that ran for near enough the whole length of the street. It must have been about 30 feet high and behind it was a big cotton mill. At the end of the wall there was a spur of canal, which joined to the main Bridgewater canal and served as a quay for boats to load and unload to the mill.

There were plenty of houses along the road, but there were also other factories… and then the paper shop, a chip shop, a little corner shop for groceries and, then, at the top there was a big church and a school. At the other end of the street, you were on the main road from Eccles to Liverpool.

Our house didn't have electricity until the mid-50s so we had no lights or sockets or anything to plug anything into to start with. We used to have an oil lamp on the wall for light in the night-time, which the old man would light up if we could afford it. Eventually, we had electricity when I was a teenager and then the lights were on all the time… and dad spent his entire life turning round to Albert and me saying, 'Oi, turn them lights off!' But we had no other electronic devices… no oven, no washing machine, no kettle.

In fact, our only source of heat was that fire; a lovely open one, which also served as our cooker as we didn't have a stove. The house did, though, actually have a fitted bathroom indoors, rather than a toilet in the backyard, as it was built between the wars and so was relatively modern.

My brother and I slept in a bed together in one bedroom, with dad in the other one. Thankfully, Albert and I got on well, but occasionally we'd fall out, usually about summat ridiculous, and sit there in bed, next to each other, just ignoring one another like some kind of *Morecambe and Wise* sketch… with little me as Ernie and the bigger Albert as Eric. I suppose it's quite funny thinking about it, but that arrangement was typical of a young person growing up in those days in an urban environment.

That's not to say we didn't have a great childhood, actually. Because we didn't know any different, we just got on with things and had a lot of fun. Albert and I often played together, especially when younger. He preferred cricket to football, though, and we used the wall opposite the house to chalk stumps on. He soon moved on to young ladies, while I graduated to kicking balls against that wall.

Obviously, Albert's friends were that bit older than me, but when I was with them, they were respectful of my junior status and wouldn't swear, so I didn't really have that influence of bad language being spoken all the time, which actually suited me as I'm quite shy anyway. I'm far more likely to mutter something under my breath to myself and then get on with whatever it is, than start shouting obscenities left, right and centre and having a tantrum. Having said that, if Albert had had enough of me, he wasn't above saying, 'Listen why don't you just naff off and go and find someone else to bother!'

It was just the two of us kids in that house as the other three older half-brothers, as I've said, had moved on in life and we didn't really see them or keep in touch that much. Of course, as the years went on, we met each other at parties, but we didn't really visit them much because they got married and did their own things after moving out of the Eccles area. One lived somewhere in Tyldesley, and one in Salford. Ironically, it wasn't until I had moved to Stoke that I occasionally met up with one of my half-brothers, Jim, who ended up working for the British Road Service, driving big wagons from Manchester all the way to Wolverhampton. There was no M6 motorway in those days so he had to come up the A34, through Stafford and Stoke.

I used to meet him over near Trentham Gardens where there was a truckers' pull in and a big café. This was obviously well before mobile phones to arrange meetings, so he'd meet me there at a certain time late in the evening and we'd chat and have a cuppa, before he'd be off driving all night.

Other than that, I rarely saw that side of my family.

Eventually, Albert was called up into the army. Because he was 18 months older than me, he had to do his national service and he chose to do that as soon as he reached 17. So, I was left alone in the house then. I was lucky, I didn't have to do national service because they stopped it just before I would have been called up.

By the time he got out, Albert had met a young lady called Jean Linley, who he then got married to and moved out of home. He didn't live too far away, maybe a couple of miles towards Pendleton, but in urban Manchester, if you couldn't afford a bus, your only method of transport was Shanks' Pony or a bike, which meant I didn't see him a lot after that either. Especially as they ended up having three children, which kept them very busy.

THROUGHOUT THE WAR, and then afterwards, dad worked for a brickmaking and laying firm in the area of Eccles we lived in called Patricroft, near my school. It was situated within this yard which housed different firms like the brickies, a scrapyard, an office building, and then a place to make the mortar. When I was old enough, on a Saturday I'd help him a bit chucking sand in to the mixer to make cement. By doing that, I got friendly with the people who ran the scrapyard.

They had dogs to guard the yard and I went over to meet them. They had one Alsatian at first and it used to come to me, without barking at all. The boss of the firm, who I got to know very well, noticed that the dog liked me and so I ended up being paid to walk the dog. I walked it before and after school and, sometimes, I'd even go at lunchtime if there was nothing happening at school. I went everywhere with that dog and the scrapyard owner would give me half a crown for taking care of it. It also kept me out of trouble as I've never been one for sitting round doing nothing, and I'm sure if I'd kicked around with some of my mates we'd have got into a lot more high jinks than we did.

It's a bit like I was on the football pitch, I suppose, always looking for somewhere to go and something to do proactively. I had energy and drive. That's just how I was.

I'm like that at home now, still. I can't just sit down and relax in front of the TV unless it's something I really want to watch. I have to be up and about... cleaning, tidying... hoovering. You'd think I'm the perfect husband, but even that annoys my wife!

'Will you just sit down for a moment... instead of getting up all the time!' she says.

When I got older, occasionally the owner would ask me to help him move stuff around the yard, maybe some girders and stuff like that; just for two or three hours in the morning to earn some spending money. Then as soon as I got home dad would say, 'Have you been paid?' And I'd have to hand some money over for him to keep the roof over our heads and buy some basic food. So, I began to contribute to the house as it were. Dad never smoked and didn't really drink, so it wasn't him taking it off me for his own pleasure; it really was just to pay the bills.

Even so, I was never able to have a dog at home growing up, so the one at the yard, who was then joined by a couple of others who I also used to walk, became 'my' dogs. And ever since then I've always had one. Dogs are fantastic companions and a good way to get some exercise outside of the house. I've had Alsatians and German Shepherd ex-police dogs, which are great because they live a long time.

Our last dog lived until it was 15 years old. When it died, in 2017, we decided then that we were getting too old to have our own dog. But then I came up with a plan that works for everyone. My wife was actually desperate to have a young pup and we decided to get a Dachshund and share it with my step-daughter, who lives nearby, as they have a big garden and two teenage kids to play with Dotty the Dachshund all the time.

The good part is that they go out a lot. So, I have to look after it, and walk it. A lot! It's a chore… but someone's got to do it! By the way, the reason we called the dog Dotty isn't because she has spots, but because she drives both my wife and I dotty!

OF COURSE, FAMOUSLY – that is, if you already know the story – one of my dogs led to my nickname. When I first came to Stoke, I had a little Corgi which was full of beans, which meant I needed to walk him as much as possible. I walked with him from my digs to training most mornings. I think I was the only player who would bring their dog to the training ground and, sometimes, I'd ask the young lads who'd be outside the ground watching us arrive to look after it for me and then give them something for doing so, just like I'd had years earlier at the scrapyard.

Then, after training, I'd pick him up and take him into the canteen where he would jump up at the players when they were having something to eat, begging for food. They kept feeding him and feeding him, so he jumped up more. You know how it is with dogs.

Anyway, I'd called him Alfie, which was just one of those names which was quite cool and trendy in the early 1960s, and I really liked it. I never really liked the name Eric anyway, so I was quite happy with Alfie! Before I knew it the players were all calling me Alfie after my dog and the nickname has stuck for over 60 years… and now it's in the title of my book.

People, these days, think that the main influence on me choosing the name was the film *Alfie*, starring Michael Caine, who was just about the biggest British box office star at the time. But that film didn't come out until 1966 and this was several years before that, just after I got into the first team. The title of the book is indeed a reference to the song from Alfie, performed by Dionne Warwick, which begins with the lyric *'What's it all about, Alfie?'*

And, before you ask, I know that the character in the film is a womaniser and neither my dog nor I fall into that category, despite what some former players from my era might tell you! I should note that the final scene of the film does feature Alfie walking over Waterloo Bridge with a dog, so I can see why people make that mistake.

THE OTHER WAY I earned some coins, aside from walking those dogs, was by delivering papers, while Albert earned his cash working on the milk floats. Mostly we spent our hard-earned cash on food. Yes, more meat and potato pies. Even at lunchtime during the school day.

We were fairly rough and ready really, living in second-hand clothes our entire lives, so I became fascinated with nice clothes and people who could afford them, leading me later to open up a gentleman's clothing retailer while I was at Stoke.

Our school clothes were very much our best clothes, so when we got home the old man would say, 'Get them school things off because they have to last you all week'. We'd go out to play wearing our rag, tag and bobtail clothes that got worn through pretty quickly due to everything that we got up to out there on the streets.

When we got older there would be chores for us to do around the house. One of mine was sorting out the coal for the fire, which was very dirty, but I kind of liked that. I used to enjoy it when the coalman came to deliver. Our coalhole was down the side of our house, so the coalman would go down the pathway and drop the coal outside. Then my job was chucking it all down the chute so it could be used for the fire, which was our only form of heating and cooking.

My old man loved his garden. It was only a fairly small patch, but he grew both flowers and vegetables out there and often he'd get me digging trenches for plants at the weekend

It was a different type of life than somebody who came from a wealthy family. You know, because we never saw cars, if someone came to our house in a car we'd be all over the vehicle, admiring it. Wanting to sit in the front seat. It rarely happened, though!

Obviously, dad being an only parent as a father was relatively unusual. I certainly didn't have any other friends who only had a dad. When he wasn't working, to relax he liked to sit outside the house at the front and watch us playing. Every so often, he'd get me to do things because he could see that I was just running around aimlessly, so he'd give me a bit more focus by giving me a task to do.

It was quite a long way to run around the block, so dad would be leaning against the gate and say to me, 'Right, off you go!'

And I'd go running right around the block.

When I'd get back he'd say, 'Now… go back the other way. See if you can go any faster!'

I did a lot of that.

I believe, now, this stood me in good stead in terms of having stamina, and also developing a focus and determination to be the best version of myself that I could be, always trying to better my time as I got older.

Without knowing it, dad was developing my competitive nature.

MY LIFE AS a kid revolved around school and my mates. Not that I was academic, but I loved being at school, being with friends… being in the playground.

Then, we would become gangs in the evening. I mean, just the type of gangs young kids have at night. Nothing bad or malicious; most of them were told by their mom that they'd have to be in for nine o'clock or when it got dark.

Our dad was strict in that sense too, because he'd got to get up and go to work, so we had to be in whenever he said.

Being younger, I naturally hung around with my big brother. I was small and scrawny and wiry. Compared to me, Albert was the big one. He was tall and broad and bulky. So, if he told to me do something, as the younger one, I had to do it.

There were many times we had fights, but because I could run fast and get away, Albert often couldn't catch me. He was also fairly good looking. When we were teenagers, I never had any women chasing after me like Albert did. That was the advantage of being tall and that bit older, I suppose.

When Albert started doing a bit of courting in his early-to-mid teens, he didn't want dad to know, so we'd leave home together as if we were going out to play for the evening. And he would say to me, 'Right lad, you're on your own tonight!'

Off he would go! Sometimes, when I was roaming around with my pals, I'd see him with some girl or other, walking the streets arm in arm or going to the pictures. There were two cinemas that weren't too far away, and there was also a roller-skating rink which we used to go to that was near the school.

I was most at home being pally with my schoolmates after tea, messing around and mucking about having been released from the house. We knew everyone in the area. You'd be out on your bike – which I assume my father nabbed second-hand off someone – and just bump into somebody to muck around with. I also had a friend called Alan Jackson, who was a good footballer as well, and I'd get on my bike and cycle to his place and we'd lark around. Alan ended up going to Australia later on in life, so I haven't seen him in years.

People think it's grim up north. It wasn't at all as far as I was concerned. We had a great time, messing around with mates and playing outside constantly. Yes, there were piles of rubble and industrial wastelands all around, but most cities were like that in post-war Britain, not just in the north.

And we could escape occasionally too. When I was old enough, I was able to go on a day out to Southport on my bike. A mate and me cycled there and back for the day to see the sea. That was exhilarating and very different.

I never missed school. I wasn't one for playing truant and, anyway, there was too much fun to be had. School life was good. We saw our friends and learnt a bit, I suppose, not that we were the most attentive.

I went to Patricroft C of E Primary. The school was next to a big church at the bottom of our road with a police station next to it. But the discipline in our school came from the headteacher, who loved laying down the law. He was a little man and a bit of a bully, if truth be told. I had very scribbly handwriting and I used to dread being given lines. Sometimes, the teacher would tell me off for something.

'Right Skeels,' he's say. 'Eighty lines by tomorrow morning… saying, "I shall not do this" or whatever it was I'd done wrong. I'd have to go home and write them up. It was the worst possible punishment because it curtailed my time outside playing with my mates.

Then, if you didn't bring those lines in the next day, you'd be asked to hold your hand out and get the cane. That was fairly common, although I did everything I could to avoid that fate.

I quickly realised that the focus was always on the kids that chose to sit at the back of the classroom, as that was where most of the troublemakers were. That just meant, though, that you'd be watched if you sat back there, so I learnt quickly to position myself in the middle of the class, which meant I could carry on like I was at the back and have some fun without being spotted. I suppose that was an early example of being tactically aware, something I was often praised for by Tony Waddington when snuffing out danger posed by other teams and their best players.

Sometimes, though, my need to chat with my mates would get the better of me and, while the teacher was talking, I'd start messing around, being distracted. He'd hear me, and turn.

'SKEELS!!'

He'd have that tone of voice that all good teachers have, and I'd look up realising I'd got caught.

'Come to the front!' he'd say, and I'd go down to the front of the class and he'd ask me, in front of the entire class, 'Now tell me, what are you supposed to be doing?'

It was a rhetorical question and I learned pretty quickly not to answer it.

With a sigh, he'd continue, 'You're supposed to be listening to me, aren't you, Skeels?'

Now it was my line.

'Yes sir'.

No matter what I had done, it would always end up with him saying the next few words.

'Get your hand out there, lad!'

A couple of swift whacks of his cane would follow.

I can't have been all bad as I was actually given the honour of being a class prefect. You're probably thinking this was a duty that annoyed me, but far from it. I soon realised that many of a prefect's duties would allow me to get out of being stuck in the classroom, as you had to go wherever was needed to help out. For example, I remember we used to have crates of milk containing small bottles for the kids to drink.

As a prefect and milk monitor, it was my job to distribute the milk to the other classrooms, which meant I was missing lessons. So, I was always happy to volunteer for such additional duties. And there would always be at least two of us, so we'd enjoy pottering around with the crates, delivering them and taking our time chit-chatting as we went.

Carefree times.

At school I was actually quite interested in geography, which is ironic considering what happened when I began getting trials for clubs, which I'll tell you about shortly. I also liked history, and I was quite good at arithmetic, but I wasn't very good at spelling, so it's even more ironic that I've ended up writing a book.

That's the last thing that I ever thought would happen, and I'm eternally grateful that you are interested enough in my story to get this far… please keep going with me!

THE HOUSE I grew up in is still there today, but the chippy and corner shop have gone. It's now two doors down from a Domino's pizza outlet on the main Liverpool Road, but then where isn't these days?

Dad stayed in that house until he was 77, when he passed away. His funeral was the last tie I had with Eccles. Once I left to go to Stoke-on-Trent the only time I went back to see him was in the very early days at weekends after my game had finished.

I wouldn't get there until Saturday evening and, before you knew it, the weekend's gone and I was travelling back to Stoke again. I actually haven't seen any of the friends I grew up with since dad's funeral, as I can recall, and I haven't been back to Eccles for donkey's years to be honest. My home is in the Potteries now.

How did I come to be in Stoke-on-Trent? Well, by the time I got to 16 years old I had to start thinking about a job. I didn't really know what career I was going to follow, to be honest.

Hadn't got a clue.

All I really knew about was the type of work my dad did, or the factories or yards nearby that I'd seen growing up. In fact, you didn't really think about careers as such in those days; you just worried about getting some kind of job that you could earn money from and then learn some skills to improve and win promotion… which would mean more money.

Naturally, when the time came for me to leave school I went and worked in that cotton mill across the road. I had to start at the very bottom, as a labourer. I'd get these big cotton rolls that went on the back of the machines and I'd have to hump them around and stack them on a big rack. And then I'd get given little odd jobs to do until I learned to do a little bit more. That was me, always trying to be helpful, a bit like I'd end up doing under Tony Waddington at Stoke City… filling in, doing the jobs no one else wanted to do.

I earned about three pound a week and that was with the overtime, although I think if I had stayed there, I would eventually have been doing a fairly senior manual job, possibly leading into low-level manager or supervisor in time.

But I only lasted about four months, until something far more exciting came along.

Football.

Because that's when Stoke City asked me to sign for them.

Little did I ever imagine, as a boy growing up in Eccles, that I would have a career as a professional footballer and play with and against the greatest players in the world. This includes my friend and former teammate Geoff Hurst, England's hat-trick hero in the 1966 World Cup final.

CHAPTER 2

My Football Education

WAS I DESTINED to become a footballer?

Was I born with a talent for feinting to beat men time after time like Stanley Matthews?

Powering through midfield like Duncan Edwards?

Ghosting in to goalscoring positions like Dennis Viollet?

Or was I even a genius free-kick taker like David Beckham?

No... was I heck.

I was just a scrawny, rough and ready lad from Lancashire who went where life took him, knowing enough to take advantage of some of the breaks that came my way.

My footballing journey started by kicking a ball against that wall opposite my house. I did it time after time... *after time*. Just like any lad did in those days. I've always been thankful for that fairly terrible piece of urban design as, although it looked hideous to walk out of our front door and be met with a hug wall of bricks directly opposite, it at least meant I could kick a ball against it and learn to control it as it bounced back. As I say... *time after time... after time*.

Starting playing in the streets had its benefits. I learned that you needed to anticipate the way a ball might bounce off a protruding cobble or the edge of the pavement. But it also had its pitfalls. Many was the pair of trousers that saw their knees go through on those cobbles.

Dad despaired. But he also saw that I had dedication to improve.

I actually got to know the angles off every single brick in that wall, off those cobbles and the surrounding pavements and walls on our side of the street so that I could play the ball against them and know that if it hit that stone like this, it would go over there. It helped me read the bounce and spin of a ball and anticipate it. It also made me very two-footed. Even though I am predominantly right-footed, I learned to control the ball and pass it against that wall with my left foot, doing it time and again from a very young age. That stood me in great stead all through my career.

Often, I'd be out there for hours on my own, but I also spent a lot of time with one mate or another playing one-on-one, with goals made of coats or jumpers, taking turns having the ball and bearing down on the one being in goal and trying to beat them, or more often just bash past them. Controlling the ball in that situation on those cobbles was no mean feat. Other times we'd have a few other lads come up and we'd have a little two- or three-a-side game between us.

I really do think that the way I grew up helped me become a better, more versatile footballer. Not just in terms of ball control, either. For example, playing the game us kids called 'rally' meant I was always whizzing around at sustained pace, twisting this way and that way, keeping an eye out for my opposition and then keeping them at arm's length. The game was one of those where you had to avoid being tagged, or as we called it 'ticked', by one of the other players. So you'd spend hours just running around, dodging, swerving and haring away as fast as you can. It was great fun and we played it across our whole area, not just on our own street, Cawdor Street.

There wasn't a formal limit to the playing area and we'd cover at least down to the big main road at one end and the canal at the other. It was full of nooks and crannies, so if you were trying to find others and tick them you'd have to run around a lot.

Often the gang of us enjoying this game would include girls. There might be 10 or so of us playing rally and maybe three or four would be female. It didn't bother us at all. We weren't interested in girls in that sense and I certainly wasn't in the same way my elder brother was. I was too busy having my own type of energetic fun. Even when we went roller skating, which was where Albert often took his dates, it was purely for fun with my mates, despite some of them being girls.

We'd play for hours, until it got dark at night, ducking and diving down various ginnels and entries. The worst thing would be if you got caught and ticked early as it meant you had to stand around waiting while everyone else was out enjoying themselves, so you soon learned to ensure you were fast enough to get away and then clever enough not to be found. Even then, if they found you, they had to catch you up and tick you. So speed to get away was crucial. Eventually, we'd all have to go home and that was usually just how the game ended as we simply drifted off because it was getting dark outside and no one had caught you.

Of course, it really helped that the streets didn't have much traffic in them and we could roam free. You couldn't do that these days, I suppose. Although there were rarely any cars on our street, we did used to have the milk cart come along pulled by a horse to drop the milk off that we had to avoid if we were out early in the morning, but that horse served another purpose for my old man. As I mentioned earlier, dad loved his garden and for him any horse was just a source of manure for him to gather up. I say him. Of course, what happened was that when the milk cart clattered past and the horse did a poo outside on the road, once I was old enough, he'd order me do it. He'd say, 'Go and get that before somebody else gets it,' and I'd have to go out with a bucket and spade and scrape it up so he could put it on his garden.

Even when we were in the park playing five-a-side in and around the swings and roundabouts we'd actually use the equipment as part of the game. I was so determined to win the ball that I'd jump on top of the equipment to lunge and make a tackle. I may have been rough and ready but it stood me in great stead, helping my athleticism and I suppose all of the kicking the ball off the angles of the moving playground equipment, to then control it, that must have helped with eye-to-foot coordination.

I never thought I was preparing myself for a career as a sportsman, though. It just wasn't something that entered my head. All my ancestors and siblings were active folk, either farmers or in the army. So we were a fit and strong bunch, but none of them turned that into a sporting career, so I had no idea that was even possible. I was just busy enjoying myself, being a kid.

OF COURSE, WHEN you're a lad playing football in the street you dream of playing for your team, with your heroes.

I was a Manchester United fan as a kid, definitely not a Manchester City supporter; they were from the other side of the city. Naturally, every young lad who gets into football loves to dream and I dreamt of playing for United, my local team. When I could and I was old enough, I'd go and see them play.

Getting there was an experience. There were supporters' coaches which ran from the garage down by the canal, full of fans wearing rosettes and spouting colourful language. There's be these lines of charabancs parked up there and you'd just turn up and pay two bob for a ticket and they'd bus you down to the ground, and then after the game bring you back.

Old Trafford was fabulous, with an incredible atmosphere. I used to stand with my mates opposite the tunnel which was at the centre of the old main stand so we could see the whole pitch and have a view down the tunnel to see our heroes emerge. I had stars in my eyes. Even though I often dreamt about how wonderful it would be to be playing at Old Trafford, I never thought I could ever actually be a professional footballer, let alone appear at the stadium United fans now call the Theatre of Dreams.

The irony is, of course, that every time I played there I wanted them to lose. Desperately. I might have grown up a United supporter, but my loyalty was always to the team I was playing for and there was no room for sentiment. We lost on the first occasion I played at Old Trafford which was very special for me, but then drew on six of the next seven visits we made.

My only victory came on December 9, 1972 when I filled in for the injured Alan Bloor alongside Denis Smith at centre-half. Striker John Ritchie and left-back Mike Pejic netted our goals in a famous 2-0 win. Stoke hadn't beaten Manchester United at home since October 1952, over 20 years earlier. That was a tremendous feeling and came at the end of a series of eight games over the course of the preceding year, three league games, three in the League Cup and two in the FA Cup, in which we knocked United out of both cup competitions and won for the first time in two decades at Old Trafford. They were sensational games and great victories against a team which three or four years earlier had been champions of Europe and still boasted some of the best and most talented players in the world.

We weren't bad either by that stage.

And, of course, there was also that famous night when we qualified for the

1972 League Cup final by defeating West Ham 3-2 in torrential rain in a second semi-final replay after the original two-leg tie ended all square at 2-2. That titanic cup tussle in a mud-bath was also at Old Trafford, although I was an unused substitute that night.

In those games at United, I was often playing for Stoke alongside former United giant Dennis Viollet. As a youngster I had watched Dennis play for manager Matt Busby's Manchester United team in the mid-50s. Little did I realise when I was watching as a starry-eyed teenager that he would become my teammate and friend.

My favourite player as a lad was young midfielder Duncan Edwards. He was a Rolls Royce of a player, not particularly fast, but he was so strong and he would give the ball to a colleague then run into a better position to receive it back. It was simple, but so effective. I often think modern coaches can over-complicate things at times. I'd love to tell you I modelled my game on Dunc, but I was more the player who would win the ball back and give it to the likes of him, holding back in case the opposition won the ball and countered, rather than pressing on and looking for the return pass.

Two other great players who were favourites of mine were Tommy Taylor, the centre-forward, and then David Pegg, the winger, who they used to say would sell you a dummy so much you'd have to pay again at the turnstile to get back in. That was an incredible team and one which was cruelly taken from us in the air crash at Munich in February 1958. I remember seeing the headlines in the paper and reading all about it. I was stunned. It was horrific.

At that time, people thought Matt Busby would die as he had been read the last rites whilst lying in hospital in Munich, but that Duncan Edwards would survive. When Duncan died around two weeks after the crash it felt like the whole of Manchester went into mourning. Even though he wasn't a local lad, hailing from the West Midlands, Edwards had become a phenomenon for United. To lose him and all those other players, officials and the journalists who also died in the crash . was devastating.

But my opportunities to go and watch the Busby Babes, as Matt Busby's young, all-conquering team of the 50s was known, became limited as, by the time I got to the age of 15, well before the Munich disaster, I had begun playing regular, organised Saturday afternoon football myself.

I STARTED OUT, naturally, in the school team. I was always picked because I was a decent player, with lots of energy, so I got selected even though I was a bit younger than most of the team to start with, and before long I was made captain. So, I knew I was good compared to my peers and those slightly older than me. Back then I was a little inside-forward, dribbling or playing passes through to the wingers or centre-forward, and then getting into the box to snap up chances.

I used to love scoring goals. It became my forte, which again is ironic because it would turn out to be the last thing anyone would remember me for in my professional career.

I enjoyed myself playing football as a kid, but I found it all the better being at the hub of things, being central and being in the action, rather than being on the wing and waiting all the time for the ball to come out to me. I needed to be involved. I was a grafter, but at that level I also had good skill, especially with all that background on the cobbled streets.

I wasn't one for boasting about just how good I was as a player at school or anything, but I was one for standing up for myself, and others. Just occasionally that would result in a fight, for the right cause that is. Usually, this wasn't actually for myself. I used to fight on behalf of lots of lads at school who got bullied. They'd come to me as prefect and I'd start off by trying to talk to whoever it was that had been having a go at them and tell them that if they do something like that again I'd be packing them off to the headmaster and then they'd be in trouble. But they'd only get the one chance at that option. I enjoyed scrapping, it didn't bother me at all, and if whoever was bullying some kid thought they were cock of the north and told me to get stuffed when I challenged them, then it would be a red rag to a bull and I'd lay into them and scrap on behalf of the victim to sort out whichever bully needed it. It was just my sense of justice.

I'm not saying I won every fight, but it was a matter of principle that I didn't back down and more often than not I just got stuck in. So, I suppose that I was like that in football too, although not in a literal fighting sense. It was what made me a good leader on the pitch and why I was made school team captain.

Despite my size, I was never frightened of anybody in football even though they were better players than me and looked a bit more physical and athletic than I did. Even back then playing for the school, when I was a couple of years younger than the rest of the team, right through to when I made my initial appearances for Stoke in the first team, I was confident in my own abilities. What I learned, though, was never to actually fight on the pitch. That wasn't my style as a professional.

I was tough, but not violent. I would wind up the opposition with my tenacity, my determination and by winning the ball off them in tackles and headers, by anticipating and intercepting, by being fitter and smarter than them; all the things I learned growing up in Eccles.

MY FOOTBALL BOOTS were huge and bulky, nothing like boots are now. They had big studs, a long leather tongue up to my ankle and once they got wet in the sludge, they felt like massive, heavy lead weights on your feet. Often the pitches were a total mud-bath. Even when playing professional football they could be terrible.

I'm not joking when I say that sometimes the pitches I played on at the school playing fields were actually better than the ones I played on professionally. Derby County's Baseball Ground was renowned for being dreadful, although Stoke's was often just a sea of mud as well, so playing on such awful pitches as a lad was a good starting point and helped me build stamina in my legs to power through it while others laboured.

Mind you, I knew no different then. And I certainly never complained, even when having to clean all that muck off my boots, which I did every Sunday morning before going out to play for the day. Because they were leather, I should have put dubbin on them to protect them, but I couldn't afford such luxuries as that as I didn't have the money to pay for it. Instead, I cleaned them with water and wiped them down with a cloth and then put them by the fire to dry out. I only ever had one pair of boots at a time, never a spare second pair. I'm not sure how dad ever afforded them; they wouldn't have been bought new anyway, but he made sure I had some boots to wear at least.

Being the early 50s, the school kit we had to wear was that really heavy material, with orange and black diagonal stripes, the school colours. When it was wet and windy and you got all muddy, you'd have to take your gear home with you and get it washed. Well, we didn't have anything fancy like a washing machine at our house, so I had to put the kit in a pan full of hot water on the fire, let it boil, then fish it out and hang it over the fire to let it dry.

It was the same when I was playing for my first men's team, the Albion. Their colours were black and white stripes and I remember the day when the washing went wrong, when the lighter colour went half dark and then the following week I didn't realise quite how bad it was until I put the shirt on just before we were going out to play.

I remember looking down at it and thinking, *oh heck*.

When I was lining up with the rest of the team, their kits were all immaculate and mine was a completely different shade… grey not white. The lads looked at me and said, 'Bloody hell, Skeelsy… what happened to your shirt?!'

It was quite embarrassing and didn't go down well at all with my teammates, who constantly took the Mickey out of me during the game. They didn't let me live that one down for a while.

Eventually at weekends I found playing for the school team on Saturday mornings wasn't enough. So, I also started to play games on a Saturday afternoon for another local team as well. I could play game after game because I was so fit and energetic and, to be honest, there was nothing else I wanted to do.

But before I joined the Albion, I started playing for the Adelphi Boys Club in Pendleton. It wasn't just a football club, there was boxing and athletics and it was also a kind of social club; one of those fantastic places that keeps young kids busy. I liked the set up at the club, which I only really went to initially just to see what was going on. Their coach just asked me to train with their team, and I enjoyed it. Then I got into their side and started doubling up; playing for the school team in the morning, then for my new club in the afternoon. The standard wasn't hugely different, but it was another game of organised football for 13- and 14-year-old me to take part in.

It turned out to be an opportune choice as, while I was at Adelphi Boys Club, I got my first chance at what you might think of as the big time. We played this one game against Stockport and after the match someone approached me and took me completely by surprise by saying, 'Lad, would you like to come down to Stockport for a trial?'

Stunned, I replied, 'A trial?'

The feller says, 'Yeah… a trial. At Stockport,' as if it was Manchester United or some other huge team I should be impressed with. I was quite excited actually, but my reaction probably wasn't showing that on my face.

The problem was, despite my enjoyment of geography at school, I didn't actually know where Stockport was and I didn't like to tell this scout that!

I'd grown up in Eccles all my life to that point and never actually left, other than to go into Salford or, on rare occasions, into Manchester itself. I think I'd seen Stockport on bus timetables or on the destination board at Manchester Piccadilly the few times I'd been there, but suddenly I was imagining this exotic place that didn't have heaps of rubble still strewn around the place from where bombs had destroyed houses and created wastelands, or where urban slum clearance was paving the way for new council estates in the late 50s. Shows how little I knew!

As well as my dearth of knowledge about its location, I didn't like to tell this scout I didn't have any money, so I probably couldn't afford to get there… wherever it was, anyway.

Thankfully, it turned out that Stockport wasn't too far away from Eccles and I travelled down to trial with them, which went well, so I signed up on youth forms. It was the middle of the 1954/55 season and I thought I was doing quite well, even though County were struggling in the Third Division North. They were, after all, a Football League club.

THE TROUBLE WAS to get to Stockport. With not having any transport myself, I had to get a bus from Eccles to Salford, then one from Salford to Manchester… and then one from Manchester to Stockport. For training, I would be doing this in the early evening rush hour on Tuesdays, then the reverse journey fairly late at night.

On a Saturday, I didn't have to be at Stockport until 12 o'clock, but for me that actually meant getting up early to make certain I could get the bus and ensure I was early, rather than late.

Rather than being enjoyable, it was a struggle. I enjoyed the games, but there was also never any sort of encouragement from the coaches to make me think I could progress and play at a higher level. I felt like I was just one of the load of youths that would come together and battle for starting places for the matches we played. It was hard to get to know the other lads too as we only met once a week, for matches; so it wasn't as if you could get really friendly with them.

All this meant that, after the end of the season, I decided not to re-sign again and I told them it was too much travelling for me and, anyway, my old man wanted me to help with his work at weekends, which was partly true as I was now 15.

So, it seemed my opportunity to be like Edwards, Taylor and Viollet had gone. I went back to playing local Saturday football.

OVER ON MY side of Salford, the skyline was dominated by the distinctive chimney of the Albion Cotton Mill at Pendlebury. From that local landmark had come the name of my first proper club; simply called the Albion.

I'd played for Adelphi Boys for about a season before that opportunity came up at Stockport. But when I decided not to return to County, I also didn't go back to Adelphi Boys because I wanted more structure and coaching at football, which was something I'd had a taste of at Stockport, and anyway I had to get two buses to get across to Pendleton on the other side of Salford, which was almost the same issue as getting to Stockport, so I joined the Albion. Initially I went to watch their matches on a Saturday afternoon, as they played in a nearby park which I could walk to – no more buses – and then I started chatting to people and eventually someone told the manager that I was a good player in the school team, had played well that morning and had had a trial at Stockport or whatever, so fairly quickly I was asked to play for the Albion men's team. I remember their manager asking me if I'd like to come and play for them? I was so excited. I mean, I didn't really care whether the team was good or bad, I just wanted to play.

The Albion played in the Eccles and District League; a full men's league, so I was stepping into the world of senior football despite having only just turned the tender age of 15. Some of my teammates were in their mid-to-late twenties, possibly even older. Those ageing ones tended to like me, though, because I had so much energy and was so keen I would dash around covering plenty of ground, being their legs for them.

I was also just happy to play, so I would turn out anywhere they wanted me to. I didn't care and wasn't precious. Little did I know that that attitude was also going to be key to my professional career, because it was that quality which endeared me so much to Tony Waddington at Stoke City a few years later.

As an inside-forward I loved scoring goals, like everyone did, but I could turn my hand at anything and before I knew it I was playing at full-back, striker... even winger at times. It was a good footballing education. I'd only ever played inside-forward before and was always one of the best and most influential players in the school team or at Adelphi Boys, but now I was dropped in to plug gaps as the manager needed me. Being young and enthusiastic, I was happy to oblige.

The only position I never wanted or never tried out for was being a goalkeeper, which is not surprising really given at five feet eight inches I really was not tall enough. It was indeed also the only position I never played in professionally.

The Eccles and District League was an unforgiving place to play. The tackles were tough and the pitches weren't great. They were corporation pitches, with six marked out in this park. They were probably trimmed no more than once a month and sometimes the markings had disappeared into the gloop. Quite often, there was no visible penalty spot even at the start of a game and there would definitely be no nets, so when you blasted the ball past the 'keeper to score, you'd have to run miles to go and fetch it back again. But it was actually really good fun and I enjoyed the challenge of matching up to fellers significantly older than me.

The older I got and the more I filled out, even if I didn't grew any taller than five feet eight inches, the more I got to play in my preferred position and by the time I was 18 I was well-established and settled, enjoying life and my Saturday afternoon games. Thoughts of a career in football were long gone from my head.

So, there I was, happily playing away for about three seasons, growing up, earning a few pennies, enjoying myself playing for Albion, when one day my life changed.

IT WOULD HAVE been sometime in early 1958, not long after I'd turned 18, when, after an Albion game had finished, I was once again approached by a random feller as I walked off the pitch, covered in mud.

In fact it wasn't just me who got pulled to one side, but another young player in the Albion team, whose name I'm afraid I can no longer remember, but both of us were pleased to learn that we were being talent-spotted by a scout named Reg Savage. I had no idea who Reg was when he introduced himself, but it turned out he was an Eccles man who had played in goal for a local works team, Taylor Bros, before being spotted by a scout himself. He first turned out for nearby non-league Stalybridge Celtic, but then signed for First Division Leeds United, aged 18, in 1931, before making 79 appearances for them in the latter half of the 30s. During the war he joined the RAF and, whilst stationed in Lancashire, he picked up wartime cup medals with Blackpool, for whom he guested without formally signing up.

In that team was a certain Stanley Matthews, then a Stoke City player, although stationed alongside Savage as a PT Instructor in the RAF in Lancashire for much of the war. Shortly after, he signed permanently for Blackpool. And, of course, I would eventually end up as a teammate of Stan's at Stoke.

Had I known that, as he walked towards me on that pitch in 1958, I think I'd have spontaneously combusted!

Reg had retired after a stint at Nottingham Forest after the war was over and had become a scout, sending players to a range of northern and midlands clubs, and earning some money on the side from his actual job as a butcher. He had taken over his father's shop in Swinton, not far from where he'd grown up in Eccles, but his Saturday afternoons were spent watching amateur football, eyeing the young talent, which is when he came across me.

I always assumed I eventually ended up at Stoke because of Reg's contacts with the club, through knowing Stan during the war, but I honestly don't know that for sure. People, especially men, just didn't talk about 'why' in those days. They just told you where you had to be and you did it. That's just how it was.

And in any case, it wasn't to Stoke that Reg sent me at first.

He wasn't one for dilly-dallying around with niceties, was Reg. He just said to us, 'Lads, are you two alright to go for a trial?'

The other lad was speechless. I'd been here before, though. Borne of all that prior worldly experience, I said, 'A trial?'

And the scout said, 'Yeah'.

And I said, 'Where at?'

And the scout said, 'Birmingham'.

'Birmingham?'

'Yes… Birmingham.'

You can tell I knew exactly what I was talking about, can't you?

One thing I did know was that Birmingham City were in the First Division at this time, a far cry from Fourth Division Stockport, as they now were, so I was getting quite excited about this opportunity as Reg spoke. But at the same time I was thinking how far it is going to be to get there because, thanks to my schoolboy geography, I vaguely knew that Birmingham was quite a bit south of Manchester.

The scout says to both of us, 'Yeah, I'll sort it out for you. I'll let you know'.

Well, obviously, we didn't have a phone at home, given that we had no electricity at all, so all I could do was wait. I wondered for a while if anything was going to happen, but then Reg arrived this one evening to simply tell me where to be and when, and who to ask for when I got to Birmingham. I took him completely on trust. It's how things were in those days. No agents or mobile phones or anything.

SO I WENT down to Birmingham, with this compadre, on the train together. We arrived, got changed and played in a trial game and we both did all right, so we were offered amateur terms, which meant we'd get our travelling expenses but not be paid for playing, although we'd be in and around the reserves so could get ourselves noticed and maybe earn a pro contract if the rest of the season went well.

I knew straightaway this was a fantastic opportunity at a top-flight club with a good manager that was going places. It allowed me to even start thinking about leaving Eccles for the first time in my life, not that I had huge ambitions of becoming a massive football star or anything, but there was a tangible possibility I wouldn't be stuck on building sites or in cotton mills for the rest of my life.

I jumped at it, even though it meant a bus to Manchester Piccadilly, then a train down to Birmingham New Street for both midweek training and Saturday games. As I was an amateur, I didn't stay down there and I wasn't training full-time, but those few months did give me a great taste for what being a professional would be like, and I loved it.

I did okay at Birmingham over the remainder of the 1957/58 season, although I only played about seven or eight games for their A team, but I am sure had things worked out differently I could have progressed there. But here's where the fickle nature of football threw me my first career curveball, and it wasn't a particularly good one.

The Birmingham manager was a gentleman named Arthur Turner, who actually used to be Stoke captain in the great team before the war starring Freddie Steele, Stanley Matthews and Frank Soo. Turner was the central midfielder when the team finished fourth in the First Division, Stoke's highest ever finish, with him as captain under manager Bob McGrory in 1935/36. Turner had then been sold to Birmingham for £6,000 in 1939, aged 30, and rose to become manager at St Andrew's, after initially returning to Stoke after retiring from playing and becoming assistant manager to McGrory and then his successor Frank Taylor in the early 50s.

This was my introduction to the brutal nature of football business. Birmingham under Turner had just had their greatest ever season, 1955/56, finishing sixth in the First Division, something they haven't achieved since, and reaching the FA Cup final, only to lose 1-3 to Manchester City in that famous game in which goalkeeper Bert Trautmann broke his neck, but played on to ensure his team lifted the cup.

The club had also entered the first ever Inter-City Fairs Cup, an early European competition which saw Birmingham selected to represent the second city after the likes of Aston Villa and Wolves refused to let their players be merged into a representative XI, akin to the one London clubs like Arsenal, Spurs and Chelsea allowed to happen. The competition was actually played across a period of 18 months and Birmingham, under Turner, reached the semi-final, only losing to Barcelona 1-2 in a replay in Basel after the initial two-legged tie ended in a 4-4 draw. The Catalans went on to hammer the London XI 8-2 in the final.

And yet, for some reason, the Birmingham chairman Harry Morris thought that wasn't good enough and announced that he had asked Bristol City manager Pat Beasley to become joint manager alongside Turner in January 1958. Not surprisingly, this led to Turner moving on over the summer of 1958. He would join Headington United, later to change its name to Oxford United, in January 1959 and lead them from non-league into winning election to the Football League in 1962, when Accrington Stanley FC were liquidated and dropped out of the Football League. He was a much under-rated manager, was Arthur Turner.

WITH ALL OF that going on during the close season over the summer of 1958, as Turner's future hung in the balance before his eventual departure, it meant that us amateurs were completely forgotten about. Irrespective of the fact that we never really met him, we were seen as the previous manager's signings, his protégées for the future. Because all football contracts, even amateur ones, then were just for the season, I just didn't get offered anything at all.

So back I went to working on a building yard, then moving in the summer to the cotton mill behind the brick wall, while playing local football on a Saturday at the Albion in Eccles once the 1958/59 season started again.

Another opportunity had slid away from me in Birmingham.

Maybe it wasn't meant to be for me? Maybe this would be my life and before I knew it I'd be like the men whose legs I had been for the last few years, grateful for some dreamer of a whipper-snapper doing my running for me?

Lightning couldn't strike for a third time for me, could it?

After a couple of months, in late September 1958, as me and him whose name I may one day remember trudged off the pitch at the end of another Albion game… there was Reg Savage emerging again, from amidst the spectators on the side of the pitch.

I knew what was coming by now.

Reg opens up with, 'Lads, would you like…'

And I say, 'Where this time, Reg?'

'Stoke… it's not as far as Birmingham!' he says.

'I know,' I replied.

For once, I actually knew where Stoke was as I'd been through it every time I went to Birmingham on the railway. Not that I'd ever got off, but I also knew it was where pottery was made, as I'd seen the potbanks out of the window of the train. See, that education didn't go to waste.

So, we got on the train and went.

The rest, as they say… is history.

That's how I came to join Stoke City.

There is, though, this rumour, or should I call it an 'old wife's tale', if I'm allowed to in this day and age, that I wrote a letter begging for a trial at Stoke.

In fact, nothing could be further from the truth. It's a load of old tosh that I've seen repeated in some of those books you see about the club listing players and their appearances with a brief biography. I don't know who made it up, but completely fabricated it has been. I'm just glad I can set that record straight.

And that's most of the controversy in this book dealt with!

I just went where old Reg Savage told me to go. If it hadn't been for him, I would never have become a professional footballer, never moved to Stoke and never had the life that I have.

Thanks Reg!

A fresh-faced me ready to take on the world after signing terms with Stoke City. And, all these years later, with Stoke City owner and chairman Peter Coates celebrating the club's 150th anniversary in 2013. What the Coates family have done for the club and the area has been unbelievable.

CHAPTER 3

Proud to be a Potter

AS MY 19TH BIRTHDAY approached, early one Saturday morning in October 1958, me and my Albion colleague travelled to Stoke by train. Once again Reg Savage had arranged everything for us, popping over to the house on Cawdor Street one evening to fill me in on the details.

It was another journey into the unknown, this time to a club that was in the lower reaches of the Second Division, but which I knew of mostly through former player and legend of the game, Stanley Matthews. Despite being 43, Stan was still a phenomenal player. He'd actually won what turned out to be his final cap two years earlier against Denmark in Copenhagen, but there was a lot of controversy when he wasn't selected to go to the 1958 World Cup in Switzerland for which that Denmark game was a qualifier.

England bombed in that tournament, failing to win a single game and going out following a fairly stale 0-1 defeat to the Soviet Union. Many thought Matthews should have been there. I knew Stan had also been awarded the first ever Footballer of the Year trophy in 1948 and was also voted the first ever Ballon d'Or winner, or European Footballer of the Year as it was back in 1956, when he won its inaugural edition, beating Real Madrid's Alfredo Di Stéfano in the voting.

I also knew he didn't play for Stoke any longer; more's the pity, as he had been at Blackpool since 1947.

SO, THAT WAS all I knew about Stoke City, really. I certainly didn't know how to get from the station to the ground, even though I knew you went past it on the train as you left Stoke station to head towards Birmingham, so we clubbed together and took a taxi. This was the life I'd like to get used to! Hardly a baby Bentley with a drinks cabinet in the back, though, was it?

We had been selected in the Stoke youth team as triallists and we were playing Notts County. It wasn't on the main pitch in the stadium, though; the game was played out on the small training pitch at the back. We lost 0-1. But I was always remember that match because, not only was I playing my first game for Stoke City, but I played against The Magpies' young star striker Jeff Astle, who scored the only goal. Jeff was actually about 18 months younger than me, so he was still only 16 at this point, and was clearly a phenomenal talent. He would actually turn professional on his 17th birthday in May 1959 and become a first team player the following season. I would spend a lot of my career trying to stop him scoring against us after his transfer to West Bromwich Albion in 1964.

In that trial match I played more as a central-cum-attacking midfielder, so I wasn't directly up against him, but it was the first time I came across anyone who was that much better than those of us around him, and we just knew he was going to have a hugely successful career. It was obvious. I remember in 1969/70, Jeff finished as the leading goalscorer in the First Division with 25 goals and earned himself a place in the England squad at the 1970 World Cup in Mexico. That was well deserved. By that time I had spent the best part of six years trying to keep him quiet.

Back in 1958 I was much more concerned about having impressed Stoke's hierarchy enough to be asked back.

Tony Waddington was the assistant manager at Stoke and he was the man who kept an expert eye on everything that went on across the club on behalf of manager Frank Taylor. I would eventually learn to call him Waddo or gaffer, but when he approached me after this trial game he was most definitely Mr Waddington to me.

Although the team had lost, I thought I'd done reasonably well. But I knew the crunch moment was coming, although I didn't quite expect it to happen at that moment, as I was semi-naked, just getting dry as I got out of the big bath and was getting myself ready to go back home again.

Tony came over and simply said to me, 'Would you like to sign for Stoke City?'

I looked at him, gobsmacked, and came up with, 'Well… that's why I've come, like!'

He continued, 'Well, we'd like you to come and play in a few games in the A team. Do well… and there can be a contract for you'.

I somehow managed to get out a… 'Fine'.

And then he was off. That was that. I had been offered amateur terms in October 1958.

It was only after a few minutes when I'd got my stuff together and was readying myself to walk back to the station that I realised Waddo hadn't asked the other lad who'd come with me, so it was a bit of an awkward journey home. It was the end of the road for him.

Football can be a brutal game.

I WAS NAMED as a new amateur signing in my first of what turned out to be many mentions in the *Sentinel* in Stoke. I've still got that clipping which says…
'New names appearing in Stoke's third team are Jim Ledgar (20), Milton United's free-scoring centre-forward and Eric Steels (18) from Patricroft. Both have joined the amateur staff. Ledgar has been under Stoke's notice for some time. Steels came on a recent trial.'

Steels, not Skeels, you'll notice; an early introduction to how I'd have to get used to the inaccuracies of press reporters.

A few days later, I received a telegram confirming everything and, before I knew it, I was back in Stoke, all expenses paid, preparing to travel to play at holders Wolves in the FA Youth Cup in my first game as an amateur. I can still remember getting on the bus with the rest of the players and going down to Wolverhampton. We lost, but after the game Tony was pleased with what I'd done and he came and spoke to me again.

'Right… come and see me in my office on Saturday after the match.'

So, after we played a game at home the following Saturday, I went to find the office. The only problem was that I wasn't yet sure where the office actually was in the main stand at Stoke. So, there I am wandering up and down the corridors looking for Tony Waddington, and I ended up having to ask somebody where the office was? When I eventually arrived, Tony was actually waiting for me with Frank Taylor, the first team manager. It was the first time I'd met the actual manager, so I was a bit taken aback again.

Tony said those same words to me.

'Eric, would you like to be a professional footballer? Because we'd like you to sign professional forms.'

I think I was quite overwhelmed, because I couldn't actually answer at first. *Was this actually happening to me?* I didn't want to speak, especially as I was a bit shy anyway. This was everything I'd ever dreamed of being offered.

I eventually pulled myself together and replied, 'Yeah, yeah, of course!'

Waddo must have been used to dealing with shellshocked youngsters, so he just ploughed on explaining how things were going to work, talking about how I'd have to come and live in the Potteries in digs provided by the club… train, listen and learn. He never actually mentioned money at first, leaving that to the very end of his spiel.

'The contract is for a year and we'll give you a £20 signing on fee and £10 a week,' he said.

My mouth fell open.

£10 a week!

To me, this was a huge amount of money, three or four times the amount I'd ever earned before. I thought I was a millionaire!

I couldn't sign my contract fast enough. It was enough for me just to be a professional footballer. That was the main thing. But the money was a lot… well, to me anyway.

Back then, there was this strange situation in football whereby there was a nationwide salary cap, so even the top England internationals would only be getting £20 a week. This had the sporting advantage of making it a level playing field as clubs couldn't offer whatever wages they wanted to attract the best players like they can now. So, I was going to be earning half the salary of players like Stan Matthews, Nat Lofthouse, Billy Wright and Tom Finney.

That cap was only lifted in 1961 when my future teammate George Eastham took Newcastle United to court to be released from his contract and established the basic premise that players could be paid what a club thought they were worth, which has led to the modern day players' salary scenario we're all so used to now.

My old man was over the moon when I got home and told him. Somehow the news made it into the local paper. I don't know how it got in there, although

I suspect Reg Savage was ensuring people knew he'd got another one of his lads a professional contract.

I went to sleep that night knowing that my dreams… my completely unrealistic, fly-by-night dreams, had actually come true.

SO, BY NOVEMBER 1958, a couple of weeks after turning 19, I found myself back in Stoke-on-Trent again, but this time, suitcase in hand, for at least a year. That was as far ahead as I could think; partly because, as any 19-year-old, I couldn't conceive of a much longer timescale than that, but also partly because, under the 'Retain and Transfer' system in operation in conjunction with that salary cap back then, all players' contracts were only for a year. No one had job security, the theory being that we would play all the harder to keep our contract and be retained for the following season.

Yet, here I still am… in the Potteries well over 60 years later!

I hadn't got a lot of stuff to bring with me from Eccles, and I headed for my new life in Stoke knowing that the hard work was just about to start. When I arrived back at the Victoria Ground I went in to the office and the lady there explained to me where to go to get to my digs, which were just around the corner. So, I went and knocked on this door of a little terraced house a few hundred yards from the Victoria Ground and a young lad, maybe around 12 or 13 years old, came to answer.

'Hi there, are your mum or your dad in?' I asked him.

Before I knew it, this lady came to greet me, saying, 'Yes, Mr Skeels. We were expecting you'. She made me feel so welcome, gave me a key so I could come and go as I pleased and explained to me how meals would be working; they provided breakfast and evening meal, then I could do what I wanted for lunch. I remember unpacking my few things and sitting on the bed taking in what had happened. As far as I was concerned, it was heaven.

Then her husband came home from work and I met him and struck up a rapport with the family, spending hours talking about football with him in the coming months.

I'm afraid my memory has failed me as to what their names were, but they were a home from home for me and I will always be grateful to them for putting me up for what turned out to be more than two years. They were fantastic with me. The club was paying them to keep me well fed and put a roof over my head, and I felt settled immediately.

One thing I do remember is that, although the mother was a housewife, she also did a bit of part-time work at a cake shop up the road and she always seemed to be coming back with cakes, which I was very happy to help her son demolish. Diet and nutrition wasn't exactly top of the agenda for young sportsmen back in the late 50s!

There was no canteen or café at Stoke in those days, so we had to fend for ourselves in terms of getting some lunch. There was a sports club across the way with local people drinking in it which sold sandwiches, or there was a local chippie where we could get some chips. I mean how old-fashioned is that... chips after training?

Sometimes, we'd then have to train in the afternoon... with a belly full of chips.

I also remember there were times over the next two seasons when we sat in the cafe near the Victoria Ground eating a meat and potato pie, before playing in the reserves. That felt very comforting that did, as it was just like those school lunchtimes when I'd scran a pie and then charge around playing football with my mates.

I WAS VERY quiet and kept myself to myself mostly to start with, but over those first few weeks I began to get to know other teammates and some other people around Stoke who began to recognise me, which was lovely. The people of Stoke-on-Trent proved to be very supportive and kind, and that's a big reason why I still live here in the Potteries all these years later.

I immediately felt at home in the city, which was a little difficult to get to know as it is a very disparate place, with some areas feeling completely separate to others. But the red brick factories and potbanks felt familiar as they were like the area of Eccles I had grown up in and there was a sense of urban industry, workers busying themselves and the bustle of everyday life.

The thing I noticed immediately was that Potters have got a very different sort of talking thing going on. I'd be listening to them and they'd say something like... 'Skeelsy... why dids't tha not kick that bow away?'

And I'm thinking, *Bow*? What are they on about?

Turns out that's the Potteries word for ball.

It's amazing to me that we have all these regional dialects and accents in this country where people use completely different words or even say the same words differently to mean completely different things in a different way. At the club we had plenty of Scots which was sometimes a tricky accent to understand and I remember when Jimmy McIlroy signed for Stoke, he had a completely different accent again being from Northern Ireland.

The Potteries dialect can be particularly strange and even now I sometimes have to ask my missus what she means when she says a particular word, so I'm still learning. I'd found the same in Birmingham with the way the Brummies talked. I'd think I was a foreigner at times as I just had no idea what people were saying to start with, but my ear attuned and the same was true in Stoke when I got used to the dialect and their way of referring to everyone as 'Youth' or 'Duck' as general terms of endearment. I thought it was great and quickly learned to say 'Ta duck', having picked up the Potteries vernacular.

Potteries folk also had a passion for sport and people would talk with me about football everywhere I went, which was great. I began to fall in love with the place. It has treated me well over the years. I think my Lowry-esque childhood in Salford also meant I got on well with the glowering Potteries smog created by the potbanks all over the city and the smoke they belched out. The Clean Air Act, the first attempt to control smoke emissions to improve the health of those of us who lived in industrial cities, may have been passed a few years earlier in 1956, but it was taking a while to reach Stoke-on-Trent.

I REMEMBER MY first day at work clearly.

I had some breakfast at my digs, then walked over to the Vic, this young lad going into a new, exciting job and finding out who was who.

The first person who greeted me when I got to the dressing-room was Frankie Mountford. Frank was the reserve team coach and was a bit of a legend at Stoke City, having played in the great side which had come so close to winning the First Division championship title in 1946/47. He had originally been a free-scoring centre-forward as a youth at Stoke, but then converted to become a centre-half and half-back, telling everyone that he preferred kicking people as a defender to being kicked as a striker. He had only just retired, aged 36, in the summer of 1958 and been given this first coaching job, so was also finding his feet.

I remember Frank took me into the changing rooms and showed me around, giving me my kit... shirt, shorts, socks. Then Tony Waddington popped in to welcome me and told me to listen to Frank, who explained the routine to me... training started at 10 in the morning, so I had to arrive bit earlier to get changed. We then went over to the A team pitch on the far side of the training ground at the back of the stadium.

I enjoyed that first session, then I remember going back to get clean as the mud on those pitches was always thick and claggy in the autumn and winter. The changing rooms had this massive bath downstairs in a sort of dank cellar, which the staff would fill up with scalding water before we came in, resulting in the room being full of fumes at times. If it was too hot to get into, you'd just get a bucket of cold water and chuck it in. It was a very old-fashioned way of bathing, as everyone would get in the same bath together and then the joking would start. Lads would be jumping in, splashing, taking the mickey.

Initially, as I didn't know anyone, I just crept in the corner, had a wash and then got straight out, but I soon got dragged into the fun. One thing I soon learned was that the water in that bath was only changed once a week, so you can imagine the colour of it some days.

Then came a truly magical moment.

I'd worn my battered old boots that my dad had got from somewhere for that first training session, but after I'd got changed, Frank Mountford pulled me to one side. 'Go to this sports store in Stoke,' he told me. 'Tell them you are Eric Skeels from Stoke City... and pick two pairs of football boots. They will fit them for you.'

Wow, my first, very own, made-to-measure pair of professional football boots and my first pair that would be bought new, not hand-me-downs or a pair with nails for studs.

I went to the shop and introduced myself, and had these beautiful boots fitted. You'll see them in a photograph. The gentleman who served me helped me get just the right size, slightly small initially, so they were nice and tight but would relax and loosen on my feet as I wore them. They were perfect and I kept them so clean, always working on them throughout my career... whatever boots I had. I always had one pair of boots for matchdays – as best – and one for training. The only times you'd have pumps on would be in the gym and when sprinting round the ground.

Boots would develop through the course of my career as leather technology and different types of studs were introduced. Originally, we used to nail the studs into the boots, which was pretty crude and often meant studs were dangerous. Then screw studs came along which meant you could change them between short ones, at half an inch through an inch, to the longest being an inch and a half, which you'd really need on a very wet pitch like at the Victoria Ground. Of course, when you came out of the dressing-room and into the corridor you had to watch where you were walking with studs that length, because you could easily slip over and do yourself a mischief.

Mind you, solid boots like that were needed in those days because the footballs we played with were those big heavy balls with an inflated bladder in them, then tied with the lace on the top? It hurt a lot and could cut your forehead when you headed that lace, so you'd be saying to anyone who crossed it, 'Listen, when you cross that ball, make sure that when I head it… the bloody lace is away from my face'.

They would also get sodden and weigh an absolute tonne as the leather soaked up the water. When you see the balls professionals play with now, they are chalk and cheese compared to those old balls. I mean, Gordon Banks, on a wet surface, from a dead ball kick, with one of those balls… he couldn't kick it over the halfway line, even with a good kick. Now they can kick it into the other penalty area. Asmir Begovic even scored from 92 metres for Stoke against Southampton in November 2013.

Not only that, but the kit we wore was very thick and heavy at the start of my career, although the material gradually got lighter through to the mid-70s when shirts were made of much more breathable fabrics and you felt like you could run all day because it was so light compared to the heavy material which soaked all the moisture up in the late-50s and early-60s.

We didn't even have kits to change into at half-time back then either, so if we got covered with mud or soaked through in the first-half we had to stay wearing the same kit.

So, there I was with my sparkling new boots. As I lay in my bed that first night, I realised I was still recovering from the shock of being a professional footballer and getting paid for it.

If this was going to be my life, I was deliriously happy.

I SETTLED INTO my new life really well and soon my weekly routine was in place.

Play a game on a Saturday.

Sunday and Monday off.

Tuesday and Wednesday were heavy training days.

Thursday and Friday would be lighter, with a few sprints and exercises, then into the gym for a five-a-side, circuits or over the back pitch for a full practice game. We'd sometimes play attack versus defence. There would also be some tactics and, finally, the three teams – A Team, reserves and first team – being revealed by the manager.

Despite the new-found freedom with having my own key and the temptation that may have put in my way, I didn't stay out late. I was getting home early so I could sleep and be ready for training the next day. I was on my best behaviour and did any job the club wanted me to do, a bit like at the cotton mill, although I was desperate not to have to return there.

One of my duties as a newcomer was that I used to put the training kit out for the first team, then pick up all their dirty gear and towels after they had finished. Because of this, I began to get to know a few of them as I'd be hanging around making sure everything was perfect as the early arrivers began to come in and get changed ready for training. I struck up a few conversations and, occasionally, some of the senior players would ask a few of us youngsters to go out with them and do some ball skills practice, which was great.

I didn't really know any of the Stoke players when I first arrived. Not only in the sense that I hadn't met them, but the first team wasn't exactly full of household names… even in Stoke-on-Trent. The club had been in the doldrums since relegation from the First Division in 1953 and was now in its sixth season of trying to win promotion. Amongst the better-known first-teamers was Dennis Wilshaw, a former England international, who had famously scored four goals against Scotland at Wembley in 1955 in a 7-2 thrashing. But I wasn't going to be mixing with the likes of them to begin with, apart from those occasional kickabouts.

I was thrown into the A team and then, after just a handful of games, promoted into the reserves where I got to know some of my teammates very well.

I gradually got to know people as I understood that was an important part of being integrated into my group, even though, in actual fact, I was also competing with them to progress from the A team into the reserves, and then into the first team. I found it easy settling in, despite me being naturally quiet, and I began to make a few friends. At that time there were also players like Peter Bullock, Alan Philpott, Alan Bloor and Mickey Bernard coming through. Later the likes of Denis Smith, Mike Pejic and Jackie Marsh came through the same route. It was a very productive one for Stoke and I'm so pleased that the new version of youth development, Stoke City's Academy, which feeds players through into the under-23s under Kevin Russell, has begun to bear fruit at the club in the modern era. Seeing the likes of Joe Bursik and D'Margio Wright-Phillips make it into the first team, plus youngsters Harry Souttar and Tyrese Campbell work their way into the squad and become key players after joining at under-18s level, as I did, is very satisfying.

My biggest buddy was a gruff Scotsman called Ron Wilson, who progressed with me from the A team into the reserves. We played a lot together. Ron was only 16 and was in the same boat as me as he'd signed just the month before, moving down from Scotland, having played for Musselburgh Athletic, which is where he was spotted. Ron was a left-back, tough as old boots, despite his youth. We got on famously.

He had worked down a mine before being spotted, so a bit like me he was of working class stock and football was his escape from that life, as it was mine from cotton mills and manual labour. We knew we had to take our chance with both hands. Ron was in digs over towards Fenton way, but we'd meet up after training and he'd take me to the places he'd already found or been shown; the most important of which was a cafe in the middle of Stoke called Ma's cafe.

It became the hub of our social life, where we'd go to meet the gang. We did have a lot of fun together as mates, as well as on the pitch as teammates, and then as people in Stoke got to know us we'd get approached at Ma's café with people wanting to talk about football, and ask how we were getting on, when we'd be in the first team, all that kind of stuff.

Occasionally, some of the senior players would come into Ma's to have a cup with us, so that's how I became friendly with Bill Asprey, the right-back and sometime right-half. It helped that Bill had just moved to live near Manchester and so he offered to give me lifts home after the game on a Saturday. He'd drop me off at a bus station near where he lived so I could catch a bus across to Eccles.

Scots' midfielder Bobby Howitt was a nice bloke as well. He lived out towards Endon and I used to babysit for him if he and his wife wanted to go to the theatre or for a drink. I'd get the bus over there and found that I really enjoyed looking after his kids.

Forward Don Ratcliffe also got me to babysit for him, so, once this started happening, my first actual nickname, before Alfie stuck because of my dog, was in fact 'The Babysitter'. Not in reference to me looking after opposition players in my defensive role in the team, but because I actually babysat for the older players who had kids. Not exactly what young Premier League stars might end up doing these days, is it?

Once they had a cup of tea with you, the first team players would mostly just go their way as they were either courting or married, so they had their own lives to lead once the football was finished. You'd be left to fend for yourself then. So we did.

Not far from Ma's café, up some stairs, was a snooker hall. Sometimes we'd go up there and play a few frames. I got to really like snooker and am still fairly good at it. It helped me get to know other people away from football and I still keep that up. Even today, I go and play snooker every Friday night for about three hours at the snooker hall in Hanley without fail with my neighbour Norman Taylor, who lives opposite me. Before the pandemic there would be a couple of others who came too, but they have drifted away because of Covid-19 and have not yet returned. Norman keeps me active as he's a bit younger, being in his mid-sixties, and we walk together and have an occasional drink. He's great at keeping my spirits up is Norman and is very good company.

Ron Wilson wasn't a flash harry and he didn't chase the girls, but he did like to have some fun. He and another young lad who had already got into the first team, left-back Tony Allen, who often joined us in Ma's cafe and would stay around because he was our age, said they'd take me dancing at the Crystal Ballroom night club in Newcastle-under-Lyme. But before that, they told me in no uncertain terms that I needed some new clothes.

And they were right! Because, when alls you've had in childhood is second-hand clothes your dad has found in Eccles, now I had got a few bob I wanted to spend it on looking good. Although across the way from Ma's cafe there was a suits shop, which was the only place I'd spied so far that I might spend some of my early wage packets, Ron and Tony knew better. This led to my first seminal Potteries experience of going Up 'anley (that's Hanley, the commercial centre of the Potteries, for the non-converted). We'd get on the bus, go up Hanley and walk round there looking in the shop windows, as they had a Lewis's and Burton's, all those sort of shops, plus an arcade which you could just wander through and look at clothes.

I tried quite a lot on and spent some money smartening up. That felt so good. It was probably actually only about a fiver all told that first time, but I came to really like my clothes and would enjoy going out to get a new shirt or pair of trousers, becoming something of a follower of fashion.

I mean, £10 a week, less tax and insurance, was a quite a lot of money in them days. My digs, including all my food, cost £3.50 so I had quite a few quid left, although I always kept my lifestyle very low key, as even with that princely basic wage of £10 a week I had to count my pennies most months to start with. I wasn't a huge drinker because I was taking my opportunity to become a professional athlete very seriously, and anyway a pint of lager might have only been a couple of shillings back then.

Initially, I also shelled out for my train and bus fare home to Eccles and when I got there I gave the old man a few bob, as I could spare some, but soon I was getting lifts with Bill Asprey and later Dennis Viollet when I wanted to go home. Eventually, though, I stopped going back as my life revolved around the club and the Potteries.

THIS MAY SEEM slightly odd to hardened Stoke City fans, but I also got very friendly with some Port Vale players. Stan Steele was a good mate of mine. He was, like me, a player who could score goals from inside-forward or fill in at half-back. When I met him he'd just finished the 1957/58 season as Vale's top scorer in the Third Division (North) with 22 goals in 49 appearances over the season, and then smashed another 22 goals in 47 games as Vale, under manager Norman Low, won the inaugural Fourth Division title, scoring 110 goals over the campaign.

Stan and I got on really well, despite him being nearly three years older than me, and once a week or so we'd meet up to have a walk and chat. Or if I didn't have a game, but he did, I'd go up and watch him in the first team

I got to know Stan because he would come and watch Vale's reserves when they played us and then we just got talking football, and then, when I told him I came from Manchester, he said, 'Well, I'm from Stoke-on-Trent… I'll show you around'. I suppose, being a bit older than me, he was being a bit fatherly, If you like. We hit it off, despite playing for rival clubs. Most of the senior players at Stoke had been transferred in and, in any case, they were married, and weren't around in the evenings to knock around with. Stan, instead, showed me around the Potteries, explaining to me what was where and the history of the place. I'd even go into Vale's social club with him, which might seem odd, but I was always made welcome because I was with him.

I soon realised, though, that Stan was a bit of a womaniser, which wasn't really my scene. He had a reputation, let's put it that way. We did knock around with a couple of girls at times, going out on joint dates together to the pictures or whatever. But I didn't always need company. I'd sometimes go to the pictures on my own at night time. Remember people, especially working class people like those who put me up, didn't have TVs in their houses back then, so I had to go to the cinema to watch anything at all, including newsreels. I wouldn't go to the pub on my own, though. I'd draw the line at that.

So it would be with Ron, Tony and maybe Stan that I would head out for a bit of socialising. Life was fun and we got into a routine and as part of that routine, Wednesday night was the last night in the week we'd be allowed to go out before preparing for the game on the Saturday. Often that meant we wanted to make a bit of a night of it and we'd head over to the Crystal Ballroom in Newcastle, as it gave me a chance to wear my new outfits I'd purchased.

You had to wear a tie to get into the Crystal, and I remember the pub opposite used to do a roaring trade in hiring out ties to lads who were only wearing open-necked shirts. I think that was the Crystal Ballroom management's way of attempting to keep the riff-raff out. I also heard that they sometimes asked you for your birth certificate, as you had to be 20 to get in, and the rumour went round that it was easier to get into the military academy at Sandhurst than the Crystal. Once in, there was live music, often from swing bands and the like, then later bands of the 1960s, and it was open on a Wednesday night to 2am, which made it a must for us young lads.

So, we'd head over to Newcastle and be found at the bar supping an expensive pint of lager, slowly, tapping our feet along to the rhythm of the music and trying to see if a young lady fancied having a dance. I have to admit, that being youngsters, we were also kind of hoping that our mild local fame as footballers might mean a young lady or two may recognise us, or at least think we were fairly athletic-looking and come and have a chat. I thought I looked pretty good as I'd got my best clobber on, having spent all that money and got myself a sharp haircut.

All too often, though, there proved to be no return.

Still, I wasn't that bothered really, as I had a fun time dancing with the occasional young lady. In all honesty, though, my focus was totally on making progress with my footballing career.

WHEN I JOINED Stoke, I was in initially in the A team, which was effectively the third team and I did pretty well, moving up into the reserves fairly swiftly. By the end of that first 1958/59 season, I was established in the reserves, playing in the Central League as an inside-forward and it was towards the end of that campaign that Tony Waddington, who was the first team coach but was in charge of the reserves, came to me to discuss a huge and career-changing transformation he wanted me to undergo.

Unbeknownst to me, Waddo had been thinking about how best to use me and he approached me at the end of one training session. 'Right, Eric… listen. I want you to play deeper in midfield and drop further back.'

'Why's that, gaffer?' I asked.

'I think you'll be better in midfield. Being fit, you can run all day, mopping up balls and passing it off straightaway.'

So, we began to practice that in the occasional Tuesday and Thursday afternoon training sessions and I became a defensive midfielder, and then, later, a defender. I really enjoyed it as I could really affect the games by, as the opposition won the ball off us and transitioned into attack, nipping in to win the ball back. I had good anticipation and had always been good at reading games. I was also quite swift and had a lot of energy, so could use that to win the ball, then take a player on and get past them before getting us going moving forward with a pass to the forwards or wingers. The really good thing was that as an inside-forward myself, I knew what pass I needed to give in order to be able to use the ball in an attacking sense, usually on the turn.

Once I'd done that, I'd move to be available whenever a teammate who had the ball got into trouble and needed a pass out. So I drifted around just behind the attack, offering myself to be available.

Of course, what Waddo didn't know was that as part of my footballing education in Eccles, I'd already played in many positions so this wasn't too much of a problem for me, and if he thought it would get me into the first team then I was very happy to oblige.

I loved it because I was involved in the game the whole time. I really enjoyed that, being active all the time with boundless energy. Initially, he moved me to right-half, but eventually I'd play more at left-half. My days as an inside-forward were over.

This change in my position was very similar to the conversion Frank Mountford had gone through in his career, although I think we were very different players and personalities. He was really able to help me with some pointers here and there, though, as to how to position myself.

Frank would always be the one who'd come and tell you what to do and what not to do. I got on with him famously because he was rough and ready, and very funny at times. He was a super bloke who looked after me. Anything I wasn't sure of, I could ask him and he'd sort it. Or he'd be the one to ask me to do something round the club, like getting balls out, cleaning boots, folding up kit, particularly when I was just starting out.

But he could be awkward with you if you'd done something he was unhappy with. Later, when he was first team coach in the 1960s and 70s, if he got a rollicking from Waddo, and if you'd done something wrong, you'd get it in the neck from Frank, which was fair enough.

That conversion proved to be my making, so I have Tony Waddington to thank for his vision in developing my career. Not only did I now have multiple strings to my bow, I was also at the head of the queue for a place in the first team if any of the half-backs, or what we now call midfielders, got injured.

I took to my new position like a duck to water, and before I knew it I was being asked to train with the first team, which was a huge boost. I was even chosen to travel with the first team for a week-long training camp in Bournemouth in early March 1959 ahead of the Second Division game at Bristol City. We travelled down to Dorset on the Tuesday ahead of the match at Ashton Gate on the

Saturday and did a lot of ball work and tactics. It was great to get to know players like skipper Ken Thomson, midfield dynamos Bobby Howitt, Bobby Cairns and striker Johnny King. However, it was my fellow reserve team colleague Tony Bentley who got his chance in that game, playing on the right-wing. I would have to wait my turn.

Had there been substitutes back in those days, I'm sure I would have been on the bench. It's notable that that group was selected and led by Tony Waddington ahead of manager Taylor joining us for the league game on the Saturday at Ashton Gate. I held my breath while the team was announced, but I wasn't in it. As it turned out, I still had another year to wait before gaining my first team bow.

I WASN'T THE only youngster knocking on the door of the first team at that point. Another player who seemed destined to make his mark at Stoke was an exciting young striker called John Anderson. He got his opportunity slightly before me, but as a right-winger in place of Tim Coleman, rather than at his better position of inside-right, and it never quite worked out for him. John was another one of the Scots clan at Stoke, hailing from Renfrew, and from 1958 to '60 he also had to contend with doing his national service, which I didn't, being stationed in Oswestry. Unfortunately, in 1959 he had a cartilage removed and he never really seemed to fully recover from that set-back.

The same was true of England youth international Peter Bullock, who had earned the accolade of Stoke's youngest ever player when making his debut in April 1958, aged just 16 years and 163 days. But that same summer of 1959 saw Bullock crack his shin bone, for a second time, on an end of season tour of Morocco. He would miss the entire 1959/60 campaign and, like Anderson, was never really the same player, moving to Birmingham in 1962 for £10,000. It was great to see Bullock's record as the youngest ever Stoke player taken by Emre Tezgel early in 2022 when the young striker came on in a couple of FA Cup ties at the Bet365 Stadium, beating Peter by 41 days. He is certainly one for the future.

Seeing Emre take to the pitch for that historic moment against Leyton Orient, it made me cast my mind back to the day I thought I was going to make my first team debut, but didn't!

I'll always remember it... October 1959, just before my 20th birthday, and

Don Ratcliffe, who had been playing at left-half, had a sore heel and all through the week the coaches were saying he wasn't going to be fit. I'd done well in a friendly victory over Port Vale on the Wednesday and, given how well things had gone for me, I thought I'd be playing in the next league game at Plymouth on the Saturday. I really got excited when I was actually named in the team by Frank Taylor and didn't think anything of the fact that Don travelled with us down to Devon the day before the game, as I thought he was just going to be watching the game. And I knew he'd be back in the team when he was fit again.

But then, on the Saturday morning, Don recovered miraculously and declared himself fit, so he was selected and I didn't get to play. All that preparation and angst for nothing! Thanks Ratter!

The team won 3-2 at Home Park in a clash between two of the early season frontrunners and my chance had gone. As the team kept doing reasonably well, I didn't get another look in until it all started to fall apart later in the campaign.

The 1959/60 season for Stoke had started brilliantly and after the turn of the year, as the 60s dawned, we sat sixth in the Second Division table. As the team was playing well, I wasn't in the mix for my debut, until that is, the wheels came off when the team lost 13 of the final 16 games in a disastrous end to the season.

In the summer of 1959 Stoke had spent £15,000 on Burnley winger Doug Newlands, which was a huge fee for the club to fork out at that time and completely at odds with the policy of not spending which had been in place, so was a massive risk. The plan was to have Newlands on one wing and Cunliffe on the other creating chances for strikers Dennis Wilshaw and Johnny King, as well as scoring goals themselves.

It worked in the first half of the season, with Newlands scoring on his debut in the first game, a 3-1 victory over Sunderland. He actually scored eight goals in his first 19 games, but after a 4-0 thrashing of Portsmouth on January 2, 1960, Stoke won just three games in the second half of the season as the team fell apart a bit. Newlands never scored again for Stoke and was dropped after a woeful home defeat to Scunthorpe in March, before being released on a free transfer at the end of the season, which was a huge admission of a mistake. I didn't get to know Doug that much as he was gone just as I was getting onto the fringes of the first team, but I always got the impression he didn't go out of his way to make friends, which can't have helped.

This was actually a hugely transitional period for the club as, until Newlands' arrival, manager Frank Taylor hadn't been able to pay a fee for any signings for some time due to the cost of rebuilding the main stand on the Boothen Road side of the ground. Consequently, he had to get through with swap deals and bringing youngsters like me through. There was a huge changing of the guard during those first couple of seasons I was at the club as older players such as Frank Bowyer, Harry Oscroft, John Sellars, John McCue and Neville 'Tim' Coleman either moved on or retired. In Oscroft's case he was swapped with Port Vale's experienced winger John Cunliffe, with my friend and fellow reserve-teamer Peter Ford also going to Vale Park as part of that deal. We'd keep in touch over the coming years, as he was now a teammate of Stan Steele.

Of course, Frank Mountford had also just retired, so it really was out with the old and in with the new. As the season drew to a fairly drab close, the manager swapped around about half the team, giving debuts to left-winger Jimmy Wallace, half-back Bert Rayner, right-back Denis Wilson and also Ron Wilson at left-back, promoting them all from the reserves. Taylor was trying everything in a turbulent period. Thankfully, as Taylor tried and *tried* to find a blend of players to get him some results, that eventually meant me because, as ever in football, my opportunity arrived as misfortune befell others.

IN MID-MARCH THE team was on a woeful run in which they had lost six of the last eight games to completely fall out of contention for promotion yet again; something that had been a recurring theme in the past few years. Not only that, but the previous weekend's game had seen them get thrashed 1-5 at Liverpool, so changes were inevitable, although there were also several players injured after Anfield.

While all of this was going on, I kept doing my thing in training and in the reserves, trying to catch the manager's eye. I remember thinking I must be in the mix for selection given how badly things were going and then, one Friday in March 1960, I heard a whisper that centre-half Ron Andrew was injured with a broken rib, while Bobby Howitt had injured his leg up at Anfield... and Bobby Cairns was already out with a knee ligament injury. I was sure I'd be in with a shout of playing the following day at home in the Victoria Ground against Charlton Athletic, so, I was taking training even more seriously that day.

At the end of the session, when Frank Taylor announced the team, Ron Andrew was indeed unfit and Bill Asprey moved across to play centre-half and I was in at right-half in Bill's place.

I always thought that came through Tony Waddington's recommendation. I never really got to know manager Frank Taylor at all. It seemed to me that Tony Waddington was the one who did all the talking with the players, often putting his arm round you to explain what he wanted you to do, while Taylor was much more stand-offish... schoolmaster-ish if you like. He didn't Eff and Jeff, or anything like that, whereas Tony was like a man's man, so we could talk to him. Taylor was the type of manager who stayed in the office and expected information to be brought to him by the coaches. You saw him wandering around at times, but nothing more.

Taylor never once talked to me about tactics, even when he picked me, although at that point I was just so excited and determined to be selected I didn't really care. I'd been playing this new role for months now and knew what to do.

But I wasn't going to be the only debutant that day.

Taylor also had huge problems in goal, using four goalkeepers across the season. I always think that any club which has a goalkeeping crisis has a problem with a destabilised team. When Tony Waddington became manager he moved quickly to always have a great goalkeeper, like Jimmy O'Neill, Harry Gregg, Peter Shilton, John Farmer and, of course, Gordon Banks... the greatest of them all.

We always felt safe and secure with those custodians behind us, although Banksy was, in my opinion, by far and away the best and we never quite recovered from losing him in that car crash in 1972.

But, in March 1960, things weren't going well on the 'keeper front for Stoke. Veteran Bill Robertson, a former Chelsea and Birmingham City player, was very tall, but quite skinny. He was about to turn 36 and was coming to the end of his career, having racked up the most appearances for Stoke as a goalkeeper at that stage with 250, a record later broken by Peter Fox. For me, Bill didn't dominate his area at all and Frank Taylor lost patience with him after a poor performance in a 4-4 draw at Cardiff in November 1959. He never played for Stoke again and retired at the end of the season, to keep a newsagent's out in Bucknell in Shropshire.

Next to be tried was Wilf Hall, who had been Robertson's understudy for six years, but he had also been dropped after a poor display, this time in a 2-5 defeat by Middlesbrough. Wilf was quite a big bloke, as befits a goalkeeper and you could have a joke with him. He knew the city and helped me out getting to know the place a bit when I first arrived, as he was the reserve team 'keeper more often than not.

Geoff Hickson, who was the same age as me, was then given his chance. He came from Crewe, which is where Tony Waddington lived, and had been an amateur at Coventry, Liverpool and Blackburn before joining Stoke. At just 19-years-old, Geoff was too quiet to be a 'keeper, really. Although he was a good shot-stopper, he didn't dominate his area enough. He was the unlucky 'keeper to be between the sticks for that Liverpool thrashing. After that, he would only ever play once more for the club, remarkably a year or so later on the final day of the 1960/61 season against Liverpool, when we beat them 3-1. That must have been sweet revenge for him before he moved to his hometown club Crewe Alexandra on a free transfer.

So, after three goalkeepers had been discarded, we wondered what Frank Taylor would do next. He was often absent on matchdays, which I always thought was strange, as he'd be watching players he was considering signing. Little did we know that his solution to this goalkeeping conundrum was going to be one of his strangest signings yet, and perhaps most desperate given the way the club was going.

This was former Liverpool keeper Tommy Younger, a Scottish international who had won 24 caps whilst at Hibernian and then Anfield, who signed from Falkirk on a free transfer. There was nothing strange in Stoke signing a Scot you might think, far from it. But there was in signing a manager of another club!

Slightly oddly, Tommy, despite being only 30, was actually player-manager at Falkirk.

Even more oddly, Tommy had just publicly announced he was retiring from playing due to a back injury in order to concentrate on management.

The really odd thing was that Younger wasn't even in Stoke-on-Trent the day before the game, so Geoff Hickson was actually announced in the team as it didn't seem as if Younger would make it to Stoke on time.

It really seemed Taylor was desperately reacting to that thrashing at Anfield the week before.

As well as an uncertain goalkeeping situation and the half-back line being completely altered, the defence was also completely rejigged because of injury, not only to Ron Andrew, but also a thigh injury to established left-back Tony Allen. So, the makeshift back four that day included another youngster, Denis Wilson, who I'd been playing in the reserves with a lot at right-back. He'd made half a dozen appearances across the season, but never held down a regular place. That was due to the other full-back that day, the remarkable and redoubtable John 'Jock' McCue.

McCue was a hard bugger, with a tough attitude, irrespective of whether you were an opponent or a teammate, and there was no messing with him. When he told you to do something, there was a glint in his eyes which made you think, *Okay, well, I'm not going to say no.* McCue was also experienced in every way you can be; in fact, my debut game was his 500th league match for Stoke, so I could hardly contradict him if I didn't agree with him, could I? I just listened to him and got on with it.

In training, he could get a bit nasty occasionally.

I remember him flattening me once and as I picked myself up, I said to him, 'Blimey Jock, how would you like it if I did that to you?'

'Go try it if you dare,' came the reply, as he fixed me with those staring, beady eyes he had.

Now he didn't scare me, like he did so many opponents over the years, earning the nickname 'Chopper' because he always ensured that any winger who beat him got flattened as he went past him with a kick to the ankles. But he did make me decide fairly swiftly that I was just going to let the matter drop.

Ironically, despite his nickname being 'Jock', McCue wasn't Scottish at all. He was from Stoke, hailing from Longton. I never did find out why he'd been nicknamed Jock all those years before, though.

Despite him nearing 38 years of age, as he was fairly two-footed Taylor had brought him back into the team to make him a regular right-back, despite him being a natural left-back, which is where he played that day in Tony's absence. This meant that I made my debut in the same team as the man whose club record for competitive appearances I would eventually take. Between us, we played for the club unbroken from 1940 to '76.

Jock played 542 competitive games for Stoke, but including his 133 wartime appearances he did actually play more games than I would eventually, so I do appreciate that my record of competitive appearances for the club is slightly misleading, and appreciate that it is only through a quirk of how the football authorities rated the standard of competition during the Second World War, that I hold the record.

I REMEMBER THE day of my debut.

March 12, 1960… and pulling on the red and white striped shirt with the No 4 on my back in the changing room as clear as day. Its previous occupant in that Liverpool debacle had been Bill Asprey, now moved to centre-half to replace the injured Ron Andrew, who was next to me pulling on the No 5 shirt.

The thing none of us could quite believe was that our new goalkeeper had actually travelled down on the overnight train from Scotland to Crewe and was getting changed with us. Tommy Younger had made it and surprised everyone by taking his place between the posts. So, not only was the Charlton game my debut, but it was also the first match for the new goalkeeper, who must have been feeling a little tired after his journey.

The game didn't go well.

We had a host of chances, yet somehow didn't score in the first-half, while Charlton's left-winger Johnny Summers smashed a wonderful cross-shot into the far corner to put the visitors in the lead after 14 minutes. He then extended the Addicks' lead on 58 minutes, rounding Younger after being put clean through.

Frank Bowyer got a neat goal back for us, but then a Summers corner, whipped into the near post, beat the defenders and goalkeeper on the line to give him a hat-trick and Charlton a 1-3 victory.

The game was played in front of the lowest crowd of the season to date of just 9,947. Attendances didn't get any better, slumping to just over 4,000 for a home defeat by Ipswich a couple of weeks later. The club was really struggling both on the pitch for results and off it in terms of finances. Apathy abounded, brought on by the terrible run since January. Meanwhile, I was delighted that I had clearly done enough on my debut to retain my place for the next game, away at Hull, the team rooted to the bottom of the division, but that proved to be an even worse experience as we got hammered 0-4. That was the end of my first chance at cementing a place in the senior team at Stoke.

I was dropped.

Following the return from injury of Bobby Cairns, Tony Allen and Ron Andrew, I went back to the reserves for the last few weeks of the season. I'd loved my initial taste of first team action, but I clearly wasn't quite ready yet, and neither were the team performing. In fact, those defeats, starting with the thrashing at Liverpool, developed into a run of 10 consecutive defeats, a dreadful club record. A final day 2-1 victory at Bristol City was no consolation and City finished 17th in the Second Division.

The end of that season was a disaster for some players. Tommy Younger lost nine of his 10 games and never played for the club again, returning to Scotland. Aside from his back injury, which I think did still affect him, the other problem was Younger's Scots accent. It was so thick it was hard to understand him. Even some of the Scottish lads in the squad struggled!

John McCue was moved on to Oldham Athletic, as he'd reached the end of a wonderful career as a great servant to Stoke City. Frank Bowyer retired, Doug Newlands was given a free transfer, despite £15,000 being spent on him just the previous summer, while long-serving skipper and long-serving centre-half Ken Thomson also left.

This brutal cull was not made by Frank Taylor as manager, however.

Football threw me another opportunity when, in June 1960, Stoke City, perhaps not surprisingly given that terrible run of form, sacked the manager and, instead of recruiting from elsewhere, went for an internal promotion, probably also to save money knowing the board at the time.

My mentor Tony Waddington was the new gaffer.

My luck was very much in.

My first action photograph, complete with my lovely new boots (top) and the Stoke City team with the Second Division Championship trophy from August 1963: Back row (from left to right) – Len Graham (Trainer), Eddie Clamp, Bill Asprey, Jimmy O'Neil, Tony Allen, Tony Waddington (Manager). Middle row – Stanley Matthews, Dennis Viollet, Eddie Stuart, Jackie Mudie, Jimmy McIlroy. Front row seated – Don Radcliffe and me.

*The magic of modern wizardry helped to move me to the left of the photo for the front cover of this book, so I'm seated at the feet of the great Stanley Matthews.

CHAPTER 4

Mr Dependable

TONY WADDINGTON HAD been an amateur at Manchester United during the Second World War, before serving in the Royal Navy. After playing for Crewe Alexandra for seven seasons, he had joined Stoke in 1952 as a coach and had done well enough to be promoted to assistant manager under Frank Taylor.

Frankly, he pretty much ran the club, apart from actually selecting the first team, so it made complete sense for the board to appoint him to the hotseat when Taylor was sacked. You could ask, why give him the job then when he was so intrinsically involved in the team's failure over the period following relegation from the First Division in 1953? But, in actual fact, I think Waddo had felt constricted by what Taylor wanted tactically and had maybe been privately lobbying the board to let him loose on building the team up because he could see that doing the manager's bidding wasn't working.

He was also the cheap option, I suppose, but my word, what a great appointment he proved to be for the club over the next 17 seasons.

He clearly felt I had something he liked as a footballer and I came more regularly into the first team picture under him in that first 1960/61 season. He was keen on promoting youth, as he had been doing lots of work with the younger players in the reserves, and the likes of myself, Tim Ward, Peter Bullock, Bill Bentley, John Anderson, Ron Wilson, Denis Wilson, Alan Philpott and an exciting young winger called Gerry Bridgwood were all given chances by the new manager.

Again, promoting youth was the cheap option as it meant paying no transfer fees and this was indicative of the parlous state that Stoke City's finances were in at that time. This was in part because of the extremely low crowds. Apathy had set in, as I've said, and income was vastly reduced. The club was under pressure as it had an overdraft of around £100,00, which was a huge amount of money at that time.

All of that combined to hand me my chance.

Waddo first selected me for the game at Charlton on September 3, 1960 and once he gave me that first start of the season, I didn't look back. Initially, he played me at right-half, moving Don Ratcliffe to inside-right, but I would soon be moved to left-half. Waddo decided to make that move in late October 1960, when the team had been well beaten at home by Ipswich Town under the management of Alf Ramsey, who would go on to win that division, the league title the following season, and then the World Cup with England in 1966.

We lost that game 2-4, and Waddo changed things around, moving me to the left-side of midfield and playing Bobby Howitt on the right, with the man to miss out being Bobby Cairns, who never played for the club again, as Waddo's clearout continued, leaving for non-league Macclesfield Town at the end of the season, aged 32.

Most left-sided players in those days would be left-footed, but I was right-footed. There was method to Waddo's decision though as, being good with both feet, I could turn inside and open out the whole of the rest of the pitch by playing across it, instead of always playing the ball out onto the left winger. I think the manager's vision was right because, having two options kept opposing teams guessing and meant all my attacking teammates were always in play. It also created space up front as Waddo liked his wingers to play wide, making the pitch bigger and if I got down the left side, because I was fairly two-footed, I could cross the ball with my left foot, rather than always have to cut back inside and then try and cross it with my right.

So, defenders couldn't anticipate what I was going to do all that easily which gave me an advantage. I was benefitting from all those hours spent kicking those old balls around the streets and against that wall opposite our house. That cemented my place in the side as results picked up a bit. I loved being involved in the first team and was determined to do everything I could to keep my place, so was very happy to adapt.

THE OTHER KEY aspect of my game which the new manager liked was that I was very dependable. He knew exactly what I was going to do and what he could get out of me. I always think that the far more talented players in our team, like Dennis Wilshaw, Jackie Mudie, or latterly Dennis Viollet or Jimmy McIlroy, could be a 10 out of 10 one week and maybe a 6 the next. I was always a 7, often an 8… averaging a 7.5 through consistency. Teams need that blend, that mix across the positions, with flair up front and dependability in defensive positions.

That versatility was also another of my best assets. It meant that if there were injuries in our fairly threadbare squad I could be relied upon to fill in anywhere throughout the team.

Whatever position I was selected in, I'd be able to fit into the team and I think that was my most valuable ability for Waddo. I was effectively four players wrapped up into one… defensive midfielder, full-back, centre-half… and dogsbody. I could do a job anywhere. Even if he put me on the left wing, which was hardly my position of choice, I'd give him a solid 7 performance.

Basically, though, Waddo turned me into a defender.

He didn't want me to go over the halfway line. He'd want me near the big centre-half to pick up the knockdowns when he challenged the opposition forward in the air. He also wanted me to cover the full-backs if they went forward, slotting in to stop a quick breakaway via the winger. In a way, I was quite like Glenn Whelan, if I'm thinking of a modern player Stoke fans could relate my role and my style to.

Because of that combination of dependability and versatility, from September 1960 I missed just 11 games in seven seasons, earning the nickname 'Mr Dependable'.

I played in both full-back positions and a lot at centre-half later in the 60s, but my preferred position was as a defensive midfielder. In any of those positions I had key attributes which stood me in good stead.

My timing and ability to read the game and anticipate was important. For example, in midfield I would anticipate the opposition wing-half who was looking to play a through ball and intercept it by reading the pass. I also often filled in at centre-half and would time my move to jump for a high ball for when their goalkeeper was punting it long towards the forward I was marking. Often the opposition striker would be a lot taller than me, but I'd drop off and then take a three or four-step run up and launch myself so that I was above him. As he'd have his back to me, he couldn't see what I was doing and I would be above him as he tried to jump, so would win the header every time.

I suppose you could say as a centre-half I was a bit like Marc Muniesa in that sense, the relatively small Spanish defender who was actually a very good footballer with lovely feet and great timing when he played at Stoke under Mark Hughes from 2013 to '17. He partnered the giant Ryan Shawcross as centre-half a lot of the time and made it look easy.

Unlike my shy social persona, I was also very vocal on the pitch, especially when talking to my teammates, and would constantly be telling them where to go and what to do. If one of them collected the ball and had an opponent bearing down on them, I'd shout 'mind your back', so they knew. I also took to ensuring we kept the ball by often playing the simple pass, the way I was facing when I first received the ball under pressure. That bought us time and made sure we didn't lose it in the last third of the pitch where the opposition could get at us quickly.

It was my job to always be available for a pass from anyone who had the ball under pressure and could be about to lose it, so I'd always be their 'out' ball. If I was being marked, though, I'd make sure they knew it if I wasn't on. My former teammates josh me now that actually I spent most of my career shouting 'not me' when they had the ball, so I could avoid receiving it under a challenge.

But that's not the way I remember it!

I was also a voracious tackler. I loved it.

I was always someone who went in one hundred percent. I don't mean dirty at all, but I knew that if I didn't commit fully to a challenge I'd be the one that got hurt. As a youngster, Frank Mountford taught me that, always encouraging me to 'go in one hundred percent... because if you don't and the other bloke does, you will be the one to get hurt'.

I can give you a very good example. Harry Burrows was a winger who played for Aston Villa in the early-to-mid-60s. Sometimes I'd get shifted out to right-back by Waddo to do a man marking job on someone like Harry, as he was a very dangerous player, who created a lot of chances for his forwards. Harry would often come at you with the ball at pace and knock it past you, then use his speed to get to it first, relying on you not being able to turn very quickly to keep up with him. I soon learned that if I crunched into a tackle with him early in the game to put my marker down, then that would keep him quiet.

As Harry also liked to hug the touchline, it meant that if I made a good connection with the ball and man, Harry would more than likely end up skidding across the red asphalt and go flying into the paddock, which was dug slightly below pitch level. I remember the first time I did this it was a 50/50 tackle and I took him out… fairly, with both of us ending up in the Boothen Stand paddock.

Once Burrows had extracted himself from amongst the Stoke fans down there and got back onto the pitch, he stopped trying to get past me and started crossing the ball from the halfway line at a much steeper angle, rather than getting to the byline to pull it back, which was much more dangerous. He didn't fancy a return visit.

The punchline is that Harry got so fed up with that experience in Villa's visits to Stoke and so acquainted with the fans in the paddock, that he opted to join Stoke City, signing in 1965 and enjoying eight seasons in the Potteries, and becoming a very good friend of mine to boot. We still see each other nowadays, and Harry blames me, and those visits to the paddock, for his dodgy knees!

FOOTBALL HAS GIVEN me everything. It was a great life, it really was, and I never wanted it to end.

That was always my big fear. Consequently, I was more than happy to play anywhere the manager asked me to. There was no problem for me. I loved all the different challenges of the differing positions I played and, in any case, causing a problem would only more than likely put Waddo's back up and make him less likely to pick me.

So, I always took the attitude, especially in the early days, that I would do whatever was asked of me as I never wanted to do anything that could put at risk my status as a professional footballer.

I also knew I was a young bloke that hadn't been worldly at all whilst growing up in Eccles and the people I was now mixing with at Stoke were often very different to those I'd grown up with. So, I just used to watch and listen and learn from them, not only about football, but also as a person. As I established myself in Tony Waddington's new look team I became part of a much more settled defensive unit, which had some great players and even bigger personalities in it.

Tony Allen had been in the team for some time as a classy left-back. We were a very similar age, despite him making the breakthrough earlier than me. He was good on the ball, with a great left foot, although his right was, admittedly, mostly for standing on, and he liked to slide passes into the forwards. He wasn't the fastest, but he rarely fouled anyone as he could read the game well, so could get up to his winger and get a tackle in, although he wasn't over rough at all.

Tony had made such an impression, despite playing in the Second Division at the start of his career, that he had won three England caps in the Autumn of 1959 when Walter Winterbottom tried some younger stars in an experimental few line-ups featuring the likes of Bobby Charlton, Jimmy Greaves and Brian Clough. He'd done well, but, as someone playing in the lower reaches of the Second Division, he was soon displaced by a First Division star, who turned out to be Ray Wilson, then of Huddersfield, and later of Everton, who would retain the place under Alf Ramsey and play in the victorious 1966 World Cup-winning team.

If Tony was injured, I'd play left-back to fill in, but we didn't really compete for the position. He was always first choice. We became good friends, training together, learning to work together as a unit and we forged a great friendship. Tony changed in the next cubicle to me in the dressing-room and we'd talk about the games and girls and whatever took our fancy, really. And, of course, it was he who introduced me to the Crystal ballroom in Newcastle.

Bill Asprey was a good mate of mine. He was a bit like my bodyguard at times and didn't mind flying into his winger to make an impression. He ended up playing at right-back, once I established myself in the team, as I'd often be right-half or, once I moved across to left-half, Bobby Howitt would play there. Bill was very tall for a right-back, but he was not only a good defender, he could also roam forward in attack and hit a ferocious shot. I remember one in particular he scored against Plymouth Argyle in December 1960 which flew in from the edge of the area, a bit like Ben Wilmott's goal against Preston in January 2022; a full-blooded drive that rose into the roof of the net.

Spectacular.

It sticks in my mind because it was in the very first minute of the game and, within two minutes, Plymouth's George Fincham had inadvertently bundled the ball into his own net in front of an unforgiving Boothen End to put us two up. Argyle capitulated after that awful start and we went on to record a club record margin of victory, 9-0, although there were only around 6,500 fans in the ground to see it, such was our poor form before that huge victory as we'd lost three and drawn one of the previous four home games.

Bill was a big man with a big personality, who ended up as Stoke coach and then manager in the mid-80s. He masterminded Stoke's incredible escape from relegation in the 1983/84 season, which saw Alan Hudson come back to the club and prompt the side to a run of 10 wins in the last 18 games to survive on the final day of the season by thrashing Wolves 4-0, with Paul Maguire scoring all four goals.

After the game apparently, Bill stood on the empty Boothen End soaking up the atmosphere of the now quiet ground and decided there and then to release four-goal hero Maguire on a free transfer. It seemed like a barmy decision when it was announced and Bill only lasted a few months more in the role, as Stoke started the 1984/85 season so badly he was sacked as the Potters slumped to the then worst season ever in the top flight of English football. It was a sad end for him as he'd been involved at the club for over 30 years.

Between the full-backs, centre-half Ron Andrew was actually a nice bloke. Despite being both a six-footer and very Scottish, he was a bit quieter than most of the team, more like me, and wasn't a shouter and screamer. Ron had his own life away from football and I had no idea what he was like outside the changing room. He wasn't a classy player, he just did his job, but I'd always say he'd be picked in my team every week, even though he wasn't often singled out in the papers. He was very dependable. Ron was one of Stoke's sizeable Scottish contingent which also included my mate Ron Wilson, Bobby Howitt and Bobby Cairns, amongst others.

One of them, big Ken Thomson, was the captain and the boss of the team when I first broke through. He was teak tough, tall and very, *very* Scottish. My word, he could give you a right dressing down. Let's just say I learned a few words from Ken. I felt like a schoolboy when I was near him as he reminded me of the personality of my dictatorial teacher.

At least Ken didn't cane my hand, although he wasn't beyond some punishments of a different kind.

I always remember one story Don Ratcliffe told me about how Ken would 'motivate' him to get up and get on with the game if he'd been flattened and wanted treatment. Ken had perfected the art of running over to a stricken player like Don, as if to see how he was and offer some sympathy for his plight, bending over to assist him. What was actually happening was Ken was using the opportunity to insert his finger up your backside!

That would get you up and running... Don always told me he soon learned to get up very smartly if he could see Ken running over.

Thomson actually left before the end of the 1959/60 season, so my only games with him were in the reserves when he was coming to the end of his career.

As I mentioned earlier, for me, a good goalkeeper is where a good defence starts and the key player Waddo signed that first summer of 1960, once he was given the manager's job, was Republic of Ireland international 'keeper Jimmy O'Neill. Jimmy gave us much-needed stability in goal, but he also had a sparkle in his eye and was a lot of fun. He had won the Second Division title with Everton in 1953/54 so was a quality player and was still only 29, which is no age for a goalie.

Jimmy signed for £5,000 and would be a key part of our improvement over the coming seasons, showing excellent shot-stopping acrobatics and he was very good at claiming crosses, which as a defender you always appreciate.

AS A MIDFIELDER at that time in my career, I played in the engine room alongside the experienced Bobby Howitt, who was also my roommate when we played away. He was quite a bit older than me and yet another Scot. Bobby was like a mentor to me on the pitch and would talk me through the games initially, helping my positioning.

It was great for me as a young player, as he'd guide me. I relied on him a lot and I think he came to know he could rely on me as well. I'd always say to him if he went forward to help the attack, I would stay to guard the breakaway and vice versa, and we developed a great understanding, which was probably why he trusted me to babysit his kids!

I played the entire 1961/62 and 1962/63 seasons at left-half, with Bobby holding down the right-half berth, which was fair enough. He was the club captain, after all.

The player who lost out because of my introduction to the team was yet another Scotsman, Bobby Cairns. He was a very small bloke, who had a very strong accent which meant I wasn't sure what he was saying sometimes, although once he was on the pitch I soon understood him because he only communicated in swear words. Bobby and I barely played together, though, as effectively I took his place and he moved on to non-league Macclesfield aged 32 in 1961.

There were a few other fringe players in the mix in that transitional time as Tony Waddington sought to blend youth with experience. Bill Bentley was a nice bloke who was on the fringes of the first team, but ended up moving to Port Vale, like Ron Wilson did. I still see Bill sometimes at Stoke games.

Left-winger Bobby Cunliffe was a cheeky little bugger, who actually looked it too. You would never see him without a wicked smirk on his face, as if he was up to no good, which he generally was. He was actually a decent player with a good left foot when he got round to remembering that he was there to play football. He was always fun to talk to at training and had this hilarious way of back-chatting by making comments while facing away from you, to make others laugh.

Bobby didn't last long under Waddo, though, being replaced on the wing by Mr Mischief himself, Don Ratcliffe, who had a permanent smile on his face and a wicked twinkle in his eye.

Don was a local lad from Newcastle-under-Lyme, who played at left-half alongside me at right-half when I first got into the team, so we were great pals as well as teammates. He was a very established first-teamer in the prime of his career, so, once Waddo switched me, as a youngster, to left-half, he moved Don to the wing to make the most of his legendary running abilities. It was off the pitch, though, that Don made the biggest impression on us all. He liked nothing more than to play tricks on you, especially us new lads who didn't know what on earth was going on.

That big bath in the changing room had two huge boards which came down to cover over the top of it when it was shut down. Don would often leap out first and pull the boards over you, trapping you in and then bugger off… so we would be stuck in there unable to push them off from underneath. He would be laughing all the while he was pranking you.

I can hear his voice even now, echoing through the room as we struggle to get those flaming boards off!

I remember once, he nailed the toilet door open so we couldn't close it and we had to go to the loo exposed to the entire squad. Or, when you were in the showers he'd do something daft like tip cold water over you, or steal your towel so that when you came out you were running around naked trying to find it. Then he'd tell you that he'd put the towel outside and when you went out into the corridor, he'd shut the door to the dressing-room so you couldn't get back in... and, of course, the towel wasn't out there so you were now naked in the corridor with, inevitably, one of the female office workers coming towards you. I can only assume they got as used to his pranks as we did.

Don was hilarious and completely daft and would regularly do things like hide your shorts on an actual matchday. He once tied my laces in knots just before a game. That amused me rather less as I tried to unravel them as the clock ticked towards our kick-off time of 3.15pm. I remember he also once swapped my shorts with Bill Asprey's, who was about six or seven inches taller than me with a significantly larger waistline!

Murder he was! But also a bundle of fun and a smashing lad. I got on great with him and, after Bobby Howitt left, Don became my roommate on away trips.

But he was also an incredible athlete and an amazing trainer... well, most of the time.

One of our major pre-season training routines was to run from the Victoria Ground over to Trentham, which is about three miles... and then run up and down the steep, sandy hills there, near the golf course. Our trainer Frank Mountford usually took no nonsense at all and would swear – a lot – if you annoyed him.

But somehow, Don had him round his little finger.

After we'd done all that sprinting up and down the hills and banks, Frank would say, 'Right, three times round the hill lads'... and off we'd go. But Don would get to the top of the hill for the first time and stop and lean against a tree. We'd go round twice more and he'd join in again on the third circuit. Unbelievable.

We then used to have to jog back to the ground those three miles or so, while Frank Mountford would drive back in a car. Where was Don Ratcliffe? Thumbing a lift from a lorry driver who would be heading that way. You'd often see his big smile as he waved at you from a cab as you trotted back.

'I'll see you in Ma's café!' he'd shout, as he passed by. 'I'll have my cuppa before you!'

Incredibly, no bugger said nothing, because Don was a regular first team player who did the business on the pitch week in, week out. So, they tolerated all these antics and let him get away with it. Not least because it made the drudgery of training, particularly in pre-season, which can be gruelling, far more entertaining.

Amazingly, despite all these avoidance tactics, Don was still fitter than most of us. In fact, he was one of the few in the squad who could out-run me. He *really* could run. Fans used to joke that he was the only player who could play a long pass down the wing and run fast enough to catch it up before it went out of play. Another time, I remember he was dribbling fast, head down, towards the corner flag and didn't seem to be aware that he was quickly running out of pitch, when some wag shouted loudly from the paddock... 'OPEN THE GATES!' Don might as well have just kept going out of the stadium and down Butler Street.

There was one person Don didn't get on with at Stoke City and that was the trainer Norman Tapken, who worked under Frank Taylor in the 50s. Tapken had taken a great dislike to Don from the first minute he joined the club as an apprentice, often telling him that, instead of cleaning his boots, he'd better keep shining his miner's lamp as that was all he was really good for, not playing football for Stoke.

Don hated Tapken for the abuse he got from him.

The first thing Tony Waddington did as manager when he took over in June 1960 was to sack Tapken and promote Frank Mountford, who he had been working with in the reserves. I remember Don getting this look on his face when he heard this news and he dashed out to find Tapken.

'WHO'S GOT TO CLEAN THEIR LAMP NOW?!' he roared into his face.

Well, Tapken chased Don up and down the stands to great hilarity for those of us who had come out to see what Don was up to.

He didn't catch him, though!

I WAS THE opposite to Don Ratcliffe in many ways, but, though dependable in most senses I may have been, the one thing the manager couldn't rely on me for was scoring goals, even though that had been my specialism as a young inside-forward at school.

Now I was mostly involved in stopping the opposition scoring them.

As Tony Waddington had converted me to play primarily as a defender, no one was more surprised than me when I did actually score my first professional goal away at Brighton and Hove Albion. I don't remember much about it, to be honest, which may surprise you, but the match report I have a clipping of says... *'The equaliser after 35 minutes also came from a cross on the right. Ratcliffe pulled the ball back, which was turned out to Skeels. Running in to the edge of the box, his first-time, oblique shot caught the defenders off balance and flashed low into the corner of the net.'*

Sounds like a belter of a strike!

I think that the reason I don't remember that one so much is that I recall my second goal at Derby County very clearly and, if I may say so, it was special.

Again, I had Don Ratcliffe to thank for supplying what these days would be called 'the assist'. He went on a long, mazy run diagonally from right to left across the pitch, crossing the halfway line, before turning the ball back to me just inside our half.

I picked it and started to move forwards.

I was looking to lay it off, but the Derby players had marked all my teammates and seemed to just forget about me. As I strode forward, there seemed to be a bit of a parting of the defence, with at least two defenders being drawn away by that diagonal run across my path by Don Ratcliffe to create space, leaving me with a clear shot. So, about 10 yards outside the area, I looked up and smashed it right-footed from about 30 yards out.

Right-footed… and it flew low… skimming past Ken Oxford in the Derby goal and in off the far post, rebounding satisfyingly into the opposite side of the net, bulging it outwards. I remember it so vividly.

I don't think I've ever hit a ball better before or since that moment.

As that was the first goal of the 1962/63 season, in which we ended up winning the Second Division title, I'm going to claim I kickstarted our promotion-winning campaign. More of that later.

I must have given the ball some welly because I really don't know how it went in, the pitch was that heavy. Heavy pitches, thick with mud, were commonplace back then. I remember when the goalkeepers at the Baseball Ground used to kick the ball up in the air, often it came right down and splashed into the mud, sticking exactly where it landed rather than bouncing up like you'd expect it to. If you don't believe me have a look at the YouTube highlights of Stoke's win at Derby in 1975, which shows how the ball was constantly getting stuck in the dreadful mud at their ground.

I actually enjoyed playing on those muddy pitches and, as I've said, I had the energy in my legs to make it through the sludge. It was one of the reasons Tony Waddington kept on selecting me. I eventually played in every outfield position, wearing shirt numbers 2-11 for Stoke. Following that 1960/61 season in which I played 37 games as the team finished 18th in the Second Division, just three points above the relegation zone, across the rest of the decade of the 60s I played over 450 games for Stoke. In the 1964/65 season I played all 42 league games, appearing in the 2, 3, 4, 6, 8, and 10 shirts... so I was more than half a team!

One side effect of being thought of as Mr Dependable that may surprise you to learn was that it actually made my anxiety worse. Because one thing that people don't know about me is that I am a massive worrier.

Massive.

Firstly, I was anxious about being selected in the team.

That was the biggest worry.

I found myself as a young player constantly competing with experienced men like Eddie Clamp, Eddie Stuart and the irrepressible Don Ratcliffe for a place in the side, then later with signings like Calvin Palmer, Maurice Setters, John Mahoney and Mike Bernard. As each new player, teammate and rival arrived, I was thinking, *Well, that's me out, then!*

But I always seemed to be in, because I was so versatile. I could turn my hand to many positions, whereas most of those players could only play one or two. In 1965/66, for example, I wore shirt number 2, 3, 4, 6 and 8 across the 41 of the 42 league games I played, never really settling into one position for more than two months, before having to be switched by the manager to cover for one injury or another.

Later, during the epic cup runs of 1970 to '72, I wore every outfield shirt number except 9 and 11, even managing a number 14 as there were two substitutes allowed in the Anglo-Italian Cup in June 1972. Talk about adaptable! I suppose I was Tony Waddington's dream player in that sense.

So, I kept my place, irrespective of who Waddo brought in. I think he liked to keep me on my toes, keeping me competitive not only with the opposition, but within the squad. It worked. I had this inner determination and steel not to lose my place. I believe my gritty, northern, urban upbringing came through for me time and time again.

But then, once selected, different anxieties kicked in. The night before a game I would settle down into bed, but then start thinking about who I had to play against. If it was Manchester United, for example, I would start thinking about...

Best, Law… Charlton. It was frightening sometimes.

And that was just when I was tucked up in my pyjamas.

What made it worse for me was that, after a night fretting about one opponent, Waddo would come along the next morning and say something like, 'I want you in at right-back today, Eric.' So, consequently, I didn't even know for sure where I was going to be playing or who against. I was such a worrier that, instead of me thinking that as I didn't know and couldn't work out who I'd be up against as it would be pointless worrying about it, I'd lie there thinking of all of the possibilities, multiplying my anxieties ten-fold.

I would often get nervous in the dressing-room as well, hearing the hubbub of the crowd outside and the noise inside the stadium as the crowd built up, especially later in the 60s when we were in the First Division playing in front of some big crowds. As we warmed up in the crowded changing space, I'd often pop into the toilet, a jangling bag of nerves

From our dressing-room, you could stand on the bench and peer through this little window to see the crowd and, if it was a big game, against a team like Manchester United or Liverpool or Leeds, until we got onto the pitch I'd be fretting away, while others chewed on gum or tied and retied their laces to deal with the nerves.

Once I stepped across that white touchline and onto the pitch, though, all those nerves melted away and I could concentrate on the game without any problem. It was a strange thing. You'd think it would be worse when you were on the pitch with supporters shouting and screaming at you, but I found the anticipation far worse than the actual playing of the games.

GIVEN THAT I seemed to always be in the side, people often ask me if I was ever worried about being dropped. The answer is yes… I was constantly worried about it.

Firstly, from the point of view of personal pride, I always wanted to be on the team-sheet, but secondly, I needed the bonus money from making appearances and picking up draws and wins, especially after I got married because I suppose one other aspect of my dependability was having a settled home life. It was something Tony Waddington was always very keen on, as he knew it meant it was far less likely anyone would agitate for a transfer. In the early-60s I'd actually heard stories that Tottenham were after me, which Tony Allen later confirmed, but at the time this was just paper talk.

It did mean Waddo was desperate to get me settled down, though.

For being selected in the first team we earned extra appearance money and then a £4 win bonus and £2 for a draw, which made a huge difference to me. It might sound a lot of money and indeed it was in those days, as it could increase your weekly wage by up to forty percent, but even with it I didn't have money to burn. We got taxed on it, of course, which meant you couldn't save anything as either rent or mortgage payments meant so much disappeared from your wage packet. So, a win would mean the difference between a great night out that week or staying in, which meant it was a very good incentive to do well. Then, not only would you be on a high from the game on a Saturday night, but you knew you could enjoy yourself a little bit more as you had that bit more money coming in. So, we had a lot of fun on those nights out when we'd won.

In order to get hitched, though, I'd first have to meet someone and what better place than the Crystal ballroom? When I went dancing at the Crystal, unless I had my bonus money, I could rarely afford to buy a girl a drink, whereas various girls would be hanging around the bar hoping for some feller to offer to buy them one. Not because they liked him, but because nightclub drinks are blooming expensive! If I really liked someone, I'd buy her one, but never two. I just couldn't afford it.

We became masters at making drinks last, which also meant we never really got drunk as we weren't drinking a lot and it would be spread out over a long time.

There was this one night at the Crystal when I saw this girl, who was a friend of someone else I was talking with, but I only said a brief hello to her.

'Hey nice to meet you, perhaps I'll see you again sometime,' I remember telling her.

Somehow, both of us seemed to have taken a shine to each other because the next week she had found out that I was a footballer and introduced herself as Margaret Bowyer. It turned out Maggie, as I could now call her, had a connection with Stoke City because she was related to Frank Bowyer, who was a legend at the club and who had been in the team when I made my debut, although he had then been reaching the end of a distinguished career.

Frank had been part of the team that had come so close to winning the league title in 1946/47, only losing out when defeated in the final game of the season at Sheffield United, which, if they had won, would have seen Bob McGrory's team lift the title. Frank was a young player in that team and came to be renowned as a great inside-forward with a wonderful right-footed volley, although he was actually very two-footed. Frank Mountford always used to go on about his volleying.

I think in my time at the club only Jimmy Greenhoff came close to being so adept at hitting volleys first time to score spectacular goals like Frank. Frank retired in the summer of 1960, so I barely played with him. He was a quietish, typical working class man, but you listened to him when he spoke because of what he'd done.

Not only was Maggie related to Stoke royalty, but she lived behind the football ground right near my digs. The downside was that it turned out her father was a Port Vale fan who worked on the railways, which was why he lived in Stoke, rather than Burslem.

The next time I saw her, I asked Maggie out on a date. I'd have been about 21 at this point and she was two years younger than me. We got engaged in 1961 and were married in early 1962 in Stoke, with Don Ratcliffe as my best man, although thankfully he didn't hide my trousers on the big day.

Although dad obviously came to my wedding, he never came down to Stoke to watch me play. He was just happy that he had done his job in getting me ready for the world and that I'd not only got a good job, but was now married too. I didn't hold that against him at all, as I figured he needed to live his life as he wished to after bringing up Albert and me on his own. He had done a fantastic job for me, being the only parent I'd ever known. He lived out his days in that house in Eccles doing little jobs for next door neighbours and settled down to keep his garden.

As it happened, one of the directors of Stoke City owned a construction company and was, at that time, building a new housing estate up at Weston Coyney and Waddo was obviously looking to make sure I was tied down in every sense. He pulled me to one side this one day and said, 'Would you like to go and live at Weston Coyney?'

'Where the hell's that, gaffer?'

'Other side of Longton from here.'

So, Maggie and I went over to have a look. We liked the bungalow as it was a brand new house in a cul-de-sac. I bought the bungalow with a mortgage Waddo arranged, cleverly ensuring that I had to pay the mortgage directly out of my wages into the building society, so I was truly bound to the club. Bearing in mind that he must have known that the wage cap was likely to be ending fairly shortly at this point, he would have been doing everything he could to ensure he locked his players in. So, it's not surprising in a famously unstable business, he wanted to settle us down and make us feel wanted.

And it wasn't just me. Gerry Bridgwood moved in near us as the houses were built and Tony Allen was also just round the corner. We'd often go out on Saturday nights with the wives and it would always be as couples, not us players on our own drinking. Maggie and I had two children, Jeremy in 1965 and Sally-Ann in 1967. This was manna from heaven for the manager, who had what he wanted... me married and settled, and able to concentrate on playing football.

BY THE TIME I finished my career my dependability had meant I had played a club record 606 competitive games for Stoke City... 507 in the league. That beat the existing club record held by Jock McCue. That remains the record today. Even Ryan Shawcross, Stoke's modern day Premier League record appearance holder, having played throughout the decade City were in the top-flight this century, only racked up a total of 453 games for the Potters, so I think it's much harder these days in the sense that the players' welfare is much more considered and they aren't made to play 60 games a season like we were. There are also much bigger squads than in my day, with rotation being a major factor. Not that Ryan was rotated that much!

I am very proud of my record.

As I said earlier, I do recognise that McCue actually played more games for Stoke.

How ironic then that, after a decade without missing more than a handful of games, I should actually be unable to play in my own testimonial match against Derby County.

It was awarded to me alongside Tony Allen in February 1969.

A game I missed with a bruised leg!

The one that got away. This is me (wearing No 6 in the striped shirt) scoring a goal, that was eventually credited as an own goal to Fulham's Jim Langley (left of picture, lying prone). Where is the dubious goals panel when you need them...?! It was the first goal in a 4-1 win in September 1964 and is being celebrated by the delighted John Ritchie in front of Cottagers' keeper Dave Underwood (also lying prone), with Bill Asprey in the background far right.

We congratulate Stan Matthews on his incredible career in 1965, just before he retired aged 50 years young. And (from the left) myself, Bill Asprey and Harry Burrows in 1966.

CHAPTER 5

The Magic of Matthews

IN THE SUMMER of 1961, Stoke City were at one of the lowest points in their long history. For the first time since the 1907/08 season, which actually saw the club fold and have to drop out of the Football League, the average home attendance in 1960/61 was under 10,000. Tony Waddington realised that turning around the fortunes of the club was going to be incredibly difficult, but as it happened a type of luck was around the corner.

Injuries are part and parcel of football. The first time I saw a really bad one was when striker Dennis Wilshaw had his career ended after a dreadful tackle by Newcastle's centre-half Bill Thompson in an FA Cup fifth round tie in February 1961. Thompson's challenge was so forceful it bent Dennis' leg back so sickeningly none of us could quite believe how bad the break was. I remember when his sock was cut away, you could see the bone sticking out of his leg. *Uggghhhhh.*

Strangely, that dreadful challenge, in a way, sparked the revival of Stoke City. Here's what I mean.

New manager Tony Waddington was suddenly desperate for a striker and ahead of the 1961 March transfer deadline, as the fairly dismal season came to a close, he made what I think is one of the best signings in the history of the club. And it's not the player some of you may think. The first of the 'Old Crocks', as the papers would soon dub the conveyer belt of experienced professionals that Stoke signed over the next few years, was Blackpool inside-right and sometime centre-forward Jackie Mudie, who celebrated his 31st birthday just after signing for £7,000 in March 1961.

JACKIE'S ARRIVAL WAS important in two crucial ways.

Firstly, we needed him to replace Wilshaw and Mudie's vast experience brought much needed guile to our attack. Jackie scored on his debut in a 2-0 victory over Scunthorpe at the Victoria Ground and he would regularly pop up with crucial goals time and time again over the next couple of seasons. I remember him scoring a winning goal against Leeds United in February 1962, and then he finished as top scorer in the 1962/63 season with 20 league goals in 39 games, firing us to promotion.

Jackie was a very good player; small, but with good pace and he could make great runs so we could play balls through for him to run onto. He had a knack of scoring goals. He didn't score great goals from miles out, but he was always in amongst opposing defences poaching.

Calling players like Jackie 'Old Crocks' was a little unfair on them as they were generally only 29 or in their very early thirties, like he was, when they joined us, which isn't exactly ancient. But us younger ones did enjoy teasing them a bit when that moniker started appearing in print.

Secondly, that £7,000 proved money superbly spent as Jackie had played with a certain Stanley Matthews over the past decade at Blackpool, not that any of us gave that any thought when Jackie joined. It was a little piece in a bigger jigsaw puzzle that it turned out Tony Waddington was putting together. But more of that in a minute.

The leading scorer in my first full season in the Stoke City first team was Johnny King. He was a fantastic goalscorer, with a wonderful left foot, who struck over 100 goals for the Potters in the 50s, ending up as the club's fifth highest ever goalscorer with an eventual total of 113. Johnny was very heavily left-footed and quite often would move over to the right, then cut in and whack it with his left foot, scoring into the far corner. He was also a very good passer of the ball, especially with that left wand.

I only really saw Johnny at training and on matchdays as he was seven years older than me and was already married and settled when I first got into the team, so he would go home after training as he lived out Crewe way, and not join us at Ma's café much or on nights out. By now aged nearly 30, Johnny was coming towards the end and in the summer of 1961, despite finishing as top scorer in 1960/61 with 13 goals, Tony Waddington moved him on to Cardiff for £12,000, which was good money for an ageing, if experienced, striker. That fee funded Mudie's arrival, leaving some decent spare change. The club was very short of cash at that time, so Waddo, much like Michael O'Neill during his tenure as Stoke manager, had to generate funds by moving players on in order to be able to make other signings to improve the team.

Johnny was also a fantastic tennis player and after he retired from football a few years later he got close to getting through the qualifying tournament for the Wimbledon Championships. What a sportsman! He's still going now and I see him occasionally at the Bet365 Stadium on a matchday, despite him being nearly 90.

Johnny was replaced first of all by Tommy Thompson, a 34-year-old former England international forward, who signed from Preston after a great career earlier with Newcastle and then Aston Villa. Despite scoring 16 goals in 37 league games to finish as top scorer in 1961/62, Tommy was clearly at the end of his career and in fact picked up a bad knee injury which required surgery, so Tony Waddington then signed the more sprightly 22-year-old John 'Jack' Nibloe from Sheffield United a couple of months later for £3,000. But that signing didn't work out either and, as momentum built in the squad, Jack was moved on to Doncaster Rovers halfway through the following season. Sadly, Jack was killed in a car crash in November 1964 aged just 25.

Although Mudie was a success, and Thompson was a one-season wonder, Waddington was pretty much left back where he started, still needing more cutting edge in attack if we were to turn into a team capable of winning promotion, and with very little money left to play with. But it was a chance conversation at training the manager had with the injured Dennis Wilshaw which provided the final piece of inspiration and sparked an incredible catalyst for the club in both of these senses.

Dennis was a very intelligent man; he was actually a practising maths teacher and only played football semi-pro throughout his career. Whilst watching our training from the side of the pitch, leaning on his crutches, Dennis proposed to Waddo that Stoke City needed a catalyst, a marquee signing to change our fortunes from the humdrum to the spectacular. And, having signed Mudie from Blackpool, why not return to Bloomfield Road to tempt the biggest star in English football?

Why not tempt Stanley Matthews back to Stoke? His legend was such in the Potteries that it would at the very least bring the crowds back, create excitement and generate some much-needed cash to fund the growth of the team.

How right Dennis was! Waddo got to work behind the scenes, pulling off arguably the greatest transfer coup in Stoke City's history.

I FIRST HEARD about the possibility of Stan returning in the *Sentinel*. It got me so excited. Me, playing with Stanley Matthews, one of my heroes and the man I'd thought about when I knew I had got a trial at Stoke. Ridiculous.

Little did I know where this would all end. Within 15 years I'd played with Gordon Banks, George Eastham, Geoff Hurst, Peter Shilton, Alan Hudson, John Ritchie and Jimmy Greenhoff… some of the greatest players Stoke City fans and, in many cases, England supporters have ever known.

I don't know if Jackie Mudie played a part at all. I just know that the deal was done, although, when Stan's arrival was actually announced a few days later, for just £3,000, Waddo didn't sit us down and tell us. He let us find out, as I said, through the local paper. It was the start of something big and he knew it.

He was turning into quite a showman and loved nothing more than to make big pronouncements to get the public geed up. I don't think any of us realised the future plans he had for the club at that point. We were too busy being shocked and excited at Stan's return. Waddo's PR had worked.

It was all anyone in the Potteries could talk about.

Suddenly, there was this buzz and I had everybody contacting me wanting tickets, initially complimentary ones, but us players only got a few of those for each game, so eventually they were wanting to get hold of any ticket they could get at full price. But they were hard to come by even for us players. The club knew they were onto something good and were ensuring that the huge interest was put to good use.

Signing the Wizard of the Dribble really opened the floodgates for bigger and better signings for Stoke. I can only liken it to someone like Lionel Messi signing for Stoke now, right at the end of his career; a global football superstar arriving in the Potteries. It was that huge.

I know, you're probably thinking, *But Stan Matthews was 46 when he re-signed.* And you'd be right. That only goes to show you how remarkable he was.

At the time of writing this book, Stoke have recently signed 39-year-old Phil Jagielka from Derby County in the January 2022 transfer window. He'd have to play for another seven years to match Stan. That's incredible to think. You wouldn't think that signing a 46-year-old could possibly galvanise a club and a city that's been in the doldrums for a decade, would you?

But then you need to understand more about Stanley Matthews, the most famous footballer on the planet, England star and homecoming hero.

I had never known anything like it. Suddenly, there was press everywhere; we had glitz and glamour and loads of attention, and were constantly doing press photo calls and the like. You'll see a photograph of me with Stan and the 1964/65 squad in this book. I'm at the back looking at the great man as he announced his retirement, but you'll see this look of admiration combined with disbelief on my face. I still can't quite believe what happened in those three and a half years following his return.

STAN'S DEBUT WAS a great case in point.

He had actually signed just before we played away at Plymouth, but Tony Waddington, ever the showman in so many ways, chose not to select him there, saving his debut for the following home game against Huddersfield Town in order to generate huge amounts of interest. And it worked.

Like a dream.

More than 35,000 turned up to see Stan's debut on October 28, 1961, over 27,500 more than the previous home match, which we'd only drawn against Preston 1-1 in front of 8,409. So, he paid back that £3,00 transfer fee, and then some, on that day itself, especially as I reckon there were another few thousand crammed into the ground on top of that. It was astonishing. It felt like a very special occasion and the folk of the Potteries were out in force. Their hero was back.

The blue touchpaper had been lit beneath the club by Matthews' return.

We really needed it. At that point, in late October 1961, we had already played 14 games of the Second Division season and won just three of them, drawing four and losing seven to sit in 19th position, one place above the relegation zone. We had won at Southend in the League Cup first round, but then been hammered

1-4 by Charlton in the second. We were just plodding along, not being very good at all, really.

That day is one of the most vivid memories I have of specific matches from my early career. I remember as I walked down to the ground I actually couldn't get near it because of the bloody traffic! There was that many cars and buses that the whole of Stoke was snarled up. The club had told us to arrive early, but that made no difference; we got caught up in the mayhem of supporters arriving early to get the best vantage points in the stadium. Thousands of people got there over two hours before kick-off.

Having finally made it to the ground, nearing 2.30pm, stomach churning as per usual, I peered out of the little window high up in the players' dressing-room that looked out onto the street outside the main entrance and saw that there was this tumult of people, hordes of them and you could hear them shouting for Stan. It didn't exactly calm my nerves, let me tell you, but then I looked across to the old maestro and there he was calmly lacing up his boots as if it was just another day at the office.

When we went out onto the pitch there was such a buzz and a huge roar. I'd never experienced anything like it. I tell you what, I was glad to be in the middle of the pitch that day because the paddocks on either side of the ground were giving anyone who went near Stan pelters; I really do think they affected the Huddersfield players.

All the fans wanted was to see Stan on the ball and he gave them exactly that. He was magical that day and absolutely murdered their left-back Ray Wilson, who would, of course, be England's No 3 in the World Cup-winning team just four and a half years later. I'm not being funny, but Wilson just could not cope with Stan running at him with the ball at his feet. I remember watching him becoming completely unbalanced, trying to anticipate which way Stan was going to go.

Most of the time Stan would feint inside onto his left foot... then jag the ball back onto his right and beat Wilson on the outside, to cross the ball into the penalty area. He did that over and over again that day, just like he had to countless international class full-backs over his long career. Sometimes, that feint was just the merest hint, but he had such control over his balance that as soon as Wilson shifted his weight to block him, Stan was off... haring towards the byline to pull the ball back.

It was a joy to watch and the fans crammed into the Victoria Ground took in this masterclass giving full-throated support.

By the end of the game, Huddersfield took to marking this 46-year-old magician with three... yes three players and Stan still produced an incredible performance and laid on two of the goals, although the first of those, to give us the lead, was very unusual because it wasn't a piece of mercurial footwork which created an opportunity, but actually some closing down which Stan did on a Huddersfield defensive throw in. This caused the receiving player to miskick his clearance directly to the waiting Jackie Mudie, who instantly arced a cross into the penalty area where Jimmy Adam, a £5,000 signing from Aston Villa just two months before, outmuscled his marker to head home.

Don't let anyone try and tell you Stan Matthews didn't ever defend!

The second goal came from a more traditional Matthews method and set the seal on our 3-0 victory. After Tommy Thompson converted a fairly flimsy penalty award, late in the game Stan drew three Huddersfield defenders yet again, to slip the ball to the unmarked Thompson on the edge of the penalty area to shoot past visiting keeper Harry Fearnley.

It was the perfect end to a perfect day.

At the end of the game, I couldn't get off the pitch as there was this huge pitch invasion to celebrate our victory. The supporters all mobbed their conquering hero Stan, embracing the rest of us too if they couldn't get near their hero. It really was a tremendous feeling and the first time I saw and began to understand what this football club could be if we made it into a success, instead of allowing it to dibble-dabble along in the doldrums like it had been for almost a decade. Fabulous it was.

I've got a newspaper clipping from that game in which the *Sentinel* journalist N.G (Norman Gosling) wrote, *It was a moving demonstration of mingled sentiment and emotion on the occasion, the likes of which may not happen again for 100 years.* Thankfully, there were actually many more days like that to come in my time at the club over the next 15 years.

I think it was a very similar situation in 2006 when Peter Coates bought control of the club back from the Icelanders and appointed Tony Pulis as manager. Pulis achieved a very similar thing to Tony Waddington in that he galvanised the club, which had been going nowhere, and created an incredible atmosphere in the ground through bringing in star players who had all done well elsewhere, but had fallen out of favour for one reason or another. He also discovered a very special talent in Rory Delap's long throw which was a wonderful thing to behold, with the stadium baying for blood every time he hurled one into the opposition box from 50 yards away.

The atmosphere around those times was incredible; Fortress Britannia they called it. Well, back in 1961 we began to create our own fortress at the Victoria Ground once Stan returned. We had a very different style of football to Tony Pulis' teams, mind you, but we used to steamroll sides as Waddo put some pride back into the Potteries and we received tremendous vocal backing from the supporters.

It was a huge buzz. Before that Huddersfield game I was a bag of nerves because I'd become used to playing in front of 10,000 or 12,000 and, suddenly, there were 35,000 watching and the Victoria Ground had become a completely different place. People were so positive and happy. There were flags and banners everywhere. I'd never played in front of a crowd like that.

But that now meant a whole world of pressure I'd never had to cope with before. Now there was expectation, when previously there had been nothing but forlorn hope as crowds dwindled. I was incredibly nervous before games, but this was why I wanted to play football… to be better, to test myself… to achieve things. So, I was up for the challenge and learned to cope with the jangling nerves.

After that victory over Huddersfield, we won six of the next nine games to revive fortunes and truly kickstart the Waddington era in earnest. The fans stuck with us across the remainder of that season and then through the glorious next one as we pushed for promotion. I mean, earlier that season I was used to driving from home in the car and getting to the ground in about a quarter of an hour.

Then, once Stan signed, I had to leave three-quarters of an hour earlier! Money just kept coming in thanks to those increased attendances, so that could be invested wisely by Tony Waddington in better and better players. The manager had pulled off a true masterstroke. Who'd have thought signing a 46-year-old would waken up the sleeping giant that was Stoke City?

SO, HOW DOES a player of that age perform at the highest level of the game? I don't care who you are, if you play on the right wing you can take breathers throughout the game, which was how Stan played… in spurts. His stamina was, of course, not as good as it had once been, so we also needed to use him sparingly.

However, the opposition would always need to make sure they marked him so Stan would always be occupying at least one man, if not more.

For me, it was a pleasure to play with the maestro because he made it easy for me and I learned so much from him about keeping things simple. When I got the ball, I simply looked up and found Stan, who somehow would always be available. Even with the opposition full-back standing right next to him, Stan would just drop deeper and deeper until the defender wouldn't come any further forward, being worried about the ball in behind him.

Once Stan had that little bit of room, he wanted the ball to his feet as he only needed five yards or so to turn and take his man on by shuffling towards him slowly… then bursting past him with that remarkable turn of pace.

I got to learn that if the defender started shuffling backwards as Stan advanced with the ball glued to his right foot, I knew he was a goner, and could position myself accordingly. The way I learned that was by finding out in training as Stan did it to me time and time again, even though I was a young kid.

We weren't allowed to tackle him hard in training as the manager didn't want him injured, but actually I couldn't anyway!

The manager also told us that if we gave Stan the ball when he was tightly-marked, defenders would love to clatter him, so we used to feint to make a pass to him, ensuring he had players drawn to him, but then spread the play the other way out to the left because him being tightly marked meant that others wouldn't be. So, sometimes, yes, 46 to 50-year-old Stan Matthews was used as a decoy.

Stan loved having a wet pitch on which to scoot across. It really suited him to be able to zip over the grass. Pitches nowadays are like snooker tables. Back then they were often quagmires over the winter, but Stan could cope with even the heaviest of pitches as he was so slight he could hare over the ground. In fact, when it got dry again in the spring, Waddo would actually call the fire brigade in to sluice the pitch in water so Stan had the underfoot conditions that favoured him and caused full-backs to slip and slide on a sodden quagmire of a pitch.

I remember the first time the fire engine turned up thinking, *What the bloody hell is going on here?!* I got to quite like it, though, especially as the pitch was never rock hard when I fell over. Quite often I'd see the other teams come out onto the pitch to warm up and watch their faces turn in amazement as they said to themselves, *Right, I'm off to change my boots…*

As I mentioned, Stan's debut was delayed by the manager so he could generate all that interest in his first home game. The team he didn't play against away from home was Plymouth Argyle and we had lost that game 1-3.

By the time we beat the same opponents at home 2-0 on March 10, we were sitting in 7th position in the table, only four points or two wins off the second promotion spot. Our transformation had been remarkable, sparked by a 46-year-old.

But that season we couldn't keep it up and we only won two of our last 10 games to finish eighth.

WITH STOKE CITY being back on the footballing map, the club quickly became attractive to other really good players. The next one to sign, three months after Stan, in January 1962, was my actual boyhood hero from his days at Manchester United, Dennis Viollet. He was a magnificent footballer, lithe and classy on the ball and so neat and tidy.

Dennis would often come off the pitch with his shirt as clean as when we kicked off because opposition players found him ghosting past them and couldn't get that near him to tackle him.

Having my hero to play alongside meant I was in football heaven.

Following that late season dip in form, the manager strengthened with quality, experienced players again in the summer of 1962, bringing in centre-half and captain Eddie Stuart from Wolves, who took Ron Andrews' place in the team.

Eddie was the perfect gentleman and a proper professional, who was very authoritative on the pitch. If he said something to you, you listened and did it. Partly because of the size of him and, with him being a proud South African, you knew you couldn't mess with him. But he was never crude at all, being more like a schoolteacher in a way, like Denis Wilshaw. I can't think of Eddie ever getting nasty or worked up at all despite the intense pressure we were often under in the following two seasons. He'd simply tell you what he wanted from you and you knew you just had to do it. Simple as that.

Eddie always dressed smartly, wearing a shirt and tie, and he held himself very straight and erect. He had captained Wolves during their great era in the late 50s, taking over after Billy Wright's retirement, winning three league titles and one FA Cup, which he himself lifted in 1960 as skipper. He cost just £8,000 and brought huge solidity to our back line. He really was a class act, both on and off the pitch as our leader, and was a huge part in our promotion push the following season. I often think he is a player who is overlooked when people talk about that era. He really was integral to our success.

As was another arrival with Wolves connections, Eddie Clamp. Eddie had been a star in those great Wolves teams of the late-50s, alongside Eddie Stuart, playing for England in the 1958 World Cup finals in Sweden. But Clampy had spent the 1961/62 season at Arsenal, which didn't go so well for him and his former teammate Billy Wright, who had just become the manager at Highbury, let him join us for £35,000, which was actually Stoke's record transfer fee paid at the time.

Clampy's arrival was caused by another bad injury, this time to Bobby Howitt, who was hurt in a defeat at Swansea in August 1962. Waddo took the opportunity to make a statement signing, though, because Eddie was an imposing sight... 6 foot tall, muscular and with a gap-toothed leery grin that soon turned into a snarl if you were an opponent. He added to his stature by rolling his baggy shorts up high onto his waist as was the fashion in the 50s.

He had a Teddy Boy style Duck's Arse haircut and had earned the nickname 'Chopper' at Molineux. And we all knew why. Eddie was, quite frankly, a complete nutter. I wouldn't say he was completely crude, but even in training he had this look on his face which meant you kept away from him. I was glad I'd never had to play against him earlier in his career because we were in the division below Wolves. The way he looked at you, if you even misplaced a pass scared me... and I was on his team.

There were no airs and graces with Eddie. He was actually a decent player with the ball at his feet, but mostly he just won it and gave it to an attacking player, much like myself. We were a 'team' in the hub of midfield and got on famously. I really liked Clampy, but my goodness he was a character.

He was untidy and a complete whirlwind. His changing cubicle would be a total mess, like a bomb had hit it. He had fishing tackle and everything in there. I remember once I asked him what it was doing there and he shrugged and said he'd forgotten to take it home. Not exactly an answer! In fact, he'd far rather talk about going fishing than about football. As soon as he came back in after a game, he'd just rip his kit off, chuck it in his cubicle, have a quick shower and off he'd go to spend hours in solitude with his rod and line.

He was also a terrible trainer and often didn't even bother turning up. Frank Mountford would be constantly sending someone down to Wolverhampton to collect him. I reckon once Eddie got wise to that, he would sit and wait for his car to arrive as it didn't cost him anything then to make the trip! He'd then hitch a lift home afterwards.

I remember one time I was injured and standing outside the ground waiting for my mates, who I was due to sit with to watch the game. If I'd been playing I knew I'd have to be in by 2.15pm latest, but this particular day it was already 2.30pm and Eddie hadn't arrived yet. I was worried that Waddo might have to play me, even though I was injured and planning on sitting in the stand with my mates. Five minutes later, Frank Mountford actually came out and asked me if I could play as Eddie still wasn't there

All of a sudden, about 20 minutes before kick-off, Eddie turned up as if without a care in the world. He just went in, put his kit on and walked straight out of the tunnel to play, without any warm up. He never used to have massages from Frank Mountford or do any stretching at all to prepare. And this guy had played for England!

Eddie took no prisoners at all. I mean, *at all*. As an example, I'll tell you this story. In 1955, well before Clampy joined Stoke, a promising young full-back called George Bourne had his leg broken in a horrible challenge in a reserve team match by a young Welsh player called Colin Webster. Seven years later, in November 1962, this story had come to Eddie's attention and when we travelled to Swansea, who now had Webster in their midfield, he exacted revenge... Clamp-style.

As we came off the pitch at half-time at the Vetch Field, Eddie made sure he disappeared into the gloom of the tunnel alongside the unsuspecting Webster. By the time I got there all hell was breaking loose. Eddie had taken it upon himself to headbutt the poor lamb and then stick his boot in as his victim lay on the floor. I can remember just ahead of me, Clampy turning round and giving Don Ratcliffe a bollocking for not joining in with the revenge mission.

Thankfully, the referee hadn't made it off the pitch as yet. When he did, the man in black heard what had gone on and knocked on our dressing-room door, behind which we were having our half-time cup of tea trying to pretend to Waddo that nothing untoward had happened at all. I remember the manager opening the door, surprised to see the referee there, inviting him in, oblivious to what Clampy had done.

'Mr Clamp!' said the ref, sternly. We were all desperately trying to keep a straight face, with the odd giggle having to be suppressed.

'I understand that you have head-butted Mr Webster.'

Eddie was some actor. The look of astonishment on his face at this horrific allegation shamed angels. His response was equally unbelievable.

'No, sir!' Eddie quite convincingly replied.

'He hit his head on that low girder in the tunnel.'

'Oh, right,' said the ref, who of course had no actual evidence other than two completely different stories, as he hadn't seen anything himself. He could do no more and left the dressing-room, utterly bemused, to check on this version of events.

Waddo, removing his head from his hands, where it had sunk as he took in the obvious truth during the exchange between Clampy and the ref, did his characteristic 'dear, dear, dear' shake of his head once the match official had gone.

'Eddie!' he pleaded.

'That girder is at least six foot off the ground. Webster's only five foot four!'

Well, we fell about.

Clampy did once come a cropper, though, when he head-butted Blackburn's Ronnie Clayton behind the referee's back in a First Division game the following season. At least he thought it was behind the referee, but it turned out the man in black was wise to Eddie's antics and saw him. As soon as Clampy realised he'd been spotted in the act, he simply held his hand up and trotted off down the tunnel. He knew he was getting sent off.

As he spent much of that first season up in the top-flight suspended, Eddie only lasted another year before Waddo sold him to Peterborough for £5,000 in October 1964.

That was Eddie all over. He was a one-off.

I DID THINK when Clampy arrived that it might be my place in the team which was under threat, but he simply replaced the injured Howitt, who ended up retiring due to his injury after only playing a handful of games as he attempted a comeback later that season. Bobby moved back to Scotland to become coach at Greenock Morton and then manager at Motherwell, where he spent seven seasons in charge.

Indeed, through all of these arrivals of experienced, top professionals, I kept being selected. I reasoned the manager must have been pleased with me because he kept on picking me. That was really all that mattered to me.

I learned so much from those older players. Anywhere we stayed overnight before an away game, us younger players would sit with soft drinks in the lounge bar; for example at the Russell Hotel if we played away in London, and listen to what the likes of Stan, Dennis, the two Eddies and Jackie Mudie were talking about. They'd often reminisce about particular players they'd played with or against.

They were the stars and us backroom boys were the workers. I was quite happy with that scenario. And, in any case, I could only talk about playing for Stoke City and getting a bollocking off the manager or the coach! I hadn't played in FA Cup finals or for England or in World Cups.

I was often really gobsmacked about what they talked about. For example, the only person I ever came across who had a diet in that era was Stanley Matthews. He was remarkable and unusual in so many ways.

Stan's body was incredible.

He was 48 by this stage, but I used to look at him as I passed the ball to him and the only giveaway that he was that kind of age was that his hair was starting to thin and recede. Otherwise, his body was immaculate, helped by drinking only tomato juice on a Monday as he wanted his body to detox after game day on a Saturday.

That 1962/63 team had a good bond and we joked a lot, especially in the dressing-room. It was full of talent and we knew we had a good chance of winning promotion with the goals we had within the forwards. So, how ironic then that it should be my worldie of a goal at Derby, that I described earlier, which kickstarted the campaign. That 30-yard scorcher was the best goal I ever scored, but I need to own up now, though, because, great hit though it was, that was actually a really lucky goal.

Not because of the strike itself, which I repeat was magnificent, but because I was only in the area of the pitch I found myself in to collect the pass from Don Ratcliffe by accident. I shouldn't have been there at all! I was only there because the manager had called me across from the far side of the pitch towards him, to take some instructions as another player had had to go off injured for a short time and he wanted me to fill a gap. Well, as soon as the ball came to me as I trotted across, I just ignored Waddo, set off… smacked it and the rest as they say is history! Talk about luck!

The 1962/63 season would prove to be my best scoring season by far. I never scored more than one goal in any other season. So, to hit four in one campaign was amazing. I netted my first goal at the Victoria Ground in a 3-1 win over Newcastle in October, opening the scoring with a quick turn and left foot finish from eight yards; then got our second in a 2-2 home draw with Plymouth a month later.

My final goal of the campaign came in a hectic 3-3 draw at Huddersfield in the frantic run-in during late-April. This is the only one of these other goals that I remember well as I ended up in the net after racing onto a loose ball and bundling it home from about a yard. I think it would have gone in anyway, but I wasn't missing out on the chance to make sure. Over the season, only six players scored more league goals than me. I'm not claiming I was a goal-machine, though!

The reason why the end of the season was so crammed with fixtures was that the winter of 1962/63 was one of the worst on record, with snow lying deep across the country for months on end. In fact, from Boxing Day 1962, when we won 2-1 at Rotherham, with Bill Asprey roaming forward from right-back to slam home the winning goal, we didn't play another fixture until March 2. It was freezing cold and we trained indoors most of the time, although occasionally Frank Mountford would show his slightly sadistic side and we'd be asked to run all the way round the stadium in the freezing snow several times, and sometimes up and down the icy steps.

When football was able to restart, on snowy pitches as there was no under-pitch heating in those days, blue lines would be marked on the snow with powder, but after a while it would get moved or kicked away. You also couldn't really judge how to weight your pass as the ball would sometimes stick in the snow, and other times it would skip over it and you'd turn out to have hit it too hard. It was hard going, being often very cold and windy as well. Despite that, in our first game back, we beat Walsall 3-0 thanks to a Mudie hat-trick to send us top of the table and look set fair for promotion. It seemed we had weathered the weather-enforced break well.

OUR NEXT GAME on March 16, 1963 at Norwich was notable for two reasons. Firstly, the game saw the debut of another member of the 'Old Crocks' brigade, Jimmy McIlroy, who Tony Waddington had somehow managed to coax to join us in our promotion challenge from First Division Burnley for a cut price £25,000, which came as a shock to the Burnley fans who branded chairman Bob Lord 'insane' for agreeing to the sale of their favourite attacking midfielder-cum-inside-forward.

Secondly, we somehow managed to lose that match 0-6.

What a disaster that game was. We really didn't turn up at all. It was very strange. Jimmy must have thought, *Why have I come here?*

What nonsense has Tony Waddington told me about winning promotion?

Jimmy was a Northern Ireland international, who had played at the 1958 World Cup, helping his national team reach the quarter-finals by drawing 2-2 with reigning World Champions West Germany. He was regarded as one of Burnley's greatest players, having played 497 matches and scored 131 goals. He had been a legend in Burnley's title-winning team of 1959/60 and, in fact, had played in the previous season's FA Cup final, which the Clarets had lost 1-3 to Spurs; while they had also finished as runners-up to Ipswich in the league.

He was dubbed the 'Brain' of Burnley and was a very composed passer of the ball, only releasing it when he was sure of finding a teammate. His neat footwork had made him a crowd favourite at Turf Moor, and would do so at Stoke. It was such an astute signing by Tony Waddington and I've no idea how he managed to pull it off.

It was actually quite harsh to call Jimmy an 'Old Crock'. He may have been 31 years old, but he was a quality passer of the ball and had great anticipation of the areas into which he needed to put the ball, to bring a Matthews or Viollet into the game. They'd been opponents in the top flight for donkey's years, so they knew each other's games inside out in that sense. All were international standard footballers and they gave the team a huge lift. They also took turns in providing the on-pitch flair.

No star player can produce genius in every match and if you only have one star player then they can be marked out of a game. We now had a plethora of talent in attacking areas. We may have had the oldest forward line you can think of, as there was only really Don Ratcliffe who was young and could run up front, but my role in the team was made so simple by these wonderful footballers.

I just had to fetch and carry the ball out of defence and give it to one of them… then they'd go off and play their football.

Imagine it… I'd look up and see Ratcliffe, McIlroy, Mudie, Viollet and Matthews ahead of me. What a choice of who to pass to that was! Shortly afterwards, John Ritchie arrived to play centre-forward, which only increased the options I had with the ball at my feet. We must have been a nightmare for opposition teams to try and mark!

Jimmy was also a great talker, not surprisingly for an Irishman. He was always up for a good chat and loved nothing more than socialising. He soon became an integral part of our squad on and off the pitch.

After that thrashing at Carrow Road, we managed to somehow concede the first goal 20 minutes into the next home game a week later, when struggling Grimsby took the lead against the run of play. We were really in need of inspiration and found it in the form of Dennis Viollet within a minute of going behind when, straight from the kick-off, I played the ball out to Stan Matthews on the right, who slotted a through pass across the snow-flecked mud to Dennis, who swivelled and fired a right-foot shot right into the corner.

I always think it's the sign of a really good team if you can respond well to going behind. Scoring so soon after conceding gave us huge confidence and we went on to win that game 4-1. Including that victory, we won eight of nine games, with Jimmy's midfield dynamism and skills prompting Mudie, Viollet and Ratcliffe to get amongst the goals in a big way. Jimmy himself scored a couple in that run too.

Only a goalless draw on Good Friday at Sunderland split up that superb run. The Rokerites were top of the division and we played brilliantly defensively to hold them to a draw at Roker Park and then, three days later on Easter Monday April 15, we faced them at home, in front of 30,419, scoring the opener in a 2-1 victory thanks to a Dennis Viollet penalty in the very first minute. That was a crucial win, but they weren't even back-to-back games; we actually beat Cardiff at home on Easter Saturday in between those two matches against Sunderland, which proved crucial to both of our seasons, as we finished only one point ahead of them, while they missed out on promotion on goal difference and finished third. Unfortunately, I was injured over that Easter period, missing all three games. I only missed one other match in the entire season.

On my return, the next game was a 3-3 draw at Huddersfield, when I scored the goal from a yard that made it 2-2 just before half time. Little did I know at the time, but it would prove to be my last goal for five and a half years, until I scored in a 1-1 draw with QPR in September 1968.

I told you I wasn't a goal machine.

AFTER THAT DRAW at Leeds Road there was a very special friendly to celebrate the centenary of the club.

I had always known that Stoke City were one of the founder members of the Football League and therefore must be very old, but I didn't realise they had reached the stately age of 100 years. To celebrate the club's centenary, on April 24, 1963, Tony Waddington and the directors somehow managed to arrange a prestigious friendly against Miguel Muñoz's Real Madrid, who had been crowned European champions five times in the previous eight years and had just run away with the Spanish title.

That game was a fabulous experience. I remember a brass band playing as the teams emerged from the tunnel side by side, Madrid clad in their famous all-white strip which seemed to gleam under the lights. Stan Matthews, aged 48, was our captain for the evening and then I recall shaking the hands of their team, which was like a who's who of world football, including the likes of Ferenc Puskás, Francisco Gento and Alfredo Di Stéfano. It was incredibly exciting.

My direct opponent was actually Di Stéfano. The game ended up a draw and he didn't score, so I was happy. Another notch on my belt.

Afterwards, we had a lovely meal at the North Stafford hotel and champagne was flowing. But I was always the quiet one and I didn't like getting drunk, while others, such as Jimmy McIlroy were much more outgoing. But I took it all in, loving the experience. I remember various presentations being made and our guests were given gifts of Spode china coffee sets and Royal Doulton character jugs, plus a Doulton bull and matador which I am led to believe still sits in the club museum in Madrid, although I remember my opponent that night Alfredo di Stéfano telling me in fairly decent English that there was actually more bull than there should have been... the figure had clearly not been castrated.

I believe on their return, Real Madrid president Santiago Bernabéu sent a telegram from Spain thanking Stoke for their hospitality and hinting they would like a re-match. Perhaps Peter Coates should see if the invitation is still open.

The Stoke team that night was… O'Neill, Asprey, Allen, myself, Stuart, Clamp, Matthews, Viollet, Mudie, McIlroy and Ratcliffe. So, we put our full first team out for a friendly in between crucial games in our quest for promotion.

PERHAPS NOT SURPRISINGLY, after our extra-curricula exertions, we lost the subsequent home game against Middlesbrough on the Saturday 0-1 and then the subsequent two games… 2-5 at Newcastle, and 2-3 at home to Scunthorpe. Three defeats in-a-row was a disaster and we went from looking like certainties for promotion, to struggling to make one of the top two spots which would see us going up.

And our next game was against new league leaders Chelsea at Stamford Bridge.

The focus was also very much on us defenders at this point as we'd just conceded eight goals in two matches, and were headed to Stamford Bridge, where only one team, bizarrely Division Three-bound Walsall, had managed to keep a clean sheet all season long. This should have been our penultimate game of the season, but due to the postponements caused by the 'Big Freeze' we still had another three after this. However, it was a crucial match because a win for either team would pretty much guarantee promotion. It proved to be a titanic battle played in front of 66,199 fans.

This was where the qualities in our team showed through, starting with one moment in the match early on when, for me, Eddie Clamp made his most important contribution as a Stoke player.

As soon as he had arrived, Clampy had declared himself as Stan Matthews' minder and took to calling him 'Uncle'. It was about the only endearing thing I ever knew Eddie do. He became the ultimate protector of our veteran star and the best example of Clampy's enforcer abilities came at Stamford Bridge in that vital game.

Young left-back Ron Harris had been detailed by Chelsea manager Tommy Docherty to hit Stan early, to drive him back up the pitch. When he did, though, Eddie got involved, racing across to get right in Ron's face with those mad, staring eyes, wagging his finger, and saying to him, 'Do that again and I'll put you in hospital!'

It was a threat full of menace and the thing was, with Eddie, you knew he actually did mean it. Harris clearly thought that was the case and, despite his nickname being 'Chopper' as well, Ron clearly didn't fancy having his leg broken. It was very interesting to see this time, that it was merely the thought of what Eddie might do that did the trick, as his reputation went before him. Harris didn't go very near Stan for the rest of the game.

Eddie's intervention created the conditions within which we were then able to score a brilliant goal, created in part by Stan, freed from the attentions of Harris, and set up by Jackie Mudie and scored by Jimmy McIlroy, whose shot flew in off Peter Bonetti's far post.

It won us the game 1-0 and we were back on course for promotion again.

After that game, Stanley Matthews was announced as the Footballer of the Year, 15 years after winning his first award, the very first in the prize's history, in 1948. He was 48. Incredible.

BUT, ACTUALLY, THERE was one more remarkable contribution to our promotion-winning season which Stan had yet to make. We lost 1-2 at Bury in midweek, but other results meant that if we won our last home game against relegation-threatened Luton not only would we secure promotion, we would win the Second Division Championship to boot.

There were nerves aplenty in the dressing-room that afternoon, but the coolest cucumber in there was Stan. He was calmness personified. I could just tell he was building himself up for one more special contribution.

It was such a big game that the crowd was once again huge... 33,644 officially, but it felt like far more. Central TV's cameras were there and they saw Jackie Mudie score a nerve-settling goal in the first-half.

Enter Stan.

No one wants to be the player who makes the mistake that costs your team a title, or a cup or promotion. That would have been my mentality the night before such a huge game... *don't make a mistake, keep it simple.*

Stan Matthews spent all his time pre-match relaxing and thinking about how he was going to win the game for his team.

We were under the cosh a bit at the start of the second-half, as Luton tried to get something from a game which would see them relegated if they lost, but suddenly

I blocked a through-ball and it span out to Jimmy McIlroy in the middle of our half. Before I could blink, off hared Stan on the halfway line and Jimmy's through ball split Luton's defenders and skimmed across the mud to fall into Stan's stride.

Once he was away, Stan latched onto that glorious pass to scoot goalwards fully 50 yards, which was a huge sprint for him, especially as it was across the Victoria Ground mud, bereft of even a tuft of grass. As if he was 17 again, not 48, Stan left Luton's defence running in treacle behind him to waltz around 'keeper Ron Baynham, selling him a dummy to go right... then switching back left and slotting home left-footed. The goal sparked scenes of jubilation all around the ground, but especially on the Boothen End where he had scored.

It was a thing of beauty to behold after such a long, arduous and difficult season.

All my butterflies disappeared as we rushed to mob Stan, as he trotted back to the halfway line as if it was just all in a day's work. What a time to score your first of the season and it was so fitting that Stan got that goal which clinched promotion.

After the game it was unreal. The crowd invaded the pitch again and were picking us all up in celebration. We eventually made it into the tunnel and up the stairs to the directors' box, amongst the cameras, to take the acclaim of the crowd on the pitch. I remember coming out to huge cheers.

It really was quite incredible. There was an address made to the giddy crowd, swarming in exaltation across the mud, by the Lord Mayor, who proclaimed, 'Dreams have come true. Stoke City are back where they belong!'

Then, after all the fans had gone, we had champagne in the dressing-room, although teetotaller Stan left the swilling to us. I remember he told reporters after the game, 'This is one of the greatest moments of my life. It's what I came back here to Stoke for.'

What a man.

We had a great weekend of celebration, attending a dinner held in our honour at the North Stafford hotel. That was a great do, which capped my first successful season as part of a great team. I'd done well myself before, but to be part of something that was greater than that was really quite amazing.

So now, I was going to be a top flight footballer, as well as being married and with my own house. Not bad for a working-class lad from Eccles.

All thanks to Tony Waddington and Stanley Matthews.

With Roy Vernon and Maurice Setters on a Penny Farthing bike. We were doing a promo for the 'Penny Farthing' nightclub where we sometimes used to go for a few drinks and a natter.

Looking tanned and ready for action for a new season in 1968; and the Boothen Stand paddock where I often put wingers like Aston Villa's Harry Burrows (who would later become a teammate) with a well-timed, firm yet (mostly) fair tackle. And I often followed them in!

CHAPTER 6

The Waddington Wall

HAVING WON THE Second Division title to clinch promotion, our next, rather daunting job, was to establish ourselves in Division One. We now, though, had a core of the team who were used to playing at that level, albeit they were the older ones at the end of their careers like Eddie Stuart and Clamp, Dennis Viollet, Jackie Mudie and, of course, Stan.

But now we were in the top flight, Waddo could sign players who were more in their prime and the first of those was Manchester City forward Peter Dobing, for whom the manager paid a club record transfer fee of £37,500 in the summer of 1963. An England under-23 international, Dobing was only 24 years old when he joined us, so by no means an 'Old Crock'. He was also a class footballer, with a great left foot and was only available to us thanks to his club's surprising relegation the season before. Peter had regularly scored goals in the top flight for both Manchester City and his previous club Blackburn Rovers, so we knew we were getting a class act and in his first season at Stoke, he scored 19 goals in all competitions to finish as second top scorer.

He was an interesting character was Dobing. Despite being from Manchester, like me, he couldn't have been more different. He was a pipe smoker and became known as 'the pipe-smoking gentleman of English football'. He was also a bit of a loner outside football, preferring outdoor pursuits such as fishing and shooting, to knocking around with us after training. I don't think he meant to be aloof, but he was a bit, and some supporters picked up on that and made him a target, as sometimes happens with football fans, particularly at times at Stoke.

I remember when Peter suffered a broken leg against West Bromwich Albion in January 1965, ending his season, during his recovery he spent time fishing for trout in Market Drayton, near where he lived, and became a keen clay pigeon shooter. Some people didn't really like that.

They thought he should be totally dedicated to recovering his fitness and a bit of tetchiness built up which sometimes resulted in Dobing being booed, which I always thought was odd, because he was such a quality player who could win us games at times.

AS BETTER QUALITY players like Dobing began to arrive, so others moved on as the club prepared for life in the First Division. One of those was my mate Ron Wilson, who was sold to neighbours Port Vale, where he forged a good career for himself, staying for seven seasons and playing 264 games, winning promotion from the Fourth Division in 1970 and the Player of the Season award the previous campaign to boot. I was dead chuffed for him.

He was actually sold in a £12,000 package deal in November 1963 along with Jackie Mudie, the veteran forward whom Dobing was effectively replacing, who then went on to manage Vale, taking over from former Stoke City legend Freddie Steele in 1965 after a disappointing season which saw the Valiants relegated to the Fourth Division. With that slightly refreshed squad, the 1963/64 season opened for us with a very tricky game at the Victoria Ground against Spurs, who were one of the best teams in the country at that time under manager Bill Nicholson. They had won the double just two seasons before and the FA Cup the following campaign. They also boasted England's top young striker Jimmy Greaves as the spearhead of their attack.

Greavesie wasn't a worker, but had this incredible knack of always being in the right place at the right time. What a nippy finisher he was, and he proved that in the very first minute. We hadn't really kicked off and Greaves nipped ahead of me like greased lightning and shot. Although it was saved at point blank range by our debutant 'keeper Bobby Irvine, Spurs centre-forward Bobby Smith followed up to tap in… 1-0 to Spurs. Greaves was my man, so I was at fault there.

What a baptism of fire that was.

But that Stoke team was made of stern stuff and we fought back to secure a famous win, 2-1, thanks to two Jimmy McIlroy goals, the first set up by a cute pass by Stan Matthews from the left… yes left wing, and the second from a pull-back from the byline by the marauding debutant Dobing. I kept Greaves quiet for the remaining 89 minutes and we were on our way, and I knew we were going to be alright when we won our first away match 3-1 at Villa Park two days later, with Dobing getting two and Mudie one.

Despite that great start to the season, results soon took a nosedive and we didn't win at home again until November 30. In fact, the next 10 games after the opening two wins saw us draw three and lose seven and, after a 1-2 home defeat by Arsenal in early October, we found ourselves in 19th position on seven points.

We now had a very exciting frontline, but were lacking a little solidity at the back. I loved playing in the First Division, as the stands were huge and they were mostly full. The standard of football was obviously a level up, but I soon found that once I was out on the pitch I simply played my own game, just having to think that bit quicker to keep up with the best forwards and attacking midfielders in the game.

Waddo knew he could trust me to give him what he needed for 90 minutes. As new boys in the division, we had to give at least one hundred percent effort, otherwise we would have no chance. My feeling was that I always needed to put in a full 90 minutes of hard work. Then if we lost, at least I knew I had done my bit. Generally, I would tackle, win the ball and then give it to someone else to do something with. That was my *game*. Occasionally, though, I had the confidence to make some progress up the pitch and I created a couple of goals with crosses for young striker John Ritchie to rise and knock in; 'assists' I think they are called these days.

The manager didn't often criticise us, even when we'd got beaten, because he could see the effort levels were there and he trusted the quality he had brought to the club. He was given time, which is obviously far less likely in the modern era than it was then, and our form began to turn around. We hit a run of six games without defeat, including three wins, but that good form was followed by eight games with just one win, one draw and six defeats. We were becoming a 'streaky' team.

One of those defeats, on December 7, 1963, came on my first appearance at my boyhood spiritual football home of Old Trafford.

I HAD BEEN looking forward to this fixture like no other and it was quite awe-inspiring running out from that same tunnel in the centre of the main stand that I used to stand opposite in anticipation of seeing my heroes. There would be no home fans cheering me, though, as I was playing right-back in the visiting team. Not exactly how I had originally envisaged appearing on the hallowed turf when I was a starry-eyed kid, but I didn't care because I was simultaneously delighted to be playing there, yet determined to cause them problems.

The game didn't exactly go to plan.

I already knew it to be true, of course, but there is no room for sentiment in football and that day turned out to be brutal and bruising, rather than a glorious homecoming.

Earlier that season, Waddo had decided to swap myself and Eddie Clamp over, so I was now playing right-half and he was left. He never really explained why that was. But for this game, the manager moved me to right-back because Bill Asprey was injured and George Kinnell, a new £35,000 signing from Aberdeen, filled in for me at right-half, although he was really a centre-half.

United were such a good side under Matt Busby throughout the 60s. They had won the FA Cup just six months earlier with a team rebuilt from the ashes of the Munich disaster. The manager was in the process of building his third great Manchester United team featuring the attacking trio of Best, Law and Charlton, all of whom could score goals and, before we knew it, Denis Law had scored two in quick time to put United 2-0 up. The next thing I know, Waddo moved me into the middle to man-mark him, shifting Calvin Palmer, who had started at centre-half alongside Eddie Stuart, to right-back.

It didn't exactly work.

I used to be able to keep players, even really talented ones like Jimmy Greaves, quite quiet. Not by being dirty, but just by being with them constantly, hassling and harrying, so they were never free to show their class. But that day Denis Law was on fire. I now had him to mark but found myself with Bobby Charlton, who had beaten two of our midfield with a typical barnstorming run, bearing down on me.

Bobby wasn't that big, but he was dead strong and when he came on one of those runs through the centre of the field he'd just muscle past you and score. He was that powerful; like an ox. You would think you could just nudge him and he'd go over, but you couldn't.

So, as he bore down on me, I was faced with the dilemma… *Should I tackle Bobby and leave Denis unmarked, or simply stay with my man as instructed and let Charlton waltz through unchallenged?* I chose to try and tackle Bobby, who, as I went in for the challenge, just slipped the ball to Denis, completely free from my attentions, to complete his hat-trick. Law ended up scoring four of the five goals as we lost 5-2.

That was a footballing education.

When I got back home and went to my local pub, the Red Cow up in Werrington where I was living at that time, Dean Stockton, the publican, asked me, 'Bloody hell, Skeelsy, what happened with Denis Law today… he scored four against you!?'

Of course, he hadn't scored all four with me marking him, but I was getting the blame for it. Thanks Denis! In fact, the next day in the paper he got 10 and I actually was given an 8! So, I can't have been *that* bad. There weren't many games where someone that I was marking scored a hat-trick against me and technically that wasn't one, as Law had already scored two of his four goals before I got put on him!

GOING INTO THAT game at Old Trafford we'd just come off a run of three home games in which we'd scored four goals in each, but somehow only managed to win one of them. That was the previous Saturday when we had hammered Birmingham 4-1. Remarkably, the previous two home games, against Burnley and then Sheffield Wednesday, had both ended 4-4.

Young striker John Ritchie had scored seven goals across those three games, and another one in one of the two away games in between, when we won 2-0 at bottom club Ipswich Town. So, we knew we were scoring enough, but we needed to tighten up defensively. Quite simply, we were conceding far too many goals

By the time we lost to Leicester on January 11 we were back down in 19th position, just two places above the drop zone. The pressure was on us as players and the manager. This was when Tony Waddington implemented a new tactic… the Waddington Wall.

Waddo's plan was simply to make us very hard to beat, to stop conceding three, four and five goals so regularly, especially when playing away from home at some of the bigger teams like United. Those flair players we had up front were then expected to strut their stuff after we'd won the ball back and played them in. Effectively, we played one striker up front and the rest of us well behind them when we didn't have the ball, with two or three players detailed to support the line striker, usually John Ritchie, once we won the ball back.

We changed from playing 3-2-5 to 4-4-2, as the manager quickly realised we couldn't have five forwards up top in the First Division. Initially, we actually dropped the two inside-forwards back into midfield and played a kind of 3-4-3, but we found that if the ball was played up to Ritchie, and he was flicking the ball on, then the two wingers would be too far away from him as they'd be positioned out on the flanks, so it made sense to put a second striker alongside the centre-forward. Once you've got two up top, you then need to withdraw your two wingers from being so high up the pitch, especially when the opposition have the ball. Then you're left with the choice to stick with three defenders, playing slightly narrow, or go with two specialist full-backs and two centre-halves; and before you know it you end up at 4-4-2, which is how Alf Ramsey arrived at the formation with which England won the 1966 World Cup.

People say Alf invented that formation and called them, 'Wingless Wonders', but, actually, most teams in the First Division, aside from the very best ones like Liverpool and Manchester United, who would have three attackers, had basically been playing that way for a few years.

Our formation earned the nickname, the 'Waddington Wall' because we often faced up with five or even sometimes six men strung in a line across midfield, so the opposition couldn't come through us as there was just a wall of red and white striped shirts.

Often this meant they'd have to try and come over us, but then our centre-half would have a 50/50 chance of winning the ball in a header. And if that centre-half was Denis Smith, later in the 60s, I'd say it was more like a 60/40 chance with the way he competed for the ball, so it was a good tactic.

I was never a winger, but on the few occasions Waddo put me in a No 7 or 11 shirt, my role would be to come inside and be a brick in that wall, acting as an extra defender to double up on the opposing team's winger when he had the ball and closing down space. Ideally, I was looking to win the ball back and set an attack going by giving it to our best players, like Jimmy McIlroy or, later, Alan Hudson.

I didn't then go charging forward supporting the attack, I'd be immediately looking around me for the danger if the other team won the ball back and broke away at us while our attackers were stranded at the other end. That was my role irrespective of where I was deemed to be playing by my shirt number. All this obviously massively reduced our attacking options, but when you were playing away at Old Trafford, Highbury, White Hart Lane or Anfield you just wanted to frustrate the home side and try and keep a clean sheet at all costs.

None of us had a problem with this as we were playing for points to keep the club in the First Division and for us players, every point meant bonus money as well.

So, we were all up for any method of winning every week, at the very least the extra £2 for a draw we received, if not the £4 for a win. We very much had the attitude of, *If they don't score, we don't lose.*

Waddo was very good at knowing what he wanted, from his team and from each individual player. If you gave him what he asked for then you kept your place, often irrespective of the result, especially in those first few seasons up in the First Division as we would naturally lose quite a lot of games while we established ourselves. He wasn't one for grandstanding, though.

He would just come along to me and quietly say, 'Right Skeelsy. Make sure their star man doesn't have time on the ball to do what he wants'.

Whoever it was – Fulham's Johnny Haynes, Spurs' Jimmy Greaves or George Best at Manchester United – it would be my job to stop him, which meant I would be the direct opponent of some of the best players in the country in an early example of what's now known as man-marking. I've already mentioned plenty of such great playmakers and goalscorers it was my pleasure to keep tabs on, but there was also the likes of Peter Thompson at Liverpool, Johnny Giles at Leeds, Danny Blanchflower at Spurs, George Armstrong at Arsenal and, later, mercurial midfielder Alan Hudson at Chelsea.

I remember in one particular game at Stamford Bridge, Huddy got so fed up of my close attentions he kept telling me to… 'Get lost'… at least I think that's what he said, because I followed him everywhere, absolutely *everywhere*… closing him down, snapping at his heels. We drew the game and, after I'd showered and got changed, I went up into the players' lounge and wandered over to the bar. Who should be there, not surprisingly, but Alan Hudson.

'Bloody hell, Skeelsy… not you again!' he turned and said to me. 'The game's over, you know!'

I loved playing against those stars as it gave me a huge challenge, which I enjoyed accepting and succeeding at. It used to bring the best out of me. Each Sunday, I would look at the scores awarded by the journalist in the paper and see that my direct opponent's score was low… like a 4 or a 5, while mine was a 7 or an 8. That was enough recognition for me. I actually didn't mind if those stars gave me the occasional run around because they were some of the best players in the world. More often than not I'd keep them quiet, especially once we had this ultra-defensive mindset in place as I had one simple, albeit destructive, thing to concentrate on.

In fact, it used to annoy me more when I played against someone who wasn't a household name and they ran rings round me. That would hurt my professional pride. The so-called non-stars often worked me harder than some of the big names and could be more troublesome. I often found myself having to strain every muscle to keep an Alf Arrowsmith of Liverpool or Ron Boyce of West Ham quiet, fellers who weren't the biggest names in their team by any stretch, but were tricky opponents.

In truth, the manager often didn't say a whole lot more to me about what he specifically wanted me to do. For example, if he wanted me to kick Denis Law he wouldn't say it in front of the whole group, he'd come to me individually and say something like, 'make sure he doesn't get a kick!'

Code for… 'whack him early!'

Then after the game, if you'd done what he asked you to, you'd just get a, 'well played,' from Waddo and that would be the extent of our conversation.

Keeping players quiet was easier back then because we could tackle from behind, of course, coming through a player to get to the ball. Now it is a very different game and you have to stay on your feet. Some of the 'fouls' you see on the TV now don't make any sense to me at all, but that's because the threshold for a foul has completely changed. It was a lot more physical in terms of direct contact in the 60s and 70s.

You could fly into tackles without worrying what you connected with first as long as you got some kind of touch on the ball at some point. It's completely different now. Once you start going into a tackle, especially at pace, you can never stop, so you are often going to give away a foul and probably pick up a yellow or even a red card, as I remember Robert Huth doing one snowy day at the Britannia Stadium when he slid into Sunderland's David Meyler, sending him flying, while actually withdrawing a tackle but being committed to the challenge already. That would have been no more than an accidental foul back in the 60s or 70s, but nowadays it's a sending off.

In my day you could talk to referees too, and I never had any problem with them. These days, I think some referees struggle with talking to players. They just referee to the letter of the law and that actually causes problems. It isn't right.

And don't start me on VAR.

It should work, but all too often it doesn't.

SO, I BECAME a considerable brick in the Waddington Wall. Once we got used to the manager's expectations and new approach, things began to look up. Of the last 17 league games of that 1963/64 season, we only lost five. Not only that, but we actually began scoring goals again; at least John Ritchie did.

John was a tall, lanky, young centre-forward who signed from Kettering and burst onto the scene with his all-action style. He was full of energy, very good with both feet and a great header of the ball. Three months into that 1963/64 season he had been given his chance in place of the injured Dennis Viollet and grabbed it with both hands, scoring twice in a 4–3 win at Bolton.

That sparked an incredible scoring streak of 15 goals in just nine games, breaking Jack Peart's 1910 club record for scoring in consecutive matches, although only six of Ritchie's were in the league, the rest being in the League Cup. The run was rounded off in that 4–4 draw against Sheffield Wednesday by John's first hat-trick. However, while the Waddington Wall was being implemented, he then only scored once in the next 11 league games.

The dam was unstuck on that particularly poor run and our general inability to score very often, when struggling Ipswich came to the Victoria Ground on March 21, 1964. We ran riot and thrashed the visitors 9-1 to record Stoke's biggest ever top-flight margin of victory, with Ritchie netting two, Dennis Viollet grabbling a hat-trick and Jimmy McIlroy also scoring twice. That result sparked a late season run of form and we won five of the last seven games to finish 17th, comfortably clear of the relegation zone.

Ritchie dovetailed nicely with Peter Dobing, finishing as top scorer with 18 league goals and 30 in all competitions, making a huge impact in that first season up. He would eventually, of course, become Stoke's all-time record goalscorer with 176 goals.

On the back of Ritchie's goals we progressed through the rounds of the new League Cup competition, defeating Scunthorpe, Bolton, Bournemouth and Rotherham, to reach the semi-final against Second Division Manchester City. We won 2-1, winning the home first leg 2-0 before keeping the hosts down to a single goal in the return.

Stoke City were in their first ever major final!

Okay, bear in mind it was only the fourth time the competition had ever been run. And actually I don't think every club in the First Division entered that season, but still it was a heck of an achievement.

We drew the first leg of the final at the Victoria Ground 1-1, with Keith Bebbington scoring for us. There was quite a buzz for the second leg at Leicester as we had played really well in the first game and should really have been taking a lead to Filbert Street. Gordon Banks had proved to be brilliant between the posts, though, and Leicester had also defended well. But we still fancied our chances, however.

The team in the second leg was Bobby Irvine, Bill Asprey, Tony Allen, Calvin Palmer, George Kinnell, Me, Peter Dobing, Dennis Viollet, John Ritchie, Jimmy McIlroy and Keith Bebbington. We came so close, only going down 2-3, to lose 3-4 on aggregate, in a pulsating game. Our scorers were Viollet and Kinnell, with Ritchie also hitting the bar and Banksy making a fantastic save in injury time.

I do feel that achievement is never given the recognition it deserves, because that team was the first Stoke side to reach a final. Obviously, it was then eclipsed by lifting the cup in 1972 and we rightly celebrate that, but the 1963/64 team was actually a very good one on our day and finishing as runners-up was a brilliant achievement.

Another great thing was that the cup run also earned us almost £100 extra in bonuses – over an additional two months' worth of wages – so we loved it!

DESPITE THAT SNIFF of success at the end of our first campaign in the First Division, we were basically aiming to stay up for most of the seasons in the latter half of the 60s, while Waddo wheeled and dealed to bring in better players to regenerate the team. This inevitably meant that those 'Old Crocks' would eventually leave and the first to move on was Stanley Matthews... or should I say, Sir Stanley Matthews, as he was actually given a knighthood in recognition of his incredible career when he finally called it a day in 1965.

Stan actually played his final game in the First Division five days after his 50th birthday when Fulham visited the Victoria Ground. We won 3-1, with Stan setting up our second goal for Ritchie with a typically incisive pass down the inside left channel for Big John to run onto and lash home left-footed. That brought the house down.

The atmosphere and love for the great man was incredible that day. It was repeated and then some on April 28, 1965 when his benefit game was broadcast to the world from the Vic.

After 19 years of faithful service split across two stints, the club laid on an extraordinary extravaganza of a testimonial for Stoke City's most famous son. As well as the 35,000 fans in attendance at the Victoria Ground, the stadium was chock full of European television cameras and radio services from around the world.

All in all, I'm told, around 112 million people tuned in to watch 'The Wizard of Dribble' weave his magic one final time. An incredible array of talent turned out as Stan's XI played the Rest of the World... including Ferenc Puskás, Lev Yashin, Alfredo di Stéfano, Eusébio, Bobby Moore, Denis Law and John Charles. For the record, the result was a 6-4 victory for the Rest of the World.

I got to enjoy the whole experience from the stands. The momentous evening ended with Stan being carried off the pitch for the final time on the shoulders of Yashin and Puskás to a standing ovation and a rousing chorus of *Auld Lang Syne* all around the ground. Stan was also named Footballer of the Year to round off an amazing season at the end of his astonishing career.

What a way to end a glittering career.

After Stan departed, the next old timer to move on was Jimmy McIlroy, whose final Stoke game, perhaps appropriately, was against Burnley on December 27, 1965 as he moved to Oldham to become player-manager. Jimmy signed several former Stoke City teammates, including Bill Asprey, Alan Philpott, George Kinnell and Keith Bebbington and did okay for a few years, but left in 1968 to rejoin Stoke as assistant to Tony Waddington. He was then poached by Bolton and went to Burnden Park to become coach and assistant to Nat Lofthouse. Jimmy was later made an MBE for services to football and to charity. As arguably Burnley's greatest ever player, he was honoured when Turf Moor's eastern stand was rebuilt in the late-90s and named the 'Jimmy McIlroy Stand'.

To me, he was just a wonderful feller.

Dennis Viollet was the final member of that talented triumvirate to depart. He continued to play for Stoke until the summer of 1967, dropping into central midfield to play incisive passes through to the attackers to use that wonderful footballing brain of his. He announced his retirement after scoring 66 goals in 207 matches. I was delighted when, shortly after Dennis's death in March 1999, he was honoured by the club having a street near the new Britannia Stadium named 'Dennis Viollet Avenue'.

It was a privilege to know and play with all of them.

Of course, three such auspicious talents would need replacing and Tony Waddington was now shopping in a far more exciting pool of talent. Dynamic midfielder Calvin Palmer had already arrived from Nottingham Forest for £30,000 in September 1963, while Maurice Setters joined from Manchester United, also for £30,000 in November 1964. Both of them could have been direct replacements for me, but I always kept my place in the team somehow, being moved by the manager to do a job somewhere round the pitch.

Waddo began to splash significant amounts of money on transfer fees as well, setting a new club record transfer fee in buying Roy Vernon from Everton for £40,000 in March 1965. Roy was a goalscorer through and through, and had been top scorer and captain when the Toffees had lifted the First Division title in 1962/63. You wouldn't have thought it to look at him, though, as he was about 10 stone wet through. There was nothing of him. He was just like a skeleton, with no muscle or fat, mostly due to his incredible chain smoking.

Basically unless he was on a football pitch, Roy was always smoking. Yes, even in the shower after training. It was amazing to witness how he kept his fag going just out of the torrent of falling water, with his lips appearing through the jets and steam to take a drag, making the end of his cigarette glow as he did so.

A Welsh international who had played in the 1958 World Cup, reaching the quarter-final, Roy was a cracking footballer, with a lethal left foot and he knew where the goal was. He also liked going to nightclubs and he knew where the bar was in all of them. He and I would go out for a coffee, as well as a pint. He was also a gambler, who liked the horses and was constantly placing bets and asking, the second he came off the pitch, whether his horse had won… and occasionally while the game was still underway.

Gambling never tempted me. I know nothing at all about racing and only ever bet on the Ground National, just going on the name of the horses. I might risk as much as a pound each way.

At the same time as Roy arrived, my old foe Harry Burrows also joined us from Aston Villa for £27,000, probably to avoid the continual dumpings into the Boothen Stand paddock I regularly subjected him to. Harry had a great shot on him and his left foot earned the nickname 'Cannonball' because of the power he generated. Consequently, he was very good at free-kicks and, particularly, penalties. Honestly, if Harry hit a spot-kick straight at the goalkeeper and he was foolish enough to get in the way, he'd have ended up in the back of the net.

Then, the following summer, which was the glorious one in which England won the World Cup, Tony managed to pull off a fantastic transfer coup when he managed to secure the signature of winning squad member George Eastham from Arsenal for £35,000. George had a wonderful touch and a lovely left foot in particular. He was already nearly 30 when he signed, but actually spent the next eight seasons at Stoke and would, of course, score the winning goal in the 1972 League Cup final.

George wasn't the only World Cup winner to join the club, though. At the end of that 1966/67 season, Waddo pulled off an even bigger coup to secure the signature of the best goalkeeper in the world; Gordon Banks, for £52,000 from Leicester. It was bizarre that Banksy was even available.

Why would you sell the best goalie around?

THE LEICESTER DIRECTORS had decided to sell the great man because he was being supplanted by the prodigious talent of 17-year-old Peter Shilton and they realised they couldn't keep both of them happy. Gordon was only 29 and for a 'keeper that probably meant he had at least five, maybe as many as seven seasons left at the very top.

I suppose, if you're going to build a footballing wall, then the first brick you need to have in place is the one between the posts. Tony Waddington had always seen the value of having a top-notch goalkeeper like Jimmy O'Neill and Lawrie Leslie, who had signed from West Ham for £14,000 in 1963, but he had always had to buy 'keepers towards the end of their careers.

Now, in the spring of 1967, less than a year after he'd lifted the Jules Rimet trophy at Wembley on that famous day, an opportunity arose to buy the best goalkeeper around and Waddo grasped it immediately, apparently beating Liverpool to the punch.

I got on well with Banksy, occasionally playing golf with him on days off. We'd laugh and talk a lot as he was a very nice man, who treated you well despite being such a star. He would joke a lot with the whole squad, although his best pal was George Eastham. They roomed together and would often be found at the VIP bar together in The Place nightclub on our nights out.

I soon learned that Gordon was very dominant when he was on the pitch and particularly in his penalty area. He was so vocal. He would always tell me, 'When I shout "My ball" I'm coming to get the ball. Don't get in my way'.

Banksy would also shout to us to mark-up attackers as well, especially at corners. I liked that. I was happy if he was knocking me out of the way to claim the ball as I believe you need a goalkeeper to be robust both physically, and in terms of personality. They really have to be the gaffer in the box.

In the meantime, as all these glamorous signings arrived for big money, youngsters were also coming through the ranks and being blooded by the manager. Alan Bloor established himself in central defence and would eventually be partnered on many occasions by my good self, while both Mike Bernard and John Mahoney, who arrived from Crewe Alexandra, made themselves regulars in midfield.

Eventually, by 1967, as these younger players came through, Waddo moved me to full-back, mostly on the right side to replace Calvin Palmer who swapped into right-half for me, but sometimes filling in on the left as he moved Tony Allen into the centre of defence once his pace started to wane. Over the next couple of years youngsters would come through and fill those spots too, so I showed my adaptability playing across the back four and in midfield. Waddo needed my experience as a brick in that wall to get the youngsters through games and I was delighted to oblige as long as I was in the team.

IT WAS AROUND that time that one of the strangest episodes in my time at Stoke City occurred. I don't really know how or why it happened, but the manager took the decision to sell our talismanic striker John Ritchie to Sheffield Wednesday for £80,000.

This very odd sale happened in November 1966, after John had scored 81 goals in just 135 games, which was a remarkable record at any level, but to do it in the top flight made him very special indeed.

Even more bizarrely, it seemed that we weren't really looking to replace John's pace or height up front. Roy Vernon and Peter Dobing were tried as the main man leading the line, but proved too lightweight, being far better suited to playing off a tall centre-forward, rather than attempting to be one.

From my point of view, I was always playing the ball up to Big John's head and without him up there to target, we didn't have anyone to hit with those kinds of longish balls. As we were playing deep to absorb pressure and then play out quickly, without him as the focal point up top we struggled to break out as often as we had used to. It affected us greatly.

New signing David Herd, another arrival from Manchester United, only managed nine goals in his one season leading the frontline in 1968/69. Herd was signed on a free transfer, so there may have been some money issues around this weird set of circumstances that I wasn't privy to. Certainly, I felt that, given that we were struggling to score more goals than we conceded, it was a bit of a shock that Ritchie was sold.

For me, it was even stranger because Waddo had also just sold reserve centre-forward John Woodward to Aston Villa for £30,000. And both Ritchie and Woodward could have thrived on the crosses of Harry Burrows from the left wing. It just made no sense to me at all.

Perhaps not surprisingly we began to really struggle and in 1967/68 we found ourselves in a relegation scrap.

We'd experienced many heady days of success, albeit with some big ups and downs from week to week, but up to that point under Tony Waddington our direction of travel had been very much upwards. We'd stabilised in the First Division with mid-table finishes from 1964/65 to 1966/67 and the supporters were generally very happy and content, despite the occasional barracking we might get when we made a mistake.

I always knew when I was happy with my game, so criticism from fans didn't really affect me, but I must admit it's very good for your ego when you go to the pub in the evening and everyone's praising you after keeping the opposition's star man quiet.

Of course, fans would get on players' backs at times because we didn't play the most exciting football, especially away from home, but we did put in huge amounts of work rate and effort and Stoke fans always appreciate that. If I was having a bad time they might shout at me a bit, but fortunately for me my game was sort of always above the average, especially in terms of work rate, so I rarely got any sustained moans in my direction.

That 1967/68 season was something completely different. We were really poor, to be honest, struggling without Ritchie's goals and his focal point as an outlet. The team was in transition, with the likes of Terry Conroy, Denis Smith, Mike Pejic, Jackie Marsh, Mike Bernard and John Mahoney right at the start of their careers. Instead of feeling comfortable and relaxed, there was tension around the place throughout the season, especially as our home form was so terrible.

In the middle section of the season, we won just three of 11 games at the Victoria Ground, and four out of 20 overall. Fans were on our backs.

Rightly so in many ways.

I was happy to play for 90 minutes and think to myself that I'd done alright. Then I'd head off and enjoy the night, going out with my wife to have a nice meal and a drink, relaxing away from football. One advantage of not being one of the stars was that I got interrupted and bothered a lot less. In fact, there were many occasions when I overheard fans talking about me without them realising I was actually sitting right next to them ear-wigging!

After a decade or so in the Potteries at this point, though, I did have quite a recognisable face, so every so often I would be button-holed by a supporter who wanted to talk with me for 20 minutes about the game, which was fine and I didn't mind when it happened, as long as they didn't get angry and agitated. It was quite nice really and I generally got on pretty well with fans.

The same couldn't be said for Peter Dobing. He had become the target of some fairly vociferous boo boys, particularly in that season when they felt he wasn't pulling his weight. I'm afraid there's always been an element at Stoke for the past 60 years or so who like to pick a particular player and moan about him.

Often it's actually someone who has talent but doesn't work hard, or seems not to be working so hard, rather than someone who just isn't very good.

Stoke fans had a lot of division of opinion about Peter.

He had dancing feet and could totally confuse defenders with his swift control and movement. He could score goals too, either really great ones, or just plenty of them. He twice netted 19 in a season, finishing top scorer in 1966/67 and then again in 1968/69 with 10 goals. In this 67/68 season he had only scored four goals during that terrible run and supporters were not happy with him.

It didn't help that his relationship with the fans had been damaged when he refused to re-sign for the 1965/66 season, publicly demanding a pay increase, which soured a lot of fans' opinions towards him. He had finally accepted Stoke's offer three weeks late. Consequently, if he made a mistake, he got catcalls and booing very quickly.

Not many forwards are tacklers and Peter wasn't one for chasing back and winning the ball. In my opinion forwards are there to score and it's our job as defenders to win the ball back and give it to the strikers to go and do their stuff. In fact, quite often when Peter did tackle back he was so bad at it he would get booked or even sent off for a bad challenge, or because he also had a fairly short temper on him and would react to opposing players winding him up. He eventually ended up accumulating so many disciplinary points that he was hit with a record nine-week suspension in 1970, a blow which was somewhat cushioned because he had actually broken his leg at Ipswich and didn't play again until the following season anyway.

As I say, Stoke fans like nothing more than a great work ethic, which is why I got on with them so well. In my opinion, though, what those fans don't understand is that talented players like Dobing will be closely marked by the opposition as they know that they offer the biggest danger. So, it's very hard, no matter how talented you are, to break free of that kind of marking. I knew all about this because for Stoke I was the man tasked with closing down the opposition's best players.

For me, Peter was a cracking player who could score us goals. I'd run all day for him, I would. I'd happily be his legs and win the ball back so he could go and weave his magic. I think that's why Tony Waddington chose him as captain. Us workers would do our bit in order to give inspirational players like him what he needed.

He wasn't the most obvious captain material on the face of it, but, although he was quite quiet, Peter also spoke very well when he needed to. He wasn't one for handing out bollockings at all and he certainly never argued with any of his own players on the pitch. But in his own way, he could be inspirational.

Despite two fantastic 4-3 away wins at West Ham and Wolves in the autumn of 1967, the first of which saw us come back from 0-3 at half-time at Upton Park to somehow win thanks to two goals from Harry Burrows and two from Dobing, our dreadful run now meant we had just five matches left to save our skins as we had actually fallen into the relegation zone.

The pressure was really on.

The first of those games was a midweek fixture at the end of April, when we hosted the title contenders Leeds United, who were just a point behind Manchester United at the top of the league, with this game in hand.

Home games like this were when the Boothen End came to life.

It was our great terrace behind the goal which stretched back and back, and could make a tremendous noise when the fans were in great voice. Don Revie's Leeds were one of those teams we really didn't like – neither the players nor the supporters.

I remember the likes of Norman 'bloody' Hunter, Johnny Giles and their skipper Billy Bremner, who was a dirty bugger. With me being a tackler, I knew they would come for me. I did get Bremner once in that game, nobbling him by keeping my studs up in a challenge when he didn't expect it. All's fair as they say… *Don't feel sorry for him.* That Leeds team would happily kick you when you didn't actually have the ball and think nothing of it.

Often we'd play hard and then have a drink with our opponents in the bar afterwards. Not with Leeds. I never had a drink with any of them.

That night, the Boothen End was electric and Peter Dobing won the Stoke fans over with a brilliant individual performance, scoring a hat-trick against England World Cup-winning defender Jack Charlton, to give us a chance of saving ourselves from relegation. His first goal was a sublime work of genius, racing 40 yards with Charlton almost literally hanging off his back… cutting in from the byline, and slamming the ball past Leeds 'keeper Gary Sprake from what looked like an impossible angle.

I remember there being a slight pause before the crowd behind the Boothen

End goal went crazy, because they couldn't quite believe what they had seen. It was one of the best goals I saw scored in my career at Stoke, although Peter's second of the evening, just before half-time, was a 30-yard rocket which fair flew in. Two superb goals. He completed his hat-trick by lashing in a loose ball in the penalty area after Charlton missed his kick to clear, sealing a 3-2 victory which gave us the confidence to pull clear of the bottom two with a great 2-0 victory over bottom club Fulham in the following game, which relegated the Cottagers.

We finished the season with another fantastic home win on a Wednesday night, this time 2-1 over Liverpool, with Peter opening the scoring with a header. We had avoided relegation and he had been integral to that late season resurgence.

Disaster averted. Boo boys silenced.

OUR CLUB PHYSIOTHERAPIST Fred Streete was always a bit ahead of his time. He would later go on to work with Arsenal and England in the 70s and 80s, but back in 1968 Fred came up with the novel idea for sportsmen of dieting in the search for peak fitness and performance.

When you read about the kinds of programmes that Olympic athletes endure these days in sports like rowing and cycling in order to complete at the highest level, you wonder how any of us that played in the 60s and 70s got anywhere near the top of the game of football when you learn that Fred's diet programme for us players included cutting out sugar, sweets, chocolate, jam, fried foods, biscuits, cakes, puddings, fat meat, beer and, slightly surprisingly, cordial. Yes, we were having to cut those things out because they were generally an integral part of our lives, despite us being finely tuned athletes.

Instead, Fred had us eating at least one egg a day, plus portions of cheese, meat and fish, accompanied by at least three servings of vegetables, three of fruit, six slices of bread, just three teaspoons of butter a day and, very precisely... three-quarters of a pint of milk.

We could drink as much tea, coffee and chicken broth as we liked, though!

I was quite lucky, because three of the squad – Alex Elder, Tony Allen and Bill Bentley – were selected to go on a 'special chemical diet' which Fred had also devised that was designed for them to shed up to 20 pounds in just a fortnight! I don't know exactly what it entailed, but I do know they couldn't eat between meals and all alcohol was banned for them.

Phew!! I was very glad I always kept myself trim in the close season and had not added any extra pounds.

Our new-found nutritional superiority over the rest of the division didn't exactly translate into results on the pitch, though, as the 1968/69 season saw us finish 19th, one place worse off than the previous season and just three points and two places above the relegation zone. We were in a bit of a rut.

The opening game of the 1969/70 season was a horrible defensive shambles at Wolves, and we lost the game 1-3. After that, the wall was reinforced even more strongly, as I was shifted to become a sweeper, a version of the relatively new-fangled position invented by German superstar Franz Beckenbauer. Unlike 'Der Kaiser', I didn't gallop upfield beating men before threading passes through to the forwards.

I was merely a destructive implement to stop the opposition. It worked. We drew the next game 0-0 at the City Ground without Nottingham Forest laying a glove on us. Tony Waddington had hit on another defensive formula to keep us more intact at the back. We only conceded 52 goals and our two seasons flirting with relegation were put behind us as we finished ninth in the First Division.

Famously, the following campaign, as Waddo used me to plug gaps all over the team in order to shore us up, I played as a centre-forward for Stoke City Football Club.

Can you believe it?

Me… a 5 foot 8 inch defensive player.

This was at Anfield, of all places, against Bill Shankly's Liverpool, on Boxing Day 1970. Clearly, Tony had given up on all thoughts of us scoring and was looking for damage limitation, so it made sense that Waddo would opt to go ultra-defensive.

Liverpool were so good that season they were comfortably better than most teams in the division, so Tony selected a goalkeeper, eight out-and-out defenders and two attackers. I didn't know what was coming when he started telling us in the dressing-room what he wanted from us.

I remember being shocked when the manager threw me the No 9 shirt and said, 'Eric, what I want you to do is take the kick-off… then just jog back and join the back four, so we have a fifth defender.

'Play your usual game… it's just to confuse them.'

So, I was a sweeper-cum-stopper, wearing the No 9 shirt.

Now, I had a couple of mates that lived on the Wirral that were coming to see me play that day and as the team was read out they were looking at each other in the stand and saying, 'well, Skeelsy isn't at full-back... not at centre-half... or in midfield, so he can't be playing then!' When I was announced as centre-forward they just looked at each other and fell about laughing. They were utterly shocked.

Liverpool put pressure, pressure...and more pressure on us during the game, but effectively we had put six men in midfield, having none up front, and they'd have to try and get it over us by chipping it forward, and our defence were then easily able to knock it away.

We drew 0-0 in the middle of a run of six clean sheets in seven league matches. We finished 13th in 1970/71, and across those two campaigns the new team that the manager was putting together had time to evolve with exciting youngsters blended with the more experienced heads like myself into a side capable of challenging for honours.

The wall had had its effect.

That Liverpool game also meant I'd completed my full set of outfield shirt numbers. The only position I never played in for Stoke was in goal, but I'll let Banksy off. He was good enough to keep me out after all.

Chatting with Gordon Banks (top)... the best goalkeeper in the world, ever as far as I am concerned. And we're off on a road trip (as they call them in the US of A) with the Cleveland Stokers, as we were known for the summer of 1967.

CHAPTER 7

The Swingin' Sixties

THE CLUB AND my life had changed a lot from when I joined in 1958.

We now had star players, huge names like Banks and Eastham playing for Stoke, following on from Viollet, Mudie, McIlroy and Matthews; all thanks to Tony Waddington as manager. Those gates of 8,000 had been transformed into an average of just under 30,000.

It was magical to be involved in and it brought a certain status, even to us more workaday players who weren't 'names'. While sometimes our football may have been slightly dour as the Waddington Wall took full effect, life off the pitch could not have been more contrasting.

In Britain, the Sixties was an incredible decade… The Beatles, The Rolling Stones… Mods and Rockers… Bond films, nightclubs, celebrations as England won the World Cup… and there were numerous shining stars such as the Fab Four, Michael Caine, Dusty Springfield and Tom Jones, plus overseas influences, particularly from America. Motown and Elvis Presley, came to the fore.

What a time to be alive. It was as if my black and white childhood had become full technicolour.

AND, IF STAN Matthews had begun the concept of footballers as 'celebrities', then the stars of the late 50s and 60s had picked that up and run with it. England captain Billy Wright had married one of The Beverley Sisters, the trio of chart-topping singing siblings. Fulham's Johnny Haynes had succeeded Wright as the national skipper and become the first £100-a-week player, and, of course, the England team had then, under Bobby Moore's leadership, gone on to conquer the world and change the face of how the nation felt about its leading players. The likes of Bobby Charlton, Geoff Hurst, Denis Law, Roger Hunt, Dave Mackay, Jimmy Greaves and Alan Ball had become talismanic household names.

Then, of course, there was my arch nemesis as an opponent, George Best, who danced across football pitches around the country and Europe-wide, earning the nickname 'El Beatle' after one particularly incredible performance for Manchester United in a 5-1 victory over Benfica in a European Cup tie in Lisbon in March 1966.

George was a superstar. Part-footballer, part pop-star, part-model. He was a very good-looking lad, wore a Beatles haircut, and cut a swishing figure in his tight-fitting suits. He was equally as famous as John, Paul, George and Ringo, and earning plenty of extra cash from a ghosted newspaper column and advertising items as varied as aftershave, sausages, eggs and... weirdly, I remember... mackerel fillets.

The media loved him. He'd pose for photos in everything from sharp-cut suits to a sombrero to give them what they needed and he was always surrounded by girls... mostly screaming, always beautiful.

As far as I was concerned, once he was on the pitch with me, all the glitz and glamour was irrelevant. Celebrity was immaterial. All I was interested in was whether I could tackle him. That was a lot harder than it sounds, though!

Georgie was extremely tricky and would come directly at you, a bit like Stan Matthews used to, and could go past you as if you weren't there, although often Best would jink inside, rather than Stan going on the outside all the time. Best could ride tackles like no one I've ever seen, going through or even over them at times. His balance was incredible, like Rudolf Nureyev, the world's greatest ballet dancer of the age. It was incredibly difficult to knock him off the ball.

And I tried, believe me.

Best was about the same height as me and was very good with both feet, despite what you might hear about him being mainly left-footed. He was in his pomp from about 1966 to '70 and arguably the best player in the world during that period, being named European Footballer of the Year in 1968 after helping

Manchester United to lift the European Cup for the first time, again defeating Benfica in the final, this time 4-1 with Best netting a wonderful solo dribble goal to make it 2-1 early in extra-time. Those Portuguese defenders must have hated facing him even more than I did! Besty also finished as the First Division top scorer, along with Ron Davies of Southampton, with 28 goals that season and once scored six goals in an FA Cup tie against Northampton.

But George loved the high life.

He was always a drinker and with the amount of money he was earning (the whisper was he was paid around £2,000 a month back in the late-60s, which was a phenomenal amount compared to my £400ish) it meant he started to focus outside football, which became his downfall. After several 'incidents' he eventually left United aged just 27, announcing his retirement. He'd been going 'missing' regularly in the two or three years before that. But, being Bestie, he was so well-known by the public he'd be spotted out wherever he was, usually in a nightclub and often with a different young lady.

There is, of course, that quite possibly apocryphal, but likely true, story of a hotel bellboy coming into Georgie's hotel room at some point towards the end of his career with room service, including some champagne and a selection of caviar, to find him in bed with the current Miss World, then hand him a newspaper which had the headline **George Best: Where did it all go wrong?**

Both of them laughed, apparently, and, as Best himself famously later said, 'I spent a lot of money on booze, birds and fast cars. The rest I just squandered.'

Well, I was quite possibly the diametric opposite to George Best. In fact, I thought I'd arrived in the big time when I got my face on a Stoke City drinks coaster. I had a stable home life and never got offered an advertising campaign for anything as glamorous as even mackerel!

At Stoke, we did get asked occasionally to do some promotional photographs for local businesses, though.

There's one that I dug up in researching this book which shows myself, Roy Vernon and Maurice Setters on an old Victorian bike. This was to advertise the new Penny Farthing nightclub, which was one of the places where we used to go for a few drinks and a natter. It was next to what was then Hanley bus station and was renowned for dancing to Motown music. But we never got paid for those jollies, at least not in cash. We'd get free drinks next time we went in as a thank you.

Not that us Stoke players went unrecognised. We didn't, we always had people wanting to chat, but we didn't have the kind of extreme hysteria that Bestie had to cope with.

I certainly didn't live the George Best lifestyle. I just liked a quiet one with the lads after the game, then I'd be off to take the missus out on Saturday night. We were creatures of habit. A nice meal out somewhere in the city, then we'd generally end up in The Place, the nightclub in Hanley frequented by generations of Stoke City players.

The extent of my drinking exploits were getting caught up in the mayhem of Alan Hudson's time at Stoke City in the mid-70s, but more of that later.

When it came to chatting with supporters, I was quiet because I always felt I wasn't that well educated, if I'm honest, but I could always talk with someone who just wanted to chat. Generally, though, I'd let them do the talking and me do the listening until it was my turn to answer or for me to get my word in, which I would still do now and then. That's the thing with being a footballer... even back then, you were public property. It's the same for all sportsmen if they get well known. People want to talk with you. Often with fans, though, they just want to tell you *their* opinion.

They aren't really asking for yours!

Even now, when we go out for a drink, my wife says I'm still like that. I'll find a quiet corner of the pub to sit in out of the way, whereas she likes to get out there and talk. But then she doesn't have to put up with all the supporters coming up to me and wanting to talk football, when I'm just trying to relax. All too often in a pub, no sooner have I finished talking with one supporter, then another one comes along.

I don't mind, though. I'll talk to them for as long as they want to, because I like talking football with fans, but it does mean that I learned to hide myself away a bit so I wouldn't be spotted too much. So I could just have a nice quiet time with my friends or my missus.

The closest I came to being one of those glamorous stars like Bestie was when I frequented the Crystal Ballroom in Newcastle, which by the mid-60s was renowned for attracting footballers. I remember meeting Jimmy Greaves in there once, after we'd beaten Tottenham at home in our first season up in 1963.

There was by then a downstairs bar called Bali Ha'i, which was a magnet for girls because glamorous footballers would often be found there. Of course, by then I'd got married so I could stand by and watch events… errrmmm, unfold.

In those days, the girls who frequented the Crystal or the Place wore explosively short mini-skirts and often did their hair in that curious piled-high style called a Beehive, which always looked as if it might fall off.

At the Crystal I first saw people dancing on their own, doing the Twist, the Madison and the Mambo, all those Sixties dances, whereas I'd always danced as a couple. They mostly danced in groups of girls and, as a feller, you would have to take your life in your hands, and go and try and dance with them to break into the circle, if you were interested. Which I wasn't.

When I popped in, people would just say, 'Hiya Skeelsy, do you want a drink?'

And I'd reply, 'I'll just have a shandy as I'm going courting'. Or 'I'm with my wife'. Just making it clear from the off. I've always been a lager drinker because with all the running you do in training, you're hot all the time and I would get that thirsty I'd like a cold lager to cool me down. Not to say I didn't have too much some nights, I did. But that was fairly rare and never after a Wednesday before a weekend game. I wasn't remotely interested in drinking as much as the likes of Roy Vernon, who was also a big smoker as I mentioned earlier.

I couldn't afford habits like smoking and I never liked cigarettes anyway. Although there wasn't the same level of awareness of the health hazards they posed back then as there is today, I knew they weren't good for me. That didn't stop 'Taffy' Vernon. It soon became clear why he was let go by Everton manager Harry Catterick so soon after leading the club to winning the Division One title.

Roy could drink like a fish, and used to chain smoke all the way until he hit the bookies, where he spent most of the afternoon, chucking money away left, right and centre.

You could tell Roy was a brilliant footballer, or had been. But by the age of 28, when he joined Stoke, he was a spent force and in around four years at the club, in exactly 100 appearances, he only scored 24 goals, whereas at Everton he had averaged more than a goal every other game.

The Sixties may have been full of glitz and glamour, but people like Roy make me thankful I didn't get drawn into all that too much. Cancer would eventually take him early, aged just 56 in 1993.

Later in the 60s and then into the 70s, we migrated to The Place in Hanley, which was the new, pre-eminent club in the area. We'd go as a squad, but once we'd arrived there was always a difference between the senior players and lads like me. There was a sort of special VIP area of the bar where Gordon Banks and George Eastham would go to be away from the main part of the club, while I'd be in the normal bar, but I didn't mind that. It didn't bother me at all.

We'd go to The Place a lot, almost every Monday, when we'd go out as a team. Again, as a married man, I'd find myself standing at the bar watching what was going on while others chatted up ladies.

The Place, like the Crystal before, became a Mecca for partying footballers from all over the country. They looked forward to playing at Stoke so they could go out there that evening. On one level, they knew there was a lot of fun to be had and on another they could go out for a drink with an icon like Banksy, or later Geoff Hurst and Alan Hudson.

So, in our own way, Stoke City became the new-found glamour club, boasting great players like Stan Matthews, and then Gordon Banks, and a nightlife renowned country-wide. It definitely helped to recruit the likes of Hudson, Hurst and Geoff Salmons.

I remember, we even had a programme which became the envy of the footballing world called the Ceramic City Clipper. And then a local playwright called Peter Terson wrote a play about terrace culture, which was a huge and growing thing back in the Sixties. It was called Zigger Zagger after one of our Stoke supporters called John Bayley, who I still see around occasionally. It was put on across the country by the National Youth Theatre. Eventually, we heard fans around the grounds picking up the chant of 'Zigger Zagger' from the show, which it had made popular, but which had actually started on the Boothen End.

So, now Stoke City was influencing football culture across the land.

OF COURSE, ONE thing that sets a footballer apart these days is some kind of flash car; maybe a Baby Bentley, a Lamborghini or a massive Range Rover. Back in those days just having a car was a huge thing because so few people could afford them. I remember how I got my first little motor in about 1960. It was off my half-brother Jim. It was a proper beat-up, second-hand Ford Consul, but I didn't care. I was just so pleased to have a car... big time. The problem was, I hadn't actually passed my test. So, I couldn't drive it down to the Potteries.

Jim drove trucks for a living and was car mad. He kept hold of the Ford for me and would be in the garage when he was at home, working on it. When I came back to Eccles from Stoke for the weekend, I often stayed with them. Jim had a daughter and son who were just a bit younger than I was, so when I'd go round I'd always be chatting with them and watching football on telly with them. His wife was super with me, as she realised I hadn't had a mother; so she looked after me as I was still only 19 or 20 at this point.

So, I think when Jim got himself a brand new car, he wanted to pass his old one down to me. Once I passed my test, which I had to do in Eccles, so I could then drive the car back home, he presented it to me like it was his pride and joy. It was immaculate and really well serviced because that was what Jim spent all his spare time doing. It was actually a really quite cool car as well.

Jim said, 'Now look after that, because I looked after it'. So I did.

And showed it off a bit.

When I drove it the 100 yards to training the next day and parked it up, all the lads came out into the car park and surrounded me, saying, 'Bloody hell, Skeelsy, how have you got that car?'

I said, 'It's my brother's.'

'Well, have you borrowed it?'

And I actually said, 'Yes' because I didn't want them all thinking they could pile in the car with me and then expect that we'd be going on adventures, as it would get in a mess. I still had Jim's words ringing in my ears. I wanted to keep it as immaculate as when he'd handed it over. So, I told them I was borrowing it off him.

I then found out that owning a car brought new levels of worry to me, as I would be concerned that, being quite a nice-looking car, albeit aged, it would get unwanted attention if I left it on the road as there were relatively few cars around in the Potteries then. So I used to park it round the back of my digs on a parcel of ground where people hung their washing out to keep it out of sight. This was back at the start of my career when I was in my digs, just round the corner from St Peter's School, only a few hundred yards from the Victoria Ground.

I then discovered I was able to park the car on the school playground, which was better as they locked the gate at night. The downside was, of course, if I wanted to get the car out after they'd gone home, then I couldn't because the gate would be locked. That kyboshed a few nights' courting, I can tell you.

I eventually traded my car up and would next end up driving a Ford Capri, and then a Rover. I liked both of those cars so much I had another one of each during the remainder of my time at Stoke. I ended up getting to know local garage owners who came and watched the games, and they would help me source my next car, every three or four years or so. By then, cars were far less of a status symbol and were fairly common around the city, but I always liked having new cars, or should I say new cars to me, as they were usually very good second-hand ones recommended by my garage-owning friends.

Car ownership was only possible for me by then because of the lifting of the £20 maximum wage cap in 1961. There were a lot of things going on at that time in terms of improving footballers' rights, with the PFA being led by Jimmy Hill and threatening to go out on strike to get that cap lifted. But one of the main drivers had been the determination of my now teammate George Eastham to move away from Newcastle United, who he felt had treated him so badly he needed to leave.

However, under the archaic 'retain and transfer' system, he couldn't do so. George always called those contracts 'slavery contracts'. He went on strike and actually earned a living as a cork salesman in London, making a point by earning more a week doing that than as a First Division footballer.

He was eventually able to join Arsenal, who paid Newcastle £47,500 for his services, and became their captain. George was selected in the England World Cup squad in 1966, although he didn't play a game, before he joined us just after the tournament ended.

I was always eternally grateful to George because he had played such an integral part in me being able to earn decent money in my career, taking Newcastle to court in 1964 funded by the PFA to enshrine the new system in law. I only played for two seasons under the wage cap and actually was so junior at that point I didn't even reach the ceiling anyway. But afterwards I earned, as I said before, up to £100 a week plus bonuses.

Bear in mind that the average wage in the UK in 1966 was about £900 a year and you can see how life, for us nouveau riche footballers, was great, despite us not earning the kinds of riches modern players do.

The weird thing was that I still felt money was still always tight. My lifestyle and circumstances changed throughout the Sixties, as I got married and had children, and money seemed to disappear on everyday living… things for the kids and the wife, plus paying the mortgage and having those cars. I still had to be sensible when I went out, unlike Bestie. I know that the big-named players who joined us at Stoke would have been on three or four times my wage. They always tended to be, while those of us who had come up through the ranks would be on far less.

You might say I was crazy to be so loyal, but I valued being settled far more than any potential additional cash I could earn from a move.

DID I EVER have the chance to leave Stoke?

I think so, but I was never officially approached. That didn't really happen back then like it does today.

I know there was a time when Blackburn showed an interest in me and Tony Waddington was interested in their centre-half Mike England, while Rovers, who had just been relegated, were thinking how best to leverage the sale of their best player. This was the summer of 1966, but in the end, Mike went to Tottenham, who, ironically, were the other club who apparently fancied me, at least according to Tony Allen, who'd heard this on the grapevine, so that seemed to be the end of that.

I suppose I could have earned a decent hike in my basic wage had I moved on, and received a decent signing-on fee too, but I just never wanted to leave. I know some leading managers, Matt Busby and Joe Mercer used to talk about me publicly as a player that they admired and that would get reported in the newspapers.

I've got a cutting from one in which Busby went on record to say, *'Eric Skeels is a rare player indeed. He can play anywhere and still be happy.'* It was lovely for him to say that, but it didn't make me think I should demand to see the manager and ask for a transfer, much as I would have loved to play for Manchester United, my boyhood team.

It's completely different nowadays of course, with agents, and the game all being about money first and foremost. Often clubs are having to sell to survive and players can agitate for moves. Back then that just never came into it.

I heard unofficial whispers occasionally, but I didn't pay any attention to paper talk. I was so settled in Stoke and Tony Waddington made sure my head never got turned. It was lovely to think clubs like that might want to sign me, but it never came to anything because I had developed all these ties to the Potteries. Moving to another club would have meant uprooting my family and I was never going to do that.

So, if a move was ruled out in terms of earning some more money – and it wasn't as if I could get a part-time job to make some extra money as I didn't really have any regular spare hours and certainly travelled away regularly enough, so that wasn't an option – I had to come up with an alternative scheme.

So I did.

I cashed in on my, ahemmm… 'celebrity'.

Or, at least tried to.

Glamorous, I was not.

But even us 'bits and pieces' players, as I call us, had a sort of caché and could go down the route of opening a sideline business… or a spot of moonlighting, if you like. Not that I thought that I was going to become some fashion leader like George Best, but one way I could increase my income, or so I thought, was to open a gentleman's clothing shop.

I did have a kind of entrepreneurial bent within me and I'd seen some of my fellow Stoke players making a success of some sideline businesses. Of course, Stan Matthews was a different league, having endorsements and advertising opportunities left, right and centre. He was after all Sir Stanley Matthews and was clearly in a completely different league to me.

But the captain of our promotion-winning team Eddie Stuart had, as well as his restaurant, opened a ladieswear shop in Newcastle, in an arcade down the hill, and I would often go down there and talk with him.

So, when I felt I needed to have a go, myself and Stoke teammate Willie Stevenson opened a gents shirt and tie shop in the same arcade; in fact in the corner opposite Eddie. The way it happened was, I'd met this chap who was in the pottery business who frequented Ma's café and become friends with him, often playing snooker together. He was also into retail and suggested Willie and I open this place and use our names to promote it, so it was owned between the three of us.

As it happened Mike Summerbee, the Manchester City winger, had opened up a sideline in the supply chain business for this kind of gear which I'd heard about. So we got in touch and he supplied us.

Willie was another roommate of mine. You could tell he had spent time at

Liverpool, from where he joined us in 1967 for £30,000. He was quite full of himself and could be a bit niggly in training, but I got on very well with him. Well, enough to go into business together in any case.

We got some publicity when we opened the shop, which was quite small with a few racks and a changing room at the back. It did okay to start with and we even opened a second branch in London Road in Stoke. But, over time, the fact that outside on the Ironmarket in Newcastle there was a market with stalls selling similar products, albeit of a lot less quality, for a lot lower prices, meant we didn't get a huge amount of trade… although that wasn't the entire problem.

What we didn't realise is that the chap Willie and I had gone into business with had recruited his own girlfriend to work in the shop; not because she was a great salesperson, but so they could close it up and have some nookie in the backroom during the day while Willie and I were training. It will come as no surprise then that the venture didn't exactly take off. It appeared there was only one thing going up, and it wasn't our profits.

We kept asking this feller how it was doing?

And he kept saying that it needed 'some time'. In the end, after a couple of years, we had to call it a day and sell up, as we made no money at all, not that we actually lost any; we ended up breaking even on the whole thing.

OF COURSE, IT wasn't all fun, frolics and outside interests. We actually worked phenomenally hard in training. Our coach Frank Mountford would occasionally get a professional long distance road runner in to put us through our paces to increase stamina. It was bloody hard going.

The runner's name was Derek Ibbotson and he had won a bronze medal in the 5,000 metres at the 1956 Melbourne Olympics and, at one point, held the world mile record. He would train us specifically to build stamina, like marathon training in a way, but then also to be able to sprint even when fatigued. We'd be jogging, with him in front of us, then we'd have to sprint when he shouted… 'SPRINT'.

But if you were halfway in the pack, or at the back, you couldn't actually hear him, you just reacted to everyone else sprinting off. It was best to be up at the front with him, so you could react as soon as he shouted. We'd do that four times round the pitch… jog, sprint… then walk a bit. Over and over again. If you were in the stragglers you'd have to do extra, hence why I was so keen to be at the front.

Other times, he'd split us into two groups and we'd have to sprint the full length of the pitch... then half of it... then a quarter, jogging in between... then back up the other way, quarter... half... then the full length of the pitch again.

Frank could be a miserable sod sometimes and took great delight in seeing the pain on our faces during Derek's sessions, shouting 'encouragement' from the pitchside as we toiled away. He often made me laugh, though. Frank was our 'sponge-man' for a long time until the club modernised and brought in physiotherapist Fred Streete, so for the first half of my career, I would be tended to, when injured, by a bluff former collier who had almost no medical knowledge and zero qualifications.

On a matchday, Frank would be in the dugout with his sponge and bucket, containing only water... freezing cold water. When he came onto the pitch to treat you, as you saw him trotting towards you, you'd suddenly develop this urge to get up quickly because no matter what the injury or knock you had, the only treatment Frank could offer was splashing cold water onto the affected area.

Depending on what said injured area was, this could be quite uncomfortable. He'd then give you a quick drink and tell you gruffly to, 'get up and run it off'. That was it, that was your lot. Hardly advanced medical treatment.

But in its own way, it acted as a real motivator to get up and get on with the game. Remember there were no substitutes at all until 1966, so Frank needed to keep us on the pitch if at all possible. He always used to tell us about a famous game he played in the early 50s, when goalkeeper Dennis Herod broke his arm early on and ended up playing on the wing, then broke away to score the winning goal in a 3-2 victory at Aston Villa.

This was an example of how players in his day were made of sterner stuff.

My other memory of Frank was him sitting in the dugout, which was very low, cut into the paddock below the turf, so that when you were sitting down your eyes were at pitch level; the touchline level with your eyeline so you had to look up to actually see the players' legs and waistline, let alone their faces. All the while he was in there, Frank would simply swear his way through games.

Sometimes, when I was substitute and went out to warm up along the touchline, I could hear Frank continue swearing to himself all the while I was jogging up and down. He'd still be chuntering away when I got back into the dugout. Frank liked to swear a lot, and I mean *a lot*... not that he had a particularly wide range of oaths and curses. What Frank could do brilliantly was massage your legs before a game. He was very good at that, especially your calves. He'd also strap you up using a bandage if you needed some support for a small muscle tear or an ankle injury. Frank himself had played through countless injuries in his days as a half-back and latterly centre-half, so he knew a lot about getting through games carrying knocks.

When we weren't doing stamina work, we'd be up in the gym, building muscle by using the different weights or doing circuits of different types of activities. Then, the day before a game, we'd just play a few five-a-sides in the area under the Boothen End, which was just a sort of concrete section under the terracing in which we used the doors to the toilets at either end as a goal, although, as it was such a hard flooring, we didn't have goalkeepers in those kickabouts. As it wasn't really built for this purpose – there were sharp edges and the walls were very solid – you had to be careful or a rash tackle or challenge could result in an injury. Or things might escalate, and you'd be having a ding-dong.

THAT DID HAPPEN once, at the end of the 1966/67 season when we were preparing to go on a post-season tour to America. In the squad by then were two very combative midfielders-cum-defenders, Calvin Palmer and Maurice Setters. When they had been recruited, from Nottingham Forest and Manchester United respectively, I had wondered if Waddo was bringing them in to replace me as both had a lot of First Division experience, but I was never dropped in favour of them, we just all got shifted around as Calvin and I could both also play right-back, while Maurice and I could both fill in at centre-half, as well as our preferred midfield positions. Calvin was right-sided, while Maurice was left. I could play anywhere, so it kind of worked.

The thing that stood me in such good stead was my reliability and even temper to just knuckle down and get on with things. Waddo knew what he would get from me. These two were much more combustible, especially Calvin. One minute you'd be best of mates… and then the next minute, you were being ignored and you had no idea what you'd done.

And he was supposed to be on your side! It was odd at times.

Calvin was blond and very good looking, with a baby face which belied his angry streak. He was dynamic and full-blooded, and often getting in trouble on the pitch as he took no prisoners, although he wasn't as unsubtle as Eddie Clamp, the man he replaced, had been. At one stage Tony Waddington made Calvin captain, hoping that the responsibility would calm him down a bit. It didn't.

Maurice had been the Manchester United captain when they won the FA Cup in 1963, but just 18 months later Matt Busby had moved him on as Nobby Stiles established himself as first choice both at Old Trafford and then for England. I think Maurice wanted to be top dog at Stoke, which was a problem because Calvin already thought he was!

So Calvin and Maurice simply didn't like each other.

I mean, I didn't ever feel you had to be best buddies with every single squad member. In fact, the odd bit of tension can be a positive thing at times, but you had to get on with each other well enough to be able to play together.

Certainly, there was no point hurting each other!

It all came to a head one day during a five-a-side under the Boothen End, when the combative pair had a scrap after Setters went in too hard and barged Palmer roughly into the concrete wall. Calvin's short fuse sparked a full-on fistfight for a few seconds, with them rolling over and over on the rock-hard floor.

The rest of us couldn't quite believe it.

Calvin ended up getting a full fist in the face during the melée and Frank Mountford had to intervene to split them up. When Tony Waddington heard about what had happened, he barred them both from travelling to North America, but Setters apologised and Waddo allowed him to go on the trip. Palmer would do no such thing.

It just wasn't in his nature to say sorry and he stayed at home.

Calvin was eventually sold to Sunderland part-way through the following season, in February 1968, as I think the manager had given up on trying to get him to fall into line. He always held a bit of a grudge against the club after he left. To be honest, Calvin had a bit of a grudge against life. He could start an argument in an empty room and would never stand down. That was brilliant on the pitch, but caused an endless series of problems off it, resulting in the manager finally giving up and moving him on.

Strangely, for that trip to America, we were not playing as Stoke City Football Club, but were rebranded as the Cleveland Stokers for the purposes of promoting the game in the USA. We were based in Cleveland, Ohio and representing the city in the North American United Soccer Association (the immediate predecessor of the North American Soccer League – NASL, which was founded the following year).

We played that summer against many other clubs from around the footballing world, who had also taken on different names to represent cities. So, we met Wolves in the guise of Los Angeles... Aberdeen posing as Washington... Dundee United represented Dallas... and Cerro of Uruguay played as the New York Skyliners... Bangu of Brazil were Houston... Cagliari from Italy were the Chicago Mustangs... ADO Den Hague of Holland represented San Francisco... and Sunderland played for Vancouver.

Apparently, each club was paid around $250,000 for the competition (worth about $2 million today), plus prize money, so Stoke City did very well out of it and we had a wonderful few weeks or so on the shores of Lake Erie, staying in a hotel near the stadium, which was actually the home of both the local American football and baseball teams, and travelling around the continent to play the games.

We had to fly almost everywhere as North America is so huge. In fact, on any week there was no game, we'd fly down to Fort Lauderdale and train in the heat and go on the beach, rather than stay up in the cooler north, which was great.

This was the life. I wore the No 3 shirt in that tournament as, for some odd reason, John Farmer, our reserve goalkeeper, was given the No 2 shirt, instead of the more traditional 13 or 14. I played 12 of our 13 games, as we finished second in our section, just missing out by one point to Aberdeen... I mean the Washington Whips. That meant we missed out on reaching the final play-off which the winners of each of the two sections competed in. Peter Dobing ended up as our top goalscorer with seven, while Maurice Setters, who would actually find himself sold to Coventry before the start of the following First Division season, perhaps as a result of that fracas back in England, scored three.

Dobing, George Eastham and Roy Vernon were all selected in the All Star Team of the Season. It was a great trip and we went on more and more of these tours as the years rolled by, as well as welcoming some of the world's greatest teams to Stoke.

I'VE ALREADY MENTIONED that I played against Puskás, Di Stéfano and Gento, when Real Madrid came to visit in 1963. Well, five years later, I played against perhaps the greatest player in the world at that time, and certainly the best striker, Pelé, when his Brazilian club Santos came to play at the Victoria Ground in a friendly.

I don't mind telling you, I couldn't really get near Pelé to tackle him, despite running all over the place trying to catch him. I did finally manage to put a couple of challenges in, so I did win the ball off him at some point! But Santos won 3-2. Even the Waddington Wall couldn't hold out against Pelé and his teammates. They were far more tactically astute than us, as they didn't just play a rigid 4-4-2 system like we did in the late 60s. Their level of skill was also incredible. They were all so comfortable on the ball.

As well as attracting some big names and clubs to play at the Vic, Tony Waddington was always looking to see where around the world he could take us to play and spread the gospel of Stoke City, earn us a few more fans and a lot more pounds. He told us to keep our passports ready at all times, and there were occasions when we'd come in for training thinking it was just going to be a 'normal' day and, by the end of it, we'd be travelling to an airport to jet off somewhere exotic in Europe or North Africa to play an impromptu friendly. For bigger trips, like the 1967 one to North America, we had far more notice of course.

The First Division season would finish in May and we'd mostly be able to have a break and go on holiday with our families, before returning to take part in the tour which had been sorted out by our agent Charlie Mitten. He had been a senior player at Manchester United when Waddo had been in the youth team, before controversially playing abroad himself alongside Stoke's Neil Franklin when a group of players went to Colombia in 1950. That had proved a disaster, but had whetted Mitten's appetite for international travel and, after managing Mansfield and Newcastle, where he had actually been in charge during George Eastham's argument with the club over wages and contract, Charlie had then got heavily involved in overseas football and promoting tours for British clubs.

Consequently, we'd disappear off abroad with Stoke for 10 days or two weeks, sometimes longer at the end of each season to different places each summer. You never quite knew where you'd be headed next. We almost never came back on the original date, as the tours kept getting extended as Mitten and Waddo found more games for us to play. We didn't mind as we were having a fabulous time and anyway, the club gave us £2 a day spending money.

Our next big trip abroad came in May 1969, at the end of a tough campaign in which we'd only just avoided relegation, when we played a mini tour of Spain. You might think that was just some end of season jolly to reward us for averting the drop. We were based in Las Palmas, but it was far from a holiday break.

You don't play with Denis Smith and go onto any football pitch without taking the game extremely seriously. Okay, so off the pitch it was like a holiday camp being there for a few days. I loved the place. But we never took any games lightly.

That tour began with an incredible 3-2 victory over Barcelona at the Nou Camp. We were actually 3-0 up in the first-half thanks to two goals by David Herd and one from Harry Burrows! I really enjoyed playing at that stadium in front of 65,000 fans, keeping them and their star players quiet.

That game was a warm-up for Barcelona, before their forthcoming European Cup Winners' Cup final against Slovan Bratislava, so their team was a very good one, but Barca also lost that game 2-3 in Basle, a few days later.

It was a few months after that when Santos came to Stoke, so by the end of the 60s, we had beaten Barcelona in the Nou Camp, drawn with Real Madrid, and only just lost to Pele's Santos. If you'd told any of us that, as the decade dawned, and Tony Waddington had taken over an ailing, struggling club as manager, we would have just laughed!

Travelling was one very glamorous perk of being a top-flight footballer that I really enjoyed. I had barely been anywhere in the UK that was unrelated to football, so to travel all over the world to play exhibition games was manna from heaven.

Consequently, this youth from Eccles got to visit and play football in cities like Dublin, Amsterdam, Barcelona, Marseille, Monaco, Istanbul, Tel Aviv, Moscow, Accra, Buenos Aires and Kinshasa... and in countries such as Turkey, Israel, Greece, Austria, Spain, Portugal, Colombia, Argentina, Morocco, Ghana, Sweden, Russia, Australia, New Zealand and the USA.

And those are just the ones I can remember! Not bad for that scrawny Lancashire lad who a few years earlier didn't know where Stockport was.

You could say that my love of geography finally paid dividends, and indeed my knowledge of these places around the world still far exceeds the UK, aside from the location of British football clubs! In fact, I'm often now fairly insufferable if conversation turns to travel, because when people tell me about their holidays, it turns out almost always that I've been to wherever they are going to or have just visited!

A lot of it was a blur. We spent a lot of time on planes and coaches, which broke down quite a lot and we played cards to pass the time. We just had an absolute blast both on and off the pitch, with one side effect being that it made us very close as a group, which I feel stood us in very good stead, both in those seasons we were battling relegation and in the subsequent ones when we were fighting for trophies.

One thing that stands out for me was that in Turkey the stands were often set very far back from the pitch, which I was thankful for as the crowds were quite crazy, loud and vociferous.

In Moscow, we stayed in a very nice hotel, but we were not allowed out without prior written permission as this was during the heightened Soviet era. There were lots of 'stewards' at the hotel, but we were fairly sure they were KGB agents, although none of them looked like Rosa Klebb, the Bond villain in *From Russia With Love*.

When we were allowed out, they made sure we knew what time we had to be back at the hotel. We managed to do some sightseeing, like going to Lenin's tomb. In general, I was always happy to go and do the trips out that were organised rather than sit around the hotel. In Moscow, we were very conscious that when we ambled out for a walk we were being watched everywhere we went and we had to make sure we stuck together. I remember, too, that the Russians drank vodka, rather than beer... a lot of vodka, knocking it back like there was no tomorrow. I avoided that as much as I could, but we did have to toast our hosts regularly during the dinners.

Going to Australia and New Zealand in 1973 was a huge trip in every way. We had a great time, but because of the distances there would often be a lot of travelling directly after the games. We visited Western Australia, New South Wales and South Australia before moving on to Auckland, Wellington, Christchurch and Dunedin as we went from North Island to South Island.

I also enjoyed Israel a lot, but why shall remain a secret.

The one time it all went wrong on tour was in Rome when we played there in the Anglo-Italian Cup on June 1, 1971. We pulled off a remarkable 1-0 win at the Stadio Olimpico in front of 37,360 increasingly angry home supporters. John Ritchie grabbed the only goal in a tetchy game, rifling home a superb left-footed volley. The irate locals let off rockets and firecrackers during the mach, and as the final whistle was blown they rioted and invaded the pitch, tearing down the goal nets and dugouts. The police deployed tear gas, but that only seemed to inflame things further and we had to shelter inside their changing room for two hours for our own safety. Outside, the army, toting machine guns as deterrents, battled with supporters. We somehow made it to our coach and hid below the window level to avoid being spotted as it drove out of the stadium.

The following morning, Tony Waddington and chairman Albert Henshall become the first English football officials to be granted an audience with the Pope and handed Paul VI a Stoke City pennant to mark the occasion.

I just gave thanks we'd got out unscathed and alive!

LIFE WAS GREAT.

I may not have been George Best, but I was a first team regular who was now used to top-flight football and glamorous international tours. Money wasn't a problem, although I could always do with finding a way to spend less.

Which wasn't what happened at all, as it was at that point that I got to know an estate agent from Longton who after a few months told me that he'd found me a dream house out near Endon for a good price. So, I went with him to have a look.

The house was in a cul-de-sac on the edge of Stockton Brook in quite a remote location. It was a big, detached house which had this beautiful view overlooking the countryside.

He took me inside and showed me its four bedrooms, two toilets, the large kitchen and then a fabulous garden out the back with this incredible view down the bank and over the valley, where there was a pathway where people rambled and open fields with horses in. There was a huge flag paving patio on which to enjoy the sun as well.

It was stunning and I fell in love with it.

The price didn't frighten me as long as we could sell our existing house. In fact, I thought this was a steal. I got the missus over to have a look that same afternoon after she'd finished work. She loved it too and that very same day we decided to buy the house.

The club and the estate agent helped me get another mortgage and, before we knew it, we'd sold our house in Weston Coyney and the four of us were living in this luxurious mansion of a place. It was idyllic.

In fact, the only complaint Maggie had was that we didn't have enough furniture to fill the house, because it was so big!

People who came to visit us must have thought we were millionaires because the house was that stunning. I very much wasn't! But I had done very nicely, thank you, from the Swingin' Sixties.

Myself, Denis Smith and Jackie Marsh, the old and the somewhat younger defenders at Stoke City in 1970.

Flat out defending to keep out Tottenham Hotspur's Alan Gilzean (second left), alongside teammates Gordon Banks, Tony Allen (No 6), Mike Bernard and Alex Elder (No 3). Spurs' Mike England watches on in frustration.

Meanwhile, cleaning my boots from all the mud, whilst the typically muddy yet forthright Denis Smith chats with the inured Jimmy Greenhoff in the dressing-room at the Victoria Ground.

CHAPTER 8

1972 and All That

I SUPPOSE YOU could say that the first two seasons of the 1970s – 1970/71 and 1971/72 – were two of the greatest ever in the history of Stoke City Football Club. Across the two seasons we played 127 matches… 84 in the league, 19 in the FA Cup, 14 in the League Cup, six in the Anglo Scottish Cup and four in the Anglo Italian Cup.

In the league we were back established as a mid-table First Division side, but it was as a cup team that we truly flourished. We reached three semi-finals, two of which resulted in controversial defeats, and won one trophy, the first and to date only major cup ever lifted by the Potters… a glorious day at Wembley in March 1972. They were heady, exciting days as we played some fantastic stuff, having shaken off the shackles of the Waddington Wall to discover a more exciting, off-the-cuff brand of football.

I played in 69 of those games in eight different positions, wearing shirt numbers 2, 3, 4, 5, 6, 7, 8, 9, 10, 12 and 14, featuring in all three of those semi-finals in one guise or another. Just the No 11 shirt missing in the collection then in those two campaigns alone.

But I have a particular viewpoint on that period, which isn't necessarily one you may have heard before, because by this stage I was a player more on the periphery; an important part of the squad, but not necessarily the first-choice team. Put it this way, I might not have been the first name on the team-sheet, but

I was still most definitely the first name on the team-sheet when the chap who was the first name on the team-sheet got injured or suspended.

In fact, of those 69 games I featured in, 12 were as a sub, but I would say I was filling in for injured players around seventy-five percent of the rest of the time.

When you are playing that many games across a two-year period it is obviously going to be a squad game and so it proved, which was great for me and I loved every minute of the challenge of right-back one week, in central midfield the next, then as a central defender the week after.

So, I suppose the key question is how Tony Waddington rejuvenated the squad to turn us into a team that could challenge for trophies.

For me, if the return of Stanley Matthews is the biggest single transfer coup in Stoke City's history, then I'd claim that the re-signing of John Ritchie, and the pairing of the big man with new arrival Jimmy Greenhoff, who joined in the summer of 1969 from Birmingham City for £100,000, was the biggest reason why that early-70s team would go on to win the 1972 League Cup.

Not that it was all down to those two alone, obviously, but John solved the goalscoring problem we had suffered throughout the period he was at Sheffield Wednesday, while Jimmy proved to be the perfect partner for him. Clever and intelligent with his runs and passes, Jim was a classy player who was very difficult to mark. How Jimmy never won an England cap is criminal.

It really does make you think about England managers favouring big clubs. He was just a superb player who, in his pomp over the next five or six years, would have walked into any of the other teams who were challenging for trophies at that time, like Leeds, Arsenal or Liverpool.

Greenhoff and Ritchie were very much a partnership. Jimmy was great right from the off when he joined. Despite being the club's first £100,000 signing he really wasn't a bighead at all. He never showed off, he just displayed his talent on the pitch. Off it, he became one of the lads.

John just slotted back in as if he'd never been away. I think he actually did come back a better player than before he'd left. I was certainly grateful I didn't have to play against him anymore, or Jimmy!

The other key ingredient in that attack was the maturing of some younger players like Terry Conroy on the wing, and Mike Bernard and John Mahoney were becoming superb central midfield players.

Conroy and Mahoney were best mates, having signed within a day of each other in 1967. Terry was the classic cheeky Irish chappie who had spent a couple of seasons developing into a fine winger, mainly on the right, but who learnt to also operate on the left, after vastly improving his left foot with regular practice. Terry would also eventually play through the middle after John Ritchie retired. He had a great turn of pace and exuberant amounts of energy, with a shock of red hair, humongous sideburns and almost translucent white legs. His strides were very long, which helped him outrun you, as he often did to me in training. He'd get down the line fast, beat a defender, get to the byline and cross the ball in for the strikers. Alongside Ritchie and Greenhoff, he formed a devastating attacking force throughout the first half of the 70s.

Behind the scenes, TC sometimes was a villain, though, in the Don Ratcliffe mould. He'd nick your clothes from the dressing-room and hide them, sometimes swapping them around with other players. He was always really cheeky as well. Being a bloody Irishman, to coin a phrase, he could talk for England. You couldn't get a bloody word in with him. And still can't!

He was and is a smashing bloke. We still bump into each other these days at the fish shop in Newcastle, often with our wives, and we stop and a chat, although he's moved out from Trentham to Alsager now.

John Mahoney was known to us all as 'Josh' or 'Josher'. He had an incredible engine on him and also took some time to develop, but he eventually matured like a fine wine. Like TC, Josh became an international, eventually earning 51 caps for Wales, while Conroy played 27 times for the Republic of Ireland. The pair of them were inseparable off the pitch, always kicking around together and having a lot of fun.

WHILE OUR ATTACK was much more fluid and full of goals, the other major overhaul Tony Waddington made was the complete change up within the back four. By 1970 his first choice starting defence was Jackie Marsh at right-back, Mike Pejic at left-back and the two centre-halves Alan Bloor and Denis Smith.

All four were local lads and in their own way were extremely good footballers, while at the same time being blood-curdlingly efficient and sometimes brutal tacklers.

As an elder statesman, along with Tony Allen, I mentored them through and into the team, often talking them through games, as the likes of Eddie Stuart and Bobby Howitt had done with me at the start of my career. It soon became apparent, though, that these four were plenty good enough to fend for themselves as they became established as the first choice in their positions, but also as a quartet they gelled together brilliantly, marshalled by the experienced Gordon Banks behind them. They have become synonymous with the success we achieved over that period... the local back four.

Alan Bloor was already well established in the side from around 1966 as he was slightly older, only being four years younger than me. He was a left-sided centre-half who was fairly no nonsense and no frills, but read the game particularly well and was great with interceptions. He also enjoyed a challenge and was extremely strong. He was hard, but not dirty. Just really *hard*. We used to call him the 'silent assassin'. Bloor hailed from Stoke and was nicknamed 'Bluto' by the supporters, in honour of his vague similarity to Popeye's combative foe in the cartoon, which we took on and called him as well. He just got on with his job. He was a man of few words and when he spoke you took heed. It was always positive advice, something you needed to do, so when he opened his mouth, you listened. He was quiet off the pitch as well, but on it he dovetailed brilliantly with the more vocal Denis Smith, his partner in assassination and a real exponent of the art.

Denis was, how shall I put it? Incredibly combative.

He became a Stoke City legend; a man who wore his heart on his sleeve on the pitch and threw himself into challenges as if his life depended upon it, but, like me, was relatively quiet off it. He was a very hard worker, both in games and in training; a real 90-minute man. At six foot tall, there weren't many people who could outjump him and he was a good positional player from corner-kicks and free-kicks. He scored a fair few goals as well.

Denis was from Meir in the south of the city and he got on brilliantly with Bluto. They formed a really strong partnership which dealt brilliantly with the attacking forces that the likes of Arsenal, Liverpool and Leeds United threw at them. His never-say-die spirit typified Stoke City in that era and some of the things he did were breathtaking, like the time he was supposed to be injured with a bad back and turned up in the dressing-room to wish the team luck before an FA Cup replay at the Victoria Ground against Manchester United. He ended up pulling on a shirt and playing, then scoring the equaliser in an eventual 2-1 win after extra-time.

Apparently, his wife's face was a picture when she saw him coming out of the tunnel instead of sitting down beside her in the stand!

Denis never complained, despite all the injuries he racked up. He was constantly getting injured in training, never mind in a game; he was that committed. He was undoubtedly a leader in pretty much every sense, other than wearing the armband in my time at Stoke. Had he been a little bit older perhaps he could have been the League Cup-winning captain, but, of course, he did go on to skipper the club later in his career, winning promotion back to the top flight in 1978/79 under Alan Durban.

I was not surprised when Denis went on to become a successful manager, who managed well over 1,000 games for six clubs. He always fought shy of coming back to Stoke to take the manager's job here, though. I think he didn't want to risk his legacy amongst the fanbase because he is still idolised by many, and rightly so.

If you thought Denis Smith was a tough tackler, then you should definitely steer well clear of left-back Mike Pejic. Pej would kick you, as soon as say hello to you!

Unlike Denis and Bluto, Pej wasn't only an assassin on the pitch. He was constantly angry. Even with his own teammates! I mean, I got on alright with him, but he could be an awkward sod. He was always looking for an argument. He was very much his own man then and is now still, as you might know from listening to his radio co-commentary on Radio Stoke.

Pejic was compactly built at 5 feet 8 inches, a strong athlete with a sweet left foot and good pace.

He had been a left winger in his youth, but Tony Waddington had converted him to a defensive player, much like he had done with me, as he was energetic, would run all day and wasn't afraid to tackle anyone. He was good enough quality to win four England caps in the spring of 1974, but Pej was also a tough bugger and a fitness fanatic. He still is, as he is an Over-65 age-group European Taekwondo champion. Mike had other interests outside football, as he kept a farm near Leek, so we often didn't see him after training and he didn't socialise so much with us.

The right back was Jackie Marsh, who was a really good player. He was a bit like me as he was just a normal, local lad who happened to have a talent for football. He was short and squat and specialised in overlapping Terry Conroy on the right and hitting hard, flat crosses over to allow forwards to just try and get a flick or touch to direct the ball towards goal with the pace that was already on it.

Jackie enjoyed training, then lived life to the full when he went out. We used to knock around a bit after games and so forth and enjoyed each other's company. One thing about Jackie was that he wore contact lenses and during the 1972 League Cup final, with about 10 minutes to go, he actually lost one and had to scrabble around on the Wembley turf to try and find it. He ended up playing those last few tense minutes half-blind.

That back line of local lads was great. They each had a special relationship with the fans and with the club, but are also always remembered as a four. By 1969 they were starting to play together on a regular basis, bolstered with great experience around them such as Banksy, George Eastham and Peter Dobing, Harry Burrows and myself.

But if they were all fit, where was there room for me?

MOSTLY ON THE bench, I was, but often there were injuries or suspensions, especially when you had voracious tacklers like Smith and Pejic in your team, so I'd be called upon to fill in for each of the back four regularly as their full-throttle all-action styles ensured they all picked up regular injuries, particularly Denis, who became known as 'the most injured man in football', being listed as such in the Guinness Book of Records one year!

Not that having an injury often meant Smithy wouldn't start the next game. Denis broke his nose on multiple occasions, fractured his ankle, chipped his spine and I've no idea how many stitches he must have had in his career... enough to darn a lifetime of socks that's for sure. None of those injuries kept him out of the team, though.

But he did break one or other of his legs five times in his career and even a nutter like Denis can't play in plaster!

I could have been used more in midfield, but not only was John Mahoney in the midst of establishing himself as a fine footballing midfielder, but so was another youngster off the conveyer belt of youth stars at Stoke, Mike 'Mickey' Bernard. Mike had joined from Shrewsbury Town as a youth player and also came of age at the same time as the young, local back four. I did get to fill in there occasionally and, despite my age, I was always determined and fit enough to keep up with these precocious youngsters in training, never wanting to be outdone.

By 1970, Mike was first choice in the central defensive midfield role. He socialised well with the lads, but was starting a family and in fact his wife gave birth to their second child on the day of the 1972 League Cup final!

At this point, I did wonder how long my time would last at Stoke, but as long as I was first change and the manager still wanted me around, I was very happy to continue. As long as I was in and around the team – and when I wasn't filling in for one of the first choice players I was often the substitute due to my adaptability, so I was always in the squad – then I felt like I was doing a decent job for the club.

That was all that mattered to me.

BY 1970 YOU could sense that we'd got a real side coming together with all this young talent blended with the more experienced pros like Peter Dobing, George Eastham, Gordon Banks and myself. In those next two seasons we found we were more of a cup side as we weren't getting results consistently enough in the league, but we showed our potential and never-say die spirit in the knockout competitions.

As with most trophy wins, there is a process involved. They don't often come completely out of left field. We had a couple of near misses before and after that glorious Wembley win in 1972, the first being in the FA Cup in 1970/71.

It's a painful memory even today.

I played in every game of that epic FA cup run. We beat Millwall at home 2-1 in round three, then took three games to get past a Huddersfield side featuring the talismanic Frank Worthington in round four, and a replay to see off Ipswich Town in the fifth round. So, we'd already played six games – the number most teams play to actually lift the trophy, and we'd only just reached the quarter-final.

When we drew Second Division Hull, we all knew we had a great chance to qualify for the semi-final for only the second time in the club's history and the first time this century as the previous visit to the last four had been in 1899. But when we went 0-2 behind in the first-half at Boothferry Park, I've got to be honest, we were on the ropes. We weren't playing at all well and the home side, buoyed by a brilliant crowd backing them all the way, were on a high.

We needed inspiration to mount a comeback and that arrived right on half-time when a speculative long pass by Sean Haslegrave down the left-hand side found Terry Conroy, racing on to it in the clear, outpacing the defence, to then dance around 'keeper Ian McKechnie on the edge of the area and slot home from six yards into the gaping net. There were hundreds of Stokies in the crowd that day and they made themselves heard when that goal went in. You could just feel the momentum shift in that moment and there was always only one winner after half-time. We knew we could take them as we sat in the dressing-room, and we did, swarming all over them as they wilted as the game wore on.

John Ritchie first tapped in from two yards to equalise, and then got onto a perfect cross from TC, floated to the far post from the right-hand side, to head home from four yards to complete a thrilling comeback and seal an appearance in the FA Cup semi-final for the first time in 72 years

I remember that winning goal came from a controversial throw-in, which the officials were undecided which way to give… and John Mahoney basically made their decision for them, picking the ball up down by the right corner flag and throwing it to Terry, just inside the penalty area, to turn and chip the ball across for John to nod home.

I wore the No 10 in that game, but far from being John Ritchie's strike partner, because Jimmy Greenhoff was injured, I was playing in a central midfield role and Terry was playing up front alongside Big John.

Against Arsenal in the FA Cup semi-final at Hillsborough, Tony Waddington selected me at right-back with Jackie Marsh carrying a slight knock, so he was dropped to the bench. I took this as a great show of faith from the manager. He trusted me in this situation; the biggest game of most of our lives.

Only Gordon Banks and Peter Dobing had actually played in the cup final itself. I had only ever dreamed of actually playing at Wembley, but now it was a tangible reality. We were absolutely brilliant in the first-half, arguably as good as we ever were in a single half of football. Arsenal didn't get a sniff as we outfought them defensively to snuff them out completely, while, at the other end, things just went for us.

You could argue that our opening goal had a huge slice of fortune involved in it, but from where I stood, Arsenal shot themselves in the foot, just as much as we got lucky.

What happened was a right-wing corner was curled in by Harry Burrows to the near post, where it fell to Peter Storey, the Gunners' defensive midfielder. Inexplicably, he tried to control the ball and dribble out, giving Denis Smith the chance to close him down. When Storey finally realised he needed to whack it clear, Denis was on him, blocking the clearance with his left foot.

The ball was hit so hard that it cannoned off Smithy and flew at tremendous pace directly above 'keeper Bob Wilson's head and into the Arsenal net off the underside of the bar, right in front of the Potters fans gathered on the Leppings Lane terrace. You could say it was lucky, but in my opinion you mostly make your own luck. Denis certainly did that.

There was a smattering of fortune about our second goal too, although again, the real skill was John Ritchie's positioning and anticipation of a potential Arsenal defensive mistake, this time from their midfielder Charlie George. From midway in his own half, without really looking, Charlie hit a tame back pass towards Wilson. It was easily intercepted by Big John, who was lurking on the shoulder of the last defender, alert to the possibility the ball might just come his way.

When it did, he found himself put clean through by George's errant back-pass and he raced onto the ball, hurdled the floundering Wilson, who had charged out of his goal, before knocking it into the net.

John celebrated by whirling back towards the halfway line with both arms raised in delight, taking the acclaim in a moment now frozen in time for posterity as part of the John Ritchie bust, which is positioned behind the Boothen End at Stoke's Bet365 Stadium.

At 2-0 up by half-time, what could possibly go wrong?

But we weren't already in the final. We weren't at Wembley. We still had 45 minutes to negotiate and, midway through the second-half, Storey, whose mistake had led to our opening goal, made amends with a rocket of a shot from 25 yards. Peter never ever scored goals. He certainly wasn't the threat as far as we were concerned and his thunderbolt shot came out of absolutely nowhere.

We now only had a one-goal lead.

Arsenal's attacks became increasingly frantic as time ebbed away and we felt that we had repelled them all, but then came the moment of huge controversy.

Or should I say, a whole succession of them.

Five minutes of injury time had already been played in a game in which there had barely been a stoppage. Not only that, but referee Pat Partridge then awarded a controversial free kick against Mike Pejic, 40 yards out on the right. We all felt that the foul was actually the other way. For us.

Then, when the free-kick was lofted into the penalty area, Arsenal striker John Radford barged Gordon Banks in the back as he went up to collect the ball, but the referee missed the foul. In the melée which followed, Banks dropped the ball after being smashed into, and Denis Smith actually punched the ball away, which Partridge also missed.

Quite what the referee was looking at, I don't know. Thankfully, at least he was consistent in missing obvious things.

The ball was then blocked away for a corner, which was curled in from the right wing and Ray Kennedy rose eight yards out to head the ball towards the bottom corner. It was saved by a flying fist, but sadly it belonged to midfielder John Mahoney… not Banksy. Even Partridge could not miss that and awarded the penalty.

All hell broke loose at that point.

It obviously was handball, but the referee had got so much wrong beforehand it should never have got that far. Storey slid the spot-kick past a dispirited Banks and we had been pegged back to 2-2 with the very last kick.

We trudged off dispirited.

We'd been so good and yet not won.

Wembley's Twin Towers suddenly seemed a distant dream.

I am sure that if we had held on for another couple of minutes to win the first FA Cup semi against Arsenal, then win at Wembley, it would have been transformative and would have given us the kind status for Tony Waddington to deal at the very top table with Leeds, Liverpool, Manchester United and Arsenal for the very best players. Instead, we lost the replay 0-2 and were the nearly men, still searching for that first FA Cup.

We actually finished third in the FA Cup that season as the FA, in their wisdom, set up a play-off between the two losing semi-finalists and we defeated Everton 3-2 at Selhurst Park the night before the cup final. Ironically, we went 0-2 behind to the Toffees that night yet came back to win 3-2. So, the last three rounds we played in that season's competition saw the team who went 2-0 ahead fail to win.

I WAS GENERALLY very lucky injury-wise. I'd get occasional knocks, but I was rarely ever injured. Often, I'd miss training to get some treatment but I could always recover quickly, be right for later in the week and able to be selected.

I only ever had one bad injury. It happened against Leicester in August 1971 when right-back Steve Whitworth went into a tackle with me and I went down. I remember it hurt a lot. So much, in fact, that when I looked up to see Frank Mountford loping towards me with his sponge and bucket at the ready, I was struggling to get up and avoid having freezing cold water squirted all over me.

Despite the pain in my leg, the treatment was the same as always and so was Frank's advice… 'Alfie, just go on the wing and run it off for a minute,' he said… which I did.

I had to.

I was the sub and if I went off, we'd have been left with 10 men.

I was actually alright until I angled my body too far forward when trying to sprint and I felt my lower left leg become incredibly painful. I went to the turf, had some more of Frank's magic sponge treatment, and got up again. I managed to play on and even played a pass in for Peter Dobing to score the final goal in a 3-1 victory.

After the game, in the dressing-room, our director Mr Crowe, who was a surgeon at the hospital, took a look at it and said to me, 'I think it could be a trapped nerve, so go up to the hospital tomorrow if it hasn't improved'.

Based on that advice, I had a shower, got changed and went out for a meal with the missus and then we joined the lads at The Place in Hanley for some dancing. Well, I say dancing… it was mostly standing and chatting, then an end of the night smooch with the missus. I do remember at one point falling down the stairs because my leg felt so odd and collapsed a bit from under me.

I wasn't particularly drunk, so I knew it wasn't the booze which had made me stumble and fall, but I still thought at that point it was only some kind of trapped nerve or a strain. When I woke on the Sunday morning it was still feeling pretty painful, so I went up to the hospital. Unlike these days when footballers have their own doctors and specialists to call upon, I had to sit in the waiting room with everyone else, awaiting my turn. Eventually the nurse called me through, checked me over and said that I should have an X-Ray. So back I went to the waiting room to wait for that.

My wife's brother was coming over to visit and I was supposed to meet him, so after the X-Ray was taken I told the nurse I was off to go and find him, but she told me that Mr Crowe wanted to see me. He sat me down.

'Eric, I'm going to put you in plaster!'

'You what?' I replied, aghast.

I actually thought he was talking about somebody else, not me.

He said, 'You've fractured your leg. It's a hairline fracture, but it's clearly visible on the X-Ray, so it's got to go in plaster and you're going to be out for a while'.

I was completely shocked. This had never happened to me before. I was admitted to the hospital and was in plaster up to the top of my leg before I knew it.

I was in plaster for about six weeks, but thankfully that was the only serious injury I ever had. Ironically, it was a completely innocuous tackle, the type I'd gone into a million times before in matches, but this one somehow led to me being in plaster. Ending up being kept in the hospital to get plastered up put paid to my social afternoon.

Recuperating afterwards, I just had to rest to start with. Then, eventually, I started going down to watch training, leaning on my crutches like Dennis Wilshaw had all those years before, just with no contribution to make over seismic signings to transform the fortunes of the football club.

After the plaster came off, I initially just started walking around, then doing some light jogging on my own before returning to training without any tackling and building myself up with gym sessions. I had to go back to have further X-rays several times and eventually they said I could train properly.

Just as I got back into contention for selection in early December 1971, almost four months after getting injured, another semi-final was fast approaching, this time in the League Cup against West Ham United. Ron Greenwood's team was full of stars, like England World Cup winners Bobby Moore, Geoff Hurst and Martin Peters, plus winger Harry Redknapp and midfielders Trevor Brooking and Billy Bonds.

My return to fitness was timely for Tony Waddington because Denis Smith had suffered one of his regular injuries, being concussed when scoring in the 4-2 win at Bristol Rovers in the quarter-final, and was out for a few weeks.

I was thrown back in straightaway to partner Alan Bloor for the second-leg at Upton Park.

In the first-leg at the Victoria Ground, a youngster called Stewart Jump had played as I wasn't quite ready to deputise for Denis, and had struggled against Hammers' centre-forward Clyde Best, giving away a penalty which Geoff Hurst had lashed home to equalise Dobing's early goal, and then lashing in a superb strike himself from 20 yards or so to give West Ham a 2-1 lead.

I was now detailed by Tony Waddington to mark Best.

Clyde was a big hunk of a striker, and could give you a very rough time as a defender. I knew I'd have to be on my game given that I'd been out for so long and this would be my first game back.

At that time, we backed ourselves against anyone, which was a good job because it took us 12 games to win the League Cup in 1972, including three against Man Utd and four against West Ham. Getting through those two rounds alone saw us play more games than it takes any team to win the whole tournament these days, due to replays being scrapped and ties being finished on the night by a penalty shootout.

So, despite losing the first game, we were actually confident going into the second-leg. You have to think you're going to win or else you're not a sportsperson, in my opinion. We were only a goal behind and there was no such thing as 'away' goals in the League Cup at that time, so we just needed to win the game and, for some reason, we really felt confident we could do that.

I think the fact we'd come back from 0-3 down to win 4-3 at Upton Park a few years earlier helped. I remember during a five-a-side in training on the day before the match a sudden realisation came over us just how good we were. Waddo kept ramming the message home as well. *We can do this.*

Tony Waddington later told me that I was selected as Denis' replacement when he overhead experienced players Dobing, Eastham and Banks talking about how sharp I was looking in training while we were staying at a hotel in Grays in Essex for those couple of days prior to the game.

THE GAME COULD not have gone better from my point of view. Best didn't have a kick. Despite him being such a big lad, I could win plenty of headers against him by backing off and timing my run and leap to be above him before he could jump up, so I'd be heading the ball away from him to a teammate to regain possession.

Anticipation and reading of the game was so key because of my height when I was playing centrally. The best ever exponent of that was Bobby Moore, who was captaining West Ham that night. I wasn't in the same class as him, but I'd say I was the tier below Bobby, who was world class, and was pretty good at it.

In fact, Terry Conroy often says it was incredible that I could come into the team for that game after so long out and keep the likes of Clyde Best so quiet and give him such a hard time that he looked like he'd been beaten up while my white shirt was pristine. I'm delighted by that.

Thanks TC.

The match was tight and tense, but in the 73rd minute the crucial breakthrough came. Terry Conroy skipped away from Hammers' left-back Frank Lampard on the right wing, crossed beyond the far post and found John Ritchie, who controlled, swivelled and fired low, right-footed past Bobby Ferguson from six yards to level the tie... 2-2 on aggregate. The tension ratcheted up even further.

But the drama was only just beginning.

Upton Park was a tight ground, with the crowd close to the pitch, creating a great atmosphere. The locals were not happy that we had taken the lead on the night to bring it back level over the two legs and were urging their heroes on. We were under the cosh quite a bit, but dealt with it and managed to take the tie into extra-time. The tension went up yet another level again.

Any mistake would surely be curtains to either side's Wembley dreams.

And that mistake came from an extremely unlikely source, a mix up between our left-back Mike Pejic and England's greatest goalkeeper Gordon Banks, when there were just three minutes left of extra time.

A long through ball was shepherded back towards Banks by Pej, but with Harry Redknapp breathing down his neck, somehow the pair of them left it to each other, allowing Redknapp to nip in. In desperation, Banksy dived at his feet and brought the West Ham winger down. There was no argument.

It was a clear penalty. I still shudder at the shock of that moment.

I say, there was no argument. We did, of course, argue with referee Keith Walker in a desperate attempt to delay the penalty and put Hurst off as he spotted up the ball, then turned and walked back to the edge of the area.

The tension was close to blowing the roof off Upton Park at that point. The noise was unbelievable. West Ham fans cheering... Stoke fans whistling and booing. Hurst versus Banks was a contest of two of England's World Cup-winning legends of six years earlier. Then they had been teammates.

Now, they were direct foes in this split-second rivalry for Wembley glory. I could barely watch. I remember Billy Bonds couldn't watch at all, crouching down on his haunches with his head in the crook of his elbow.

Hurst was finally given the go ahead by the referee to run up and smash the ball goalwards as he had at the Victoria Ground to score from the spot in the first-leg. Gordon guessed the right way as Hurst normally blasted his penalties to the goalkeeper's right. That wasn't the hard part.

The difficulty was dealing with the pace at which Geoff leathered the ball.

Actually, on this occasion, Banksy dived slightly too far to his right and had to fling his left fist up as his body fell away, to connect with the ball and send it spinning high up and over the bar. It was unbelievable that a ball hit that hard should be able to be deflected so far off its course when the keeper was diving away from it at the point he made contact. It was a brilliant save and as far as I'm concerned, even better than Banksy's more celebrated stop from Pelé's header in the 1970 World Cup, which people say was the best save ever made.

Both were astonishing and no other goalkeeper I played with could have made them.

We leapt around, losing our heads a bit while Banksy told us to calm it down and focus on the corner which was being lined up as the fans in the ground got their heads around what had happened.

That save lifted the team and we really felt this was our tie. To be fair, it was Gordon's fault they had been given a penalty in the first place, so it was decent of him to put that right!

That was the end of the action and the tie ended 2-2 after the two legs. There were no penalties back in those days. We had to go to a replay.

Except, when that game came in early January, the two sides couldn't be separated again, this time in a far duller goalless stalemate and we had to do it all again a fourth time. I came on as a substitute for Jimmy Greenhoff at Hillsborough, but wouldn't make it off the bench in the fourth game of this epic tie, which was played in monsoon conditions at Old Trafford.

It had never stopped raining all day in Manchester, the pitch was like a quagmire and, as I watched on, the players were skidding and slipping all over the shop, but the standard of football and entertainment was top class. It all started when the West Ham goalkeeper Ferguson was injured diving at Terry Conroy's feet early on and – for reasons neither me nor anyone else has ever been able to fathom – they chose their captain and best defender Bobby Moore to take over while Ferguson was patched up.

Moore then found himself having to face a penalty when John Ritchie was bowled over in the box by John McDowell, after pouncing on his poor back-pass. Even more inexplicably, up stepped Mike Bernard, a player with one Texaco Cup penalty to his name, rather than any of our strikers to take the spot-kick. Even taking into account the conditions you have to say it was the worst penalty you've ever seen in your life, which takes a lot when you've been a Stoke fan in the last decade or so of woeful spot-kicks, but Bobby, not being a proper goalkeeper, didn't catch it and, instead, merely pushed the ball directly back for him to slot home at the second attempt.

We were ahead again, but, typically for this semi-final, West Ham came back to lead 2-1 just before half-time. Then, Peter Dobing made it 2-2 just before the break with a low right-foot drive from 20 yards at the Stretford End and we went in at half-time level, just as we had been throughout most of the previous three games.

Waddo urged the players to keep the energy levels up and beware of the mud in defence during the break. I was just hoping that I would get on the pitch, which I felt was likely given that George Eastham probably wouldn't make 90 minutes, or possible more, in these quagmire conditions.

The crucial moment came early in the second-half when Jackie Marsh launched a deep cross into the West Ham box. McDowell somehow rose out of the Old Trafford mud to nod the ball away, but his headed clearance only fell perfectly for Terry Conroy on the edge of the penalty area to catch first time, right-footed on the volley. TC's perfect technique saw the ball scoot low across the slick mud to beat Bobby Ferguson, restored to the West Ham goal after half-time, low to his right-hand side.

I still remember Terry's celebration as he stood in his white change shirt in the gleaming lights, static… on the spot from which he had lashed the ball home, waving his arms up and down in the air in exultation. That goal broke West Ham a bit. Not that they gave up, but the lade were never giving that slender lead away this time and held on to win through to Stoke's first-ever Wembley final, clinching an epic 3-2 victory, ending that exhausting semi-final tussle.

I wasn't called on, surprisingly.

I had expected Waddo to bring me on, but he left the starting eleven out on the pitch and they closed the game out, so I couldn't really argue with that.

When the final whistle went, fans streamed onto the pitch. I still remember the elation at the final whistle, the realisation that we were in the final. Despite not getting on the pitch myself, I still *felt* it.

We were going to Wembley. We might actually win something.

Even for Banksy, you could sense how much it meant. He was a World Cup winner and undisputed England number one, but I felt deep down that for him this was the culmination of proving people wrong after he had been sold by Leicester. He wanted to justify why he had moved to Stoke. Winning something would achieve that.

I always felt actually that Gordon should have been the captain of the team at that point. For me, he was the obvious candidate, but it was very rare for goalkeepers to be captain in those days as they needed others to pass messages on to the midfielders and forwards.

Peter Dobing had been skipper since the sale of Calvin Palmer four years earlier. As I said, he was sometimes an awkward character. If he took against something you said, he'd pick you up on it and he was quite reclusive and didn't go out of his way to make conversation.

When Palmer was sold, Peter actually dropped back into midfield to take over his role as well as his captaincy; that was when he was coming towards the end of his career and coincided with when we bought Jimmy Greenhoff to play alongside John Ritchie up front. Alongside George Eastham, Peter's passing ability improved our attacking play, adding excellent shooting from distance, as shown in scoring that equaliser at Old Trafford in a sea of mud.

I actually got on well with Dobbo and thought he was a nice bloke, but personally I wouldn't have made Peter captain. I think maybe Waddo's choice was influenced as a reaction to the previous skipper being Calvin, who was very 'up and at em' type.

Dobing was completely the opposite.

George Eastham would have been another candidate, especially after everything he'd been through in his career as he had led footballers in general in the fight against the wage cap. As a person, I found him a bit stand-offish, to be honest, but he was a lovely player, with a wand of a left foot. But the manager chose Peter as captain and he would go on to lift the trophy at Wembley, so you can't really argue with that, can you?

FOR ME, THE big question was whether I might get to actually play some sort of part in the game as that was very much in the balance. I knew I wouldn't be in the starting eleven, barring an injury, but I was most likely the first choice to fill in as I had so often over those two seasons.

So, when I heard news that Jackie Marsh was struggling a bit in the week leading up to the game, I allowed myself to get a bit excited. This was a once in a lifetime chance to play at Wembley, as far as I was concerned, and I was really the only option to fill in at right-back. There was some paper talk ahead of the game which focussed on whether Jackie would be fit and, of course, on the one hand I wanted Stoke to have the best chance to win the final, but on the other I would rather that happen with me in the team, which meant Jackie would have to *not* be fit.

Wanting a teammate, colleague and friend to be injured is not the greatest situation to find yourself in ahead of a massive game, but it is a fairly standard scenario in football. Even a few days before the game when we left to spend some time down at the Selsdon Park Hotel as a group to prepare, it wasn't clear which of us would be starting. Because of that, I had my wife, family and various friends travelling down to Wembley to watch the game. We were fairly lucky in that the manager ensured we got plenty of tickets to give away for this very special occasion, so we had everyone at the final we wanted.

Before we headed off down south, we did something that back in those days every club that reached Wembley did... record a cup final song!

Our song was entitled *We'll Be With You* and was penned by local songwriters Tony Hatch and Jackie Trent, who would go on to write the theme tune to the Australian soap opera *Neighbours* and also wrote the song *Colour My World*, which had been a hit for Petula Clark and later featured in the musical *Priscilla: Queen of the Desert*, amongst many others. It was great fun to record.

If you listen to it when it's played before Stoke home games today as the teams walk out, you can just about hear my croaking in the background, although, to be fair, not many of us could actually sing!

I occasionally even get asked to warble a few bars when I speak at supporters' events these days and I do the best that I can, but it is great to hear it before every home game as the teams enter the field of play. It brings back fond memories.

We'll Be With You entered the charts between the League Cup final victory and the FA Cup semi-final a month or so later, peaking at number 34. So, I'm claiming a chart hit in my portfolio of things that lads from Eccles rarely get to do.

At Selsdon Park there was quite a bit of tension around and a bit of bite in training. It became clear that Jackie was okay, so I went from thinking I may be in the starting eleven to hoping I would be selected as the substitute. As there were only 12 members of the matchday squad back then, because there was only the one sub, three of the 15 players who travelled would miss out.

Realistically, that meant one of myself, Harry Burrows, Willie Stevenson and John Mahoney would be handed the No 12 shirt. I was hoping that my adaptability and dependability would swing the manager towards me.

I probably got a clue when Waddo gave a press interview saying that on the famous, energy-sapping Wembley pitch, everyone needed to be fully fit. As I was getting on in age, it was a likely indicator that I was going to miss out in favour of a youngster like John Mahoney, which happened when Waddo read the team out.

Again, it's a fairly normal thing in football to be left out at times, but I couldn't help thinking, *I've played all those games for Stoke and I can't get into the final team.*

After all, I'd played in the semi-final against Clyde Best and kept him quiet in the second-leg to help get us there. I do think this was partly to do with what had happened in the FA Cup semi-final the year before against Arsenal, not that Waddo blamed me particularly, but it certainly didn't help my case... and, of course, I was also a year older, at 32.

I was miffed, though I wouldn't say angry.

I just felt that I was ready to do the job that the manager had relied upon me for across the past 12 years. These days, with three or even five substitutes allowed, I would have at least been on the bench, but back then I was kicking my heels in the stands. At least I didn't have John Farmer's job.

As reserve goalkeeper, he clearly wasn't going to be in the 12-man squad, so John was given the unenviable task of minding the players' false teeth on the bench at Wembley… then handing them out ahead of the trophy presentation.

But I also think you have to say, with the benefit of 50 years of hindsight, that as we won the game, with John Mahoney playing an important role coming off the bench, that Waddo got it right. But I sorely wanted to be involved and I know I could have done what Josh did that day.

At the time, I wasn't best pleased, but kept tight-lipped of course as the most important thing was supporting the lads to win the game.

COME THE DAY of the final, those of us who were not playing left the team to it in the dressing-room and went up to sit in the stand.

The game began brilliantly for us as there was an early ping-pong around the Chelsea penalty area following a Peter Dobing long throw which resulted in Terry Conroy heading the loose ball into the bottom-right corner from eight yards.

The lads were 1-0 up.

But that wouldn't last and Peter Osgood had a goal back for Chelsea just before half-time. I was slightly worried that Alan Hudson was getting more and more into the game and I wasn't available for the manager to put me on to shackle him, as I had done several times before. But actually, Mike Bernard did a brilliant job in the second-half.

With the scores locked at 1-1, Stoke looked the more likely winners, partly because the Chelsea right-back Paddy Mulligan had to go off injured. Central defender David Webb had shuffled across to fill that berth and because of that Terry Conroy had switched to play on the left. That was where the crucial goal came from.

Peter Dobing clipped a long ball out to the left wing where Terry was in acres of space. He left Webb for dead and arced a perfect left-footed cross to the far post. John Ritchie cushioned the ball back to the waiting Jimmy Greenhoff with a perfectly judged header and the striker lashed a waist-high volley, right-footed, low to Peter Bonetti's right from the penalty spot.

The 'keeper saved, but couldn't hold on to the ball.

As it bobbled out, in rushed the evergreen, 35-year-old George Eastham to slot home left-footed from five yards, with Bonetti still on the floor. The place went bananas. It turned out to be George's only goal of the season and the last of a distinguished career. He is still the oldest man to score a winning cup final goal at Wembley all these years later.

The lads held on, although Mike Bernard gave us one huge heart in mouth moment when he hit a 35-yard back-pass towards Banksy that fell fairly short and Chelsea striker Chris Garland latched onto it just outside the area. But this was where Gordon earned his corn. He flew off his line and flung himself at Garland's feet, taking the striker and ball with him in a bone-crunching challenge to save the day.

I can't repeat what Mike says went through his mind, as he realised his pass was too light to reach Banksy, but it all turned out okay in the end and the lads clung on for a famous victory.

I WAS DELIGHTED, of course, and joined in the celebrations.

But I felt slightly on the outside. It wasn't the same as being involved on the pitch. And again, I never wanted to create a scene or anything. I almost never had cross words with the manager, which was one of the reasons why he kept faith with me for so long, I think. I just got on with my job. On this occasion, though, my desire to play and disappointment at being in the stands would eventually get the better of me.

After the game, we had a big celebration do at the Russell Hotel, but it was due to be the players and wives only, no hangers-on. Well, I had my friend who owned the Red Cow at Werrington down as a guest at the game and as he wasn't allowed in. I decided to go out for a drink with him, his wife and my missus instead.

We went into the centre of London to a club and enjoyed ourselves up there and had a good night, but when we came back to the Russell Hotel, Waddo was still up.

He asked me, 'Where have you lot been?'

I was still annoyed.

'Well, my party was out there, not in here,' I told him. 'My guests weren't invited in here. Yet other players have got people who've come in. So, we went out and found our own enjoyment.'

Then I walked away.

That was the biggest fallout I ever had with Tony Waddington, but it was just letting off steam because I was disappointed at not being picked and also not being able to have my guests, who had come all the way from Stoke, allowed into the banquet. He knew that wasn't like me as I was usually the quiet one, who would listen and understand before chipping in. For me to take a stand like that was very unusual.

It was quite a tense moment because it was probably the only time I ever defied him. Up until then, I had literally done everything he had asked of me. My problem was that that hadn't proved to be enough to be involved in the biggest game in the club's history. I'd played in the 1964 final, but that was played over two legs at the clubs' grounds. This was a Wembley final.

Don't get me wrong, I was delighted the club had finally won something. It was not before time. But it did leave a slightly sour taste in my mouth on the day. I don't want to blow it up into some huge issue between us, as it wasn't. There is really no point moaning about it now, as it was 50 years ago.

My disappointment didn't last long, though.

The manager and I were soon back to normal and I was delighted to be involved in the emotional homecoming on top of the old bus which the club hired for us to display the first major trophy in the club's history to thousands of fans who clamoured off every lamppost, from every rooftop and window, and thronged every pavement all the way from Barlaston, where we got off the London train, to the King's Hall in Stoke.

It was an eight-and-a-half-mile tour in and on top of an old Lymer's bus. I think an estimated 100,000 or so thronged the streets from Rough Close via Meir, Longton and Fenton to Stoke. We all felt like kings of the Potteries that day.

We had won Stoke's first trophy in 109 years and, with the club having only been to one more major final in the following 50 years – the 2011 FA Cup final – makes it all the more special.

Though I may not have played in the actual final itself, my contribution is recognised by the club and fans as I get asked about it all the time and get invited to the anniversary celebrations when they take place, most recently the 50th which saw a series of events across four days in early March 2022 to commemorate the achievement.

I am delighted that I played my part in bringing the League Cup to Stoke in 1972.

HOWEVER, WE COULDN'T rest on our laurels for long as there was still the tantalising possibility that 1971/72 season that we could win an FA Cup and League Cup double, which had never been done before, as, a couple of weeks after lifting the League Cup we defeated Manchester United in that quarter-final replay I mentioned earlier when Denis Smith scored an equaliser in a game which he wasn't meant to be playing in due to injury.

Typical Denis.

Terry Conroy's extra-time goal – a cracking right-footed half-volley that flew past visiting keeper Alex Stepney – backed up by two more Gordon Banks world-class saves sealed progress to a second successive FA Cup semi-final against Arsenal, this time at Villa Park, the site of our replay defeat a year earlier.

Revenge was very much in the air.

I had played in the two games it took us to get past Tranmere Rovers in the fourth round of the FA Cup that season, but then had filled in for both full-backs when they'd been missing for league fixtures. But I did not have to step up for any of the other rounds, including that dramatic win over United in the quarter-final. A week before the semi-final, however, Terry Conroy got injured in a 0-3 home defeat by Leeds and I suddenly found myself selected by the manager for the match against Arsenal, wearing Terry's No 7 shirt… the one which had been made so famous by Stanley Matthews.

FOR THE SEMI-FINAL, Waddo went more conservative and bolstered midfield, introducing me to the team. In fact, I could have played at left-back as Pej was suspended, but Waddo called up Alex Elder, a Northern Ireland international defender, who had joined us from Liverpool in 1967, but had been edged out of the side by Pejic to fill that berth, while I went into the heat of battle on the right side of midfield as Josh Mahoney, another possible option, had managed to get injured against Forest.

Given the way the previous season's game had gone, it was no surprise that this was a very tetchy affair. I remember getting one particularly satisfying tackle in on George Graham very early in the game… and the tackles got meatier and meatier.

Alan Bloor was booked after just six minutes for a high tackle on Charlie George. At one stage there was a mass brawl of sorts, really just a lot of pushing and shoving in the middle of the Arsenal half after Peter Storey's studs up lunge on Mike Bernard sparked it. I just stayed on the outside looking in as fights really weren't my thing, but I always lurked round the fringes just in case I was needed.

The referee was Keith Walker again, as he had been in our West Ham League Cup semi-final. He eventually sorted that one out, but I was very confused when the free-kick went against Mike and not Storey!

It was goalless at half-time, but we didn't start the second-half well as Arsenal opened the scoring on 47 minutes when George Armstrong slotted in Alan Bloor's weak clearance.

Most of the drama surrounded Gunners' keeper Bob Wilson, though, who seemed to get more and more injured as the game wore on.

In the very first minute of the first-half, he slammed his face into a post in tipping George Eastham's deep cross over the top of the net. Then, midway through the second-half, he injured his knee collecting a cross and, before he could be replaced by striker John Radford (remember there was only one sub and it was never a replacement 'keeper, so just like against West Ham, we would find ourselves playing part of the game against a non-specialist, giving us a great chance), Denis Smith challenged Peter Simpson and the ball flew in off the Arsenal player and past the handicapped Wilson to equalise.

It was quite similar to the first goal in the previous season's semi-final at Hillsborough.

However, try as we might, we could not find the winning goal and actually John Radford proved to be a much better replacement keeper than Bobby Moore had been the previous season.

The game ended 1-1. Honours even.

Another replay, this time at Goodison Park, for the right to face Leeds in the final.

We kept the same starting line-up for the replay, so I was in again. Bob Wilson hadn't recovered from his knee injury sustained in the first game, so reserve keeper Geoff Barnett was in goal for Arsenal. *Could this be our chance?*

It certainly seemed to be when Barnett hauled over Jimmy Greenhoff in the penalty area and the striker picked himself up to slot home the spot kick – awarded by that man, referee Walker – low to the 'keeper's left. At half-time, we were still ahead 1-0 and playing brilliantly, like we had in the first-half at Hillsborough.

Wembley beckoned again.

Enter the match officials! I am sure you probably know this story, as it's 50 years since it happened, but just in case you don't, you are about to learn about the most hideous miscarriage of justice I ever witnessed on a football pitch.

Well, two, actually.

FIRST OF ALL, from a long cross floated into our penalty area, which was headed out to the edge of the box, the referee seemed to spot some minor infringement or other when Peter Dobing challenged George Armstrong for a header.

No Arsenal player appealed at all.

When I heard the whistle go, I had no idea what it was for. To say it was a soft spot-kick is a massive understatement. Even to this day, when I watch the footage back, I cannot see what the penalty is given for.

Dobbo barely makes contact with the Arsenal man.

It was ridiculous.

Of course, they scored it and we were pegged back to 1-1. But that pales into comparison with what happened next.

Around Goodison Park, there were various programme sellers wearing white coats selling to the crowd and they were allowed to continue doing that while the game was on. Because we were wearing our all-white change kit, the linesman got one of those white-coated people confused with a defender on the far side of the pitch and allowed Charlie George to play on, when he was clearly almost 10 yards offside.

By the time we realised that the whistle wasn't coming, George was away and off down the right wing, from where he crossed for John Radford to slot home at the near post.

We hadn't been able to recover quickly enough to cover the break.

That goal killed us.

Until then, it was a very balanced game, but we didn't recover from conceding such an outrageous and unjust goal. We were all stunned, rather than seething after the game.

It just felt so wrong.

The fans, however, took a different view and the supporters club banded together to purchase a commemorative wooden 'trophy' of a horse's backside to award to the linesman concerned, Bob Matthewson.

At least we had one trophy to show for our efforts over those two seasons. And there were potentially greater things to come.

The 1972/73 Stoke City squad, who had just won the first (and so far only) major trophy in the club's existence, the 1972 League Cup.

CHAPTER 9

The Working Man's Ballet

IF WE THOUGHT that pushing on and challenging higher up the league table was going to be easy, then we were wrong. We'd finished 13th in 1970/71, and then 17th 1971/72 and 15th in 1972/73, although we were never in relegation trouble at all. Even in 1971/72 we finished 10 points above the drop zone, but of course we played all those cup ties that season.

However, winning the League Cup had seen us qualify for the UEFA Cup the first time in the club's history, representing England alongside Liverpool, Manchester City and Spurs. We drew Kaiserslautern of West Germany in the first round, who had qualified by being runners-up in the German Cup the previous season, which was a very difficult tie. Given that Spurs breezed past their first round opponent – Lyn of Norway – 12-3, we certainly got the tougher draw.

We won the first leg at the Victoria Ground 3-1 in September 1972, with goals from Terry Conroy, Jon Ritchie and our new signing Geoff Hurst. Yes, somehow Tony Waddington had managed to persuade Hurst to leave West Ham, despite only being aged 30, and join us in the Potteries. Again, I think the attraction of our brand of football, playing with Gordon and being able to go to The Place on a weekly basis seemed to win out.

Actually, when he signed, Geoff did say in the press that he had joined Stoke so he no longer had to be marked by Denis Smith or had to take penalties against Gordon Banks.

I got to know Geoff very well and really enjoyed his company. We have always stayed in touch a bit and see each other occasionally at reunions and the like. I still have to pinch myself that I played with Matthews, Banks and Hurst... three of the greatest names in the English game. There's a great photo of me and Geoff at a do just before lockdown which I've included in this book. It's one of my favourites from recent years.

Geoff was still a very good player and scored a decent amount of goals for Stoke. And now we had three England World Cup stars, including the best goalkeeper in the world and the hat-trick hero from the 1966 final in our ranks. Little old Stoke City might surely have been one of the top sides in the country.

All seemed set fair, but then things started to go a bit wrong in the autumn of 1972.

Firstly, in late-September we crumbled and lost the second leg at Kaiserslautern 0-4 to go out of the UEFA Cup 3-5 on aggregate at the first round stage. I played in Germany and am the first to admit it wasn't my finest performance in a Stoke shirt. In fact, I've tried to erase it from my memory really.

WE WERE ALSO struggling at the foot of the table, just one place above the relegation zone at times, and just couldn't find our rhythm. A month after that capitulation in Germany, came far, *far* worse news.

We had just lost 1-2 at Liverpool, to a controversial last-minute goal which came from a free-kick which referee Roger Kirkpatrick waved play on after a foul, but then still went back and awarded the foul after Liverpool made a mess of their attack. We felt he had given them the advantage and they had squandered it.

Gordon Banks, in particular, was incensed by the decision and even more irate after Ian Callaghan slammed the free-kick past him at the Kop end to clinch an undeserved win. Banksy chased Kirkpatrick off the pitch and was seething about it on the bus all the way back to the Potteries.

The next day, I was relaxing at home in Endon after a tough match at Anfield when news came through that Gordon had been involved in a car crash. He'd been to receive some treatment at the ground on the morning following the game and crashed his car on the lanes on the way home, on the road towards Ashley and Market Drayton. He'd ended up in a hedge and the glass in his windscreen had smashed, cutting his face and lacerating his eye.

On the news that night it showed him being taken into hospital. We were all ringing each other, devastated at what had happened. However, I don't think any of us thought it was going to be career-ending.

It soon became obvious, though, that Gordon wasn't going to recover and in fact he had lost the sight in one of his eyes, meaning he had to retire aged 32. It was a complete shock to lose the best goalkeeper in the world, and such an integral part of our team... and our squad and our club, although Gordon did later became a goalkeeping coach at Stoke.

So, suddenly, Tony Waddington had a huge hole to fill behind the back four which he didn't expect to have to deal with. Initially he tried to fill it with John Farmer, who had been Banksy's understudy throughout his time at the club. John had come into the team as a youngster aged 18 in 1966 and played quite a few games in the 1966/67 season, but ended up being relegated to acting as back-up by Banksy's arrival.

I liked John personally and thought he did his job pretty well. Being very tall made him good in the air, but I didn't think he was quite as good at getting down to low shots as Gordon had been and he certainly wasn't as agile as Banksy. He also didn't do a lot of talking in the penalty area and I felt that was an issue once he took over from Gordon, who was a great talker and organised the defence.

It wasn't quite the same with John in goal and the defence wasn't as solid. Off the pitch, John was a bit of a loner and didn't gel into the squad at times, although he was good mates with Jackie Marsh and Mike Pejic. He lived out on a farm near Leek, not far from Mike.

The manager also signed Mike McDonald from Clydebank as a back-up to John after Gordon's crash, although he had first tried to sign Scotland international keeper Bobby Clark from Aberdeen, but abandoned that in late October 1972, sticking with Farmer in the meantime, with McDonald now the understudy, making the occasional appearance.

We were undoubtedly weakened by this whole situation and it was a very difficult time both personally and professionally for all of us.

THERE WERE ALSO changes in midfield as the manager decided that John Mahoney's progress meant that he could raise some cash by selling Mike Bernard to Everton for a club record £140,000 not long after the League Cup final victory.

Josh could run all day, was a good passer and a Welsh international midfielder.

It was just a matter of whether he fitted into Waddo's plans, which he hadn't always up to that point. When he did get into the side, he proved what a great player he was. He eventually fully took over from me when I finally became a centre-half and then bit-part player from 1974 to '76. And of course, Josh was the player Tony Waddington chose to be the substitute at Wembley for the 1972 League Cup final ahead of me. Not that I held that against him, of course.

Although Josh did very well, Waddo wanted more flair from midfield, which was why he sold Bernard, as he and John were quite similar to each other, so eventually he made another superb, landmark signing, prizing Alan Hudson away from Chelsea in January 1974 for a new club record fee of £240,000.

Huddy was a one-off as a footballer... a revelation.

He could beat a man easy enough with some skill and pace, and was always looking to be positive. He played the most brilliant throughballs at times. Often, they matched the runs of players like Ritchie, Greenhoff and Conroy, but sometimes even those fabulous players couldn't read the genius of Hudson. Alan was also very good at playing one-twos, even across the mud of the Victoria Ground. I remember there was a banner which appeared at the Vic sometime in the 1974/75 season which said... **Alan Hudson walks on water.**

Exactly right, in more than one way.

But he was also an incredible character, which was partly why Chelsea had decided to sell him as his regular run-ins with the manager eventually forced their hand. As with Gordon Banks, Waddo was poised to clinch his signing as soon as he heard such a brilliant player was available, as he felt that Huddy was the final piece in the puzzle to turn our outstanding side into one which could challenge at the top of the First Division.

Alan's debut against Liverpool was described by the visiting manager Bill Shankly as, 'The greatest debut I have ever seen'. In his second game, Huddy ran the show against his former team Chelsea and ended up being tripped for the penalty which Geoff Hurst rammed home to secure a 1-0 win. We then went on a run of losing just two of the last 23 games of the season to fly up the table and finish in fifth position.

We played some brilliant football in that second half of the season as Huddy brought the different talents of the team together, with the ball seemingly glued to his feet at times, or on a piece of string before he sprayed it around the field at will, landing it perfectly at a colleague's feet or into space for them to run onto.

The media loved us because we were purists and we played football that was so attractive to watch. Non-partisan people loved the way we played with freedom and joy. There were no restrictions placed upon us in an attacking sense by the manager. We rarely had a team talk from Waddo in those days. It tended to just be focussing on certain opposition players that were dangerous, rather than anything about how we were going to be asked to play. We all knew our jobs.

Or in my case, I knew about half a dozen different ones I could turn my hand to.

I think Jimmy Greenhoff summed it up well when he said that as an attacking combination they didn't know what any of them were going to do with the ball, so there was no chance any defender trying to stop them did! Our attacking play was instinctive and exciting with Huddy in the team.

So, if you were to ask me who my top three signings Tony Waddington made were then, after Stan Matthews and the Greenhoff and Ritchie partnership (I know it's a cheat, but they come as a pair), I'd have to go for the imperious Alan Hudson as my third choice, not necessarily in any kind of order, you understand, because his arrival took our team to another level.

HUDDY'S ARRIVAL ALSO gave me, personally, a new lease of life.

By the time he joined in January 1974, I was already 34 years old and was very much a bit-part player at that point, having made 30 appearances in 1972/73, but just seven in five months in 1973/74 before Huddy signed. With Alan being such an attacking midfielder, Waddo wanted a bit more of a solid base in midfield and so he threw me back in and I formed a great partnership with him.

I played eight times with him towards the end of that season and we just clicked. We won six and drew two of those games as Huddy's mercurial talent was unleashed within the context of our fabulous attacking talent. We were the form side in the division and it really was a team that was even more than the sum of its considerable parts that spring.

But there was this flip side with Alan.

The second he was off the pitch, all he wanted to do was drink. He was always out in some bar or nightclub or whatever. Sometimes he played like a god despite the effect of the drink, sometimes it affected his football because he would have a hangover from the night before.

The 70s were a very different era to the modern approach to football of diet, nutrition and health.

Back then, Tony Waddington tolerated the drinking.

In fact, that's not quite the full truth… Waddo actually helped Huddy a lot of the time, indulging him because he was the shining star of our team. Waddo liked a drink himself and, when Huddy first arrived, the club put him up in the North Stafford hotel, which was the manager's favourite watering hole. So, Waddo would go and have a drink with Alan every night before heading back to Crewe on the train from the station just over the road.

It became a regular occurrence, exacerbated by Alan not having a wife or girlfriend when he arrived, thus being at a loose end as soon as training finished, which was a lethal state of affairs at times. I remember a few occasions on which people asked me if I'd seen Huddy at all and I knew I had to cover for him, and just denied that I'd seen him point blank, whereas I knew I'd seen him heading for some bar or other, often accompanied by one of his teammates who had less self-control than me.

I enjoyed Alan's company. He is a smashing bloke and I got on well with him. There was always a lot of fun going on when Huddy was around as he made the most of life. To be fair to him, he also trained like a demon. He could be drunk as a monkey on a Tuesday night, but then he'd be out at 10am training as hard as anybody the next morning. Waddo indulged him in part because of that. As long as he delivered the goods, then everything was fine.

In fact, the manager's approach to our social activities was always very hands-off. There was the rule that you didn't go out after Wednesday before a game, but other than that it wasn't enforced particularly. Waddo just trusted us not to go drinking, but you couldn't say that to Alan Hudson.

It just didn't work.

If Huddy was drinking a cup of tea, you'd better check it was actually tea in that cup, not something stronger. I know that Waddo knew what he was like, so it was a deliberate acceptance on his part.

One thing I do recall is that, despite being the star, Huddy was also an expert at getting other people to buy drinks for him; either other players or the public. He was always at the bar, but never putting his hand in his pocket, just cadging.

Later, after football when I had my pub in Newcastle, I'd be out with the darts team, playing an away match, and I'd come back to find Huddy at the bar.

Somehow, even though I hadn't been there all evening, I'd managed to buy him his drinks! There would be a tab behind the bar and muggins here paid it.

It was weird, because he must have been on very good money and he would have been used to London prices, but now he was living in Stoke where everything was much cheaper, yet he still seemed to be skint, so I have no idea what he did with all his money, no idea at all. Even Alan couldn't have drunk it all away.

Huddy's main partner in crime as a drinking buddy was another new signing, Geoff Salmons, who arrived from Sheffield United in the summer of 1974 for £160,000. He and Huddy clicked straightaway because Geoff also liked a drink.

Sammy had been a big timer in his team, much like Huddy. They'd now come to a fairly quiet city, unlike London and Sheffield, so they were out together every night as they were both put up in hotels and had no family or ties. I'd been put up in digs don't forget, but my situation was completely different to theirs. They had joined as big money signings in the pomp of their careers.

Sammy had a superb left foot and could beat a man and get crosses in from the wing or come inside and have a go himself. He dovetailed beautifully with Huddy and replaced George Eastham's guile and passing from the left flank brilliantly.

With those two additions, Tony Waddington now had the personnel to play a game true to his own principles. To reinforce this, in training he gave Alan Hudson a bright yellow bib to wear in practice games. He was the only one to wear this colour, which enabled him to stand out so the players could practice looking up and finding him. Every player on his team, including the goalkeeper, would be instructed to find him at every opportunity.

When we won the ball back, Alan dropped into a deep-lying midfield role, so far back that opponents who had been told to mark him would not be keen to get out of position by following him. That created space.

My job was very simple… just give it to Huddy in space as soon as I won it. He was brilliant at making himself available and I just played nice simple passes.

He kept telling me to pass it to him over and over again, but then he'd also say, 'Just because you've given it to me, don't think your job is over… I might need to give it back and move, so I can receive it again.'

So, I was always alive to getting a quick pass back.

Alan also liked me to pass the ball to him so he could take it on the half-turn, control and beat a man in one movement. Huddy was a master at that even on the muddy 70s pitches, especially at the Victoria Ground. So, in a way I became his right-hand man in creating space for him to play in, just like I did with Stan, but in a different way, adapting to the game of each of those genius footballers it was my privilege to play with. I didn't have to do anything else apart from find Alan, who was always there, fairly deep, to receive it.

Huddy was great with me and for me when he signed for Stoke, rejuvenating my career. I probably got an extra two seasons' contract because of him.

In my opinion, Huddy is the only player I've ever seen who could hold a candle to my favourite player when I was growing up, Duncan Edwards. He really was a phenomenal talent. How Huddy only won two England caps is an absolute mystery. Yes, he liked a drink, but then almost every footballer in England in those days did, some as much as Huddy!

But it was probably more his outspokenness which counted against him. It couldn't have been his talent, because in my opinion Alan was the best midfielder of his era for his first two or three seasons at Stoke. I remember his England debut, against World Champions West Germany in a friendly, in March 1975.

Huddy was head and shoulders the best player on the pitch, yet he won just one more cap. I feel that the England managers of that time often only really looked to the big clubs, meaning Huddy and Jimmy Greenhoff missed out on representing their country. You can't tell me that players like Ray Kennedy and Paul Madeley, who both won more caps than Alan in that era, were any better than him. They just played for Liverpool and Leeds United respectively.

I often wonder, would Gordon Banks have been picked for England if he had started his career at Stoke?

TONY WADDINGTON CALLED our football the Working Man's Ballet, a title Huddy later used for his autobiography. Or should I say his first autobiography.

I think he's done three. He always did talk a lot! My humble life will only just fill the one tome, you'll be glad to hear, but then compared to Alan I was always very much a shrinking violet.

There was this one time I got embroiled in his shenanigans, though. Because we'd become good mates, Huddy would often ask me to go for a drink. But, usually, I had this sixth sense which told me when it was time to go home.

Not on this occasion.

We were in London the night before a game against Arsenal in December 1975. I was injured and so wouldn't be playing, but still went down for the weekend. As he knew I wasn't going to get in trouble because I was injured, Huddy wanted my company.

'Come on, Alfie, we're going out'.

Before I knew it, I found myself with Huddy and Sammy, the two stars of the team, in this bar in central London on the Friday night before the game, chit chatting away with them. As if from nowhere, we were joined by these two girls who we plied with drinks and Alan and Sammy got friendly with. We were chatting and drinking all night, but then, around 11.30 or 12 o'clock, Huddy and Sammy said they wanted to go somewhere else, but at that point common sense kicked in for me.

'No, I'm going back!'

I didn't want to get on the bad side of Waddo by being blamed for being out and encouraging them the night before a game. As Huddy was his blue-eyed boy, I knew I'd get it in the neck.

So, I got a taxi back, crept through reception and into the hallway of the Russell Hotel, but who should I find walking towards me... but Tony Waddington.

'Eric (I knew I was in trouble if he called me Eric, not Alfie), have you been out?'

'Yes, gaffer,' I replied.

'Have you been with Huddy and Geoff Salmons?' The obvious next question.

Well, I wasn't going to give them away, so I said, 'Oh yeah, we've just been wandering about'. Like Huddy and Geoff were known for just taking the air...

'Well, where are they?'

Perfectly good question. I had to think on my feet.

Unable to dig them out of a hole, but unwilling to throw them into it, I said, 'Well, I wasn't feeling too clever, so I've come back,'... and wandered off quick back to my room before the manager could ask any further awkward questions.

I have no idea what time they got in or if Tony waited up for them, but there were no consequences that any of us saw, even though the whole squad knew what they'd been up to.

The next day, we beat Tottenham.

Huddy was the best player on the park and Geoff scored the equaliser as we came back to win 2-1... even though they had been out all night.

I remember when we were travelling back on the train after the game. Alan, Geoff and myself were sitting together at a table when along comes Waddo up the aisle checking on all the players. He stopped and took a look at the pair of them, huffing and puffing as he often did when he was agitated about something someone had done.

Eventually, he says, 'What am I going to do with you two?'

They looked at each other knowing they'd been rumbled, but before they could reply, he continued... 'Anyway, what are you drinking?'... and he ended up buying them a couple of beers for the journey home.

Typical Waddo, indulging them entirely.

I think in general they just got away with murder. I often wonder what would have happened if Waddo had been a bit firmer with Huddy. He could have been one of the true greats.

Regularly, when we used to get off the train at Stoke station, we'd walk straight over the road and go in the North Stafford hotel opposite. Waddo would buy us more drinks there. It became quite a frequent occurrence. You'd never see that these days.

It backfired the following season when Huddy crashed his car on the way home after a session a few days before the UEFA Cup first round tie against European giants Ajax of Amsterdam at the Victoria Ground. Shaken, Huddy wasn't himself as we drew 1-1 at home then went out two weeks later when we could only draw 0-0 away, despite dominating and nearly sneaking an incredible away win in a superb performance.

I think that was the thing with that team and the likes of Hudson, Salmons, Conroy, Greenhoff, Hurst and all those great players... Waddo couldn't really tell them how to play football. They were the cream of talent, so really he just concentrated on keeping them motivated, keeping them happy. I always felt in those social situations he would speak with the stars, but he hardly ever spoke to me socially.

That's just how he was, keeping his best players onside.

He could be charm personified when he wanted to be, especially with the big time players, but it meant the rest of us would sometimes feel ignored. Whereas, he would often tell me exactly what he wanted me to do on the pitch and he knew I'd do it.

There were other players, like the local back four of Smith, Bloor, Marsh and Pejic who he would also spend most of his time discussing football with because he needed them to be defensively organised. They had come through the ranks at the club, though, whereas the stars had come in at the peak of their careers.

All he'd ever say to me outside discussions about tactics or how to play the game was the occasional, 'Hiya Alfie, are you alright?'

That was it. He could sometimes just walk past me without even saying hello. I tended to only get spoken to when he wanted me to do something specific, or, socially, as part of a wider group in a hotel when we were playing away from home. I didn't really like that side of him, to be honest.

It's not a gripe because Tony Waddington made my career, selecting me over 500 times. I am eternally grateful to him. I'm just telling it like he was with me.

MANCHESTER UNITED CAME to Stoke for a rearranged game just two days after they had been relegated by defeat to Manchester City at Old Trafford in April 1974, although it had turned out that even if they had won that Manchester derby they would still have gone down. We won that game 1-0 thanks to a John Ritchie goal to top off our brilliant end of season run.

Who'd have thought all those years ago that the great Manchester United would be relegated from the First Division before little old Stoke City were?

I was sad in a way, but my experience told me that the teams which deserve to get relegated end up going down. We were fighters. United had a team of ageing stars which had not been replenished and when Matt Busby retired in 1969 there was only one way the club was going... and that was downhill rapidly.

Successive managers could not halt that slide.

Forty years later, that cycle would be repeated when, after 27 seasons of Sir Alex Ferguson's reign, successive United managers can not keep them at the top like he had and they have been struggling ever since. Of course, Premier League money means that struggling for Manchester United these days doesn't mean relegation, it means the humiliation of playing on a Thursday in the Europa League or losing the final of that competition on penalties.

The kind of humiliation, I'd gladly cope with!

Winning that game not only meant my boyhood team were sent down to the Second Division with a final humiliation from us, but also that, in finishing in fifth place, we had qualified for the UEFA Cup based on our league position. We would be competing in Europe once again.

There is one other thing I need to address, which is the small, or in fact not so small, matter of my 1970s moustache. I can't ignore it.

There is photographic evidence. It was one of those El Bandido-style 'taches which were poplar in the 70s. People said I looked like a Mexican bandit. I suppose in a way I did, because I had modelled myself on the American film star Charles Bronson, who often played cowboys or Mexicans in Wild West films.

It had seemed as if everyone had one, so I'd started to wear one and people kept telling me I looked just Bronson, especially when I was tanned in the summer after one of our trips away. I loved it. It was the time of discos and nightclubs, *Saturday Night Fever* and long locks, and I fitted right in.

My moustache was groomed, as was my hair, by the same barber I had for 20 years who became a big mate of mine. His name was Sid and he would come to watch our matches, even at one stage coming down to Stoke and cutting the directors' hair. In fact, I still go to see his son now at Sid's the hairdresser, although their barber's shop is no longer in Hanley, but is now on the road out to Leek just past the university.

I still enjoy going in and getting the newspaper and reading it while I'm waiting, then talking about football with people, as I have for over 60 years.

I've been having my hair cut by one of those two since 1958.

Celebrating my final goal for Stoke in one of my last games to rescue a 2-2 draw with Wolves as we went for the title in March 1975.

The boys of '72 reunited when Stoke faced Chelsea in the Premier League in 2017. Back row – myself, Jackie Marsh, Denis Smith and Terry Conroy. Front row – Mike Pejic, George Eastham, Mike Bernard, Gordon Banks and Harry Burrows.

CHAPTER 10

Land of Smoke and Water

AFTER 14 YEARS OF hard work, glory and several near misses, Stoke City under Tony Waddington were now serious contenders for the league title. Any side which goes on a run which sees them only lose two of 23 games, has to be considered so. We were on a massive high, were the form team in the country and had a squad of players that could take on any of the top sides going into the following 1974/75 campaign, the first one in which we would have Huddy from the start.

For that season, I thought my role was set to be very much bit-part, as I was now almost 35 years old. But, as it turned out, I played over half the games, as injuries took a huge toll on our title challenge as the campaign unfolded. Four players broke their legs that season… John Ritchie, Jimmy Robertson, Mike Pejic and Denis Smith.

At one stage it seemed as if broken legs were happening on an almost weekly basis. In fact, Peter Dobing's career had been ended by a broken leg sustained against Coventry in September 1972, so really we lost five key players entirely from that 1974/75 title campaign at different stages. That's half a team.

Add to that Alan Bloor suffering a crippling back injury, which kept him out for the entire season. Terry Conroy missed most of the first half of the campaign with one of his perennial knee ligament injuries. And Jimmy Greenhoff broke his nose in a game at Birmingham.

Despite all of those set-backs, with Alan Hudson propelling us forward from midfield with his dynamism and vision, Tony Waddington's version of the beautiful game reached its zenith week after week as we cut a swathe through the league once again, playing some lovely football.

At that time the song the Boothen End sang about the team went like this:

Land of smoke and water
Home of Stoke City
High, higher and higher
On to victory

WE FIRST HIT the top of the table on November 30 following a 1-0 win over Leicester, amidst a run of four wins and a draw in five games. That draw was a frustrating one as we only conceded the equaliser to a controversial Kenny Hibbitt penalty against Wolves in the 90th minute, given for a trip by Denis Smith on John Richards. A crucial point dropped, as it would turn out.

That game at Molineux was the debut for our new star goalkeeper Peter Shilton, a club record signing and a world record fee for a 'keeper of £325,000. I played in the latter three games of that run… at Wolves, against QPR in a 1-0 win at the Victoria Ground which saw Geoff Hurst score early on, and then the following week against Leicester as we hit the top with a Denis Smith left-footed piledriver four minutes from time.

It was the first time in 37 years that Stoke had been at the head of the First Division table. That late winner flew past Shilton's replacement in the Foxes goal, Carl Jayes, who had a wonderful game that day and was unfortunate to be on the losing side, but then seemed to disappear from view, unable to follow his eminent predecessor who was now very much our man.

We could boast the best goalkeeper in the country once again.

We had started the season really well and were always in the upper region of the top half of the table, but had been prone to conceding a few goals… drawing 2-2 with both Newcastle and Spurs, and 3-3 at Chelsea. I think those games caused Waddo to give in to his desire for star players, and top-level goalkeepers, which is completely understandable, because, despite John Farmer being a good goalkeeper, he did make a few mistakes, especially one at Chelsea which handed a last-minute equaliser to the home side, meaning another crucial dropped point.

That was the straw that broke the camel's back and Shilton became the latest landmark signing.

As a teenager, Shilton had displaced Gordon Banks from the Foxes first team, forcing his sale to us. What irony then that Shilton should join us in November 1974 and within 10 days of his arrival help us rise to the top of the table, something that Banksy had never managed to achieve. Had Waddo's bravado in securing the signature of the England goalkeeper come good again already?

OF COURSE, SHILTS is a legendary figure in English football, still holding the record for England caps with 125 and jointly holding the record of 10 clean sheets at World Cup finals with France's Fabien Barthez.

He played nearly 1,400 games in his career, and yet his time at Stoke would not prove to be the finest, despite us challenging for honours in his first season. For example, as I was mentioning earlier, as soon as he arrived at the Victoria Ground, despite us doing so well, he lost his place in the England team to Liverpool's Ray Clemence. Bizarrely, he played just one international game in his first two seasons with us and then won his place back at the end of his third season, the one in which the club was actually relegated from the First Division, just after I left.

Figure that one out!

We had always felt safe and secure with Banksy behind us. It was never quite the same once he had gone. Banksy was, in my opinion, the better 'keeper and we never quite recovered from losing him in that car crash in 1972. Shilton was very good, but not quite as brilliant and game-changing when playing for us as Gordon was.

So, I don't feel his signing really paid off.

Peter was a big lad and you had to get out of his way when he came out as he would clatter everyone if he was coming to take a cross, which is fair enough and that was definitely an improvement on John Farmer. However, he did slightly unsettle the back four in terms of balls played through or over the top and coming out to sweep them up. He was far less good at that than Gordon had been.

A bigger problem was off the pitch.

Shilton was also a funny one in terms of mixing in with the group. On his own, Peter was good company, but he didn't really gel with us when we were going out, so we didn't create such a bond as we had with Gordon. The other thing was, he clearly thought he was the best – to the point of being obsessive sometimes – which is fine when you're playing, you need a very positive mentality, of course you do, but there was a bit too much of that about him when we were socialising too.

It made a difference off the pitch and that was reflected on it.

Fine margins.

Because of his self-obsession, Shilts and Alan Hudson didn't see eye to eye a lot of the time, as they were two Alpha males, vying to be the leaders of the group. There was something of a personality clash, although I can state for certain that I don't think Shilts would have been lending Huddy any money. He was far too miserly for that! He was also something of a gambler, although I wasn't aware of that at the time.

Because I'd never bet on anything more than the Grand National once a year, I didn't frequent the betting shops it now appears Shilton was going to. I never gambled because I didn't know anything at all about horses. From what I now know about Shilts' gambling losses, it turns out… neither did he!

He's lost a fortune over his lifetime.

Gambling is, of course, an addiction, a type of illness. I know that now. Back then, I always felt that if I'd put a bet on a horse and it lost, I would feel that loss so acutely that I wouldn't go to sleep at night. Money has always been too hard to come by and I had too much riding on my pay packet to fritter it away. It was just the mentality I had, probably ingrained in me from my childhood in Eccles.

And if I had placed a bet on a race which was going to happen the next day, I literally wouldn't sleep at all with worrying about it, so I just chose not to get involved, especially because I didn't want to have to be explaining gambling losses to my wife.

THE LAST GAME in that five-match unbeaten run following Shiltons's arrival and going into the heavy winter programme saw us defeat Birmingham 3-0 at St Andrew's, a match which was notable for Jimmy's broken nose, but also for his absolutely superb volley on the turn from the corner of the penalty area, lashing it over Blues 'keeper Dave Latchford into the far top right corner.

If you haven't seen Jimmy's goal on YouTube, I recommend viewing it. Magical skill and a heck of a shot. A worthy goal for a team who sat at the head of the First Division.

We were on a roll.

But we then lost three games in-a-row as a crazy season saw us drop to 7th place with a host of clubs vying for the title at this halfway point of the campaign. The last of those was on Boxing Day in a match against Coventry which saw Jimmy Robertson stretchered off with his broken leg just a minute into the game.

I was dropped during that poor run, but as the injuries mounted I knew I'd be needed again, and lo and behold I got back in the team for a frustrating goalless draw at the Victoria Ground in the return fixture against Birmingham... and retained it for the rest of the season.

Overall, I played 22 games, most of them during that second half of the season, and a lot of them at centre-half alongside young Alan Dodd, as both Alan Bloor and Denis Smith were out.

Doddy was a quietly spoken lad, but a tremendous athlete. He was also incredibly fit and was a far fiercer competitor than his mild manner would suggest. He reminded me of myself quite a bit, although physically he was several inches taller. He never really raised his voice or anything like that, but, when you've got other players in the team that are gobby, you tend to keep quiet and let them get on with all their chat and nonsense and just do your job. That's what Doddy and I did... the young and the old.

Being taller than me, Alan acted more as the centre-half, making challenges, while I mopped up and covered in case his centre-forward won the header. We dovetailed well together.

I mentored Alan through games, although he soon blossomed into a tremendous player, who was particularly outstanding in how he read the game, intercepted and then passed the ball, often directly to Alan Hudson, who took Doddy under his wing in a footballing sense.

Doddy was also a really nice bloke. Because he was relatively shy, young Alan didn't aspire to the drinking feats of older Alan. He lived in a rural area on the other side of Leek in the Moorlands and was a bit of a farmer type, so, once he had finished training, he was off to work up where he lived.

Alan and I played together in central defence in one of the most pivotal games that season, on February 15, 1975 at home to Wolves. That proved to be one heck of a game. We went 0-2 down; first to another Kenny Hibbitt penalty after 25 minutes, and then Frank Munro made it 0-2 in the 47th minute.

But then came the late fightback, showing we were made of stern stuff. First, in the 87th minute, Terry Conroy scored amidst a goalmouth scramble to make it 1-2. Then, just a minute later, the dramatic equaliser was scored by yours truly!

Yes, at the grand old age of 35, and after a gap of almost six and a half years since my previous goal in a 1-1 draw with QPR in September 1968, I found the net once again. I remember that goal as clear as day.

We were desperately attacking the Butler Street end. A corner kick was cleared out to me and I just instinctively hit it from just inside the left-side of the penalty area.

The ball went through a sea of legs and billowed the back of the net to complete a wonderful comeback to nick a draw. It was my seventh and final goal for the club. I was so surprised, I went on a little run and dance in celebration, caught up in the drama of the moment as much as anything, which was captured in a photograph we have managed to locate and include in this book, showing me being rugby tackled to the ground by John Mahoney (No 4), hotly pursued by Jimmy Greenhoff (No 8), Geoff Salmons (No 11) and Ian Moores (No 7) with the Boothen End and main stands in the background going crazy.

But the drama wasn't over yet as, just a minute later, we lost yet another player with a broken leg when Mike Pejic went into a challenge with Wolves' Steve Kindon.

Pej being Pej, he limped through the remaining moments of the game, only discovering the true extent of his injury when he returned to the dressing-room. This time, Dr Crowe managed to diagnose him immediately and he didn't end up dancing at The Place like I had a few years earlier to make it worse

Even though we didn't win, that point took us top of the division. We were set fair, although there were actually only four points covering the top 11 teams in an incredibly tight season. We had won the previous two games, 4-0 against Manchester City and then 2-0 at Spurs.

Both performances were amongst the best we ever gave, as was a victory at Derby in mid-March on a complete mud-bath of a pitch, which saw Jimmy Greenhoff score both goals as we came from behind to win 2-1 against a key title rival on their own pitch.

We were now in a position when, with nine games left, we could win the league.

Not everything was going our way, though. We had lost in early March at Middlesbrough to drop to third, with Boro then just two points behind us.

The previous week had seen us draw at lowly Luton, when we not only had what we thought was a perfectly good goal disallowed when the ball was cleared, and were convinced it had crossed the line, but we also missed a penalty when Geoff Salmons shot wide from the spot.

Then, in our next home game against Ipswich, Denis Smith became the fourth player that season to suffer a leg break. To cap it all, we lost 1-2 to drop to sixth. The terrible luck with penalties, refereeing decisions and especially injuries was threatening to really derail our title challenge.

I WASN'T IMMUNE either. Playing in your mid-thirties means you are just far more prone to injury. It also takes longer to recover and the cumulative effect of the knocks takes its toll as well. I regularly had cortisone injections in my Achilles to get me through the periods when we were playing two games a week. There were some seasons, particularly in the early 70s, when we occasionally played three a week.

The injections eased the pain so you could play through it, but come the following morning you'd be back to square one or even worse in terms of the agony it caused.

Consequently, I think any player in the 70s would rarely be going out to play feeling one hundred percent There was always some kind of niggle going on. Back then, the appearance money and win or draw bonus was so important to us and the squads were that small that we were a very valuable commodity to have on the pitch and clubs would do anything they could to get us out there, while we needed to be in the team to earn that extra bit.

You simply just had to get on with it and then, after the game, you could have another massage from Frank Mountford. Then Dr Crowe would administer your next painkilling injection in time for the following game.

Yet, despite all those injuries, we still fought on with our rapidly-reducing pool of players. This inevitably meant that young, fringe players such as Alan Dodd began featuring. But there were several others who came into the team to plug gaps as well.

Up front, Ian Moores replaced John Ritchie as the main striker, after Big John's career-ending leg break at Ipswich. Ian was very young and quite a quiet lad. He was very tall and awkward to mark, but he didn't have the same chemistry with Jimmy Greenhoff that Ritchie had had. He did a decent job, scoring twice in that thrashing of Manchester City, but he wasn't as robust as John and was eventually sold in August 1976 for £75,000 to Tottenham.

Midfielder-cum-winger Sean Haslegrave was a nice little player who'd always give you a good 90 minutes, but he didn't always come looking for the ball as much as Terry Conroy, who he often filled in for.

Midfielder Steve Waddington was actually a nice lad, but as his old man was the boss you felt a little bit under the cuff when you were speaking to him and you were a little bit frightened of doing anything to him in training, like whacking him if he annoyed you, as his dad was the manager. Mind you, he never ever said to me 'I'm the manager's son' or anything like that.

Then there was defender Kevin Lewis, who I got on very well with. I used to look after him in training once he got into the squad as we got on so well. He was a very chatty feller, so chatty in fact I'd call him a Scouser, even though he was from Hull.

Terry Lees was another back-up defender. Along with Kevin, he played a few games in various different positions as the season wore on because, due to those injuries piling up, eventually only Jackie Marsh of the first choice back four was available.

I thought Terry was a bit like myself and I encouraged him a lot as a youngster, as I saw him as my orphan boy that I could make a difference to. He played for various English clubs after Stoke, but then moved to Holland and played for Sparta Rotterdam, amongst others. Terry remains a very big mate of mine nowadays and we see each other quite a lot.

He's done well for himself financially. After he finished football, Terry and his wife bought a place in Spain and now they've just sold it after renting it out for many years. They also had some property in the UK which he and his wife have done well from too. I'm really pleased for him.

He often comes round with tickets for me for the game up at Stoke and we go together. He is also a dog lover, like I am, and we get on alright. He was always a great talker, but you can't shut him up these days when we meet! We rattle on at each other when we sit down with a coffee.

I think being stuck at home during the pandemic has meant that I haven't had an active brain, so I have found I've been forgetting faces and names and memories, which hasn't exactly helped when writing this book. Terry keeps on at me that I need to get out of the house more and I keep telling him that the one thing I wish I could forget, but somehow haven't, is his face!

But seriously, he is a smashing bloke and has been a brilliant friend and being that much younger brings a real verve into my life in these post-pandemic times. We get on great.

DESPITE THE INJURIES, things began to really go for us at this point, not least because Terry Conroy had returned from his injury in terrific form. In a barnstorming run from the end of March, TC scored eight goals in five games.

He was absolutely on fire. Although everybody really thinks of TC as a winger, he was actually playing as a striker through the middle at that stage due to the career-ending leg break John Ritchie had suffered at the hands of Kevin Beattie in September 1974.

Annoyingly, though, we only won three of those five matches, drawing the other two away at West Ham and Arsenal, losing the lead in both matches. After that game, with five matches to go, there were just five points between the team in first place, Liverpool, who had 45 points, and the team in ninth position, Manchester City.

We had 43, just two points off top spot, but sitting in fifth position.

We then had two home games against Liverpool and Chelsea, which saw us play some superb football, knocking the leaders off the top of the table with a brilliant and memorable performance on Easter Monday in front of almost 46,000 fans at the Victoria Ground to record a 2-0 victory. That left us in third place, but only on goal average, with Liverpool and Everton slightly ahead of us, and Derby slightly behind us, all on 47 points, with Ipswich only a point behind.

The top five teams were separated by just one point with only three or four games left each. It was an incredible and tense run in.

With just three games remaining for us, with the way the fixtures fell, we knew if we won all three, we would more than likely win the title. As it turned out that was exactly true. Had we won all three we'd have lifted the First Division trophy.

Instead, we failed to score another goal in any of those three fixtures, losing 0-2 at Sheffield United and then drawing 0-0 twice, against Newcastle and then at Burnley, to end the season disappointingly in fifth, four points behind eventual title winners Derby County.

But there was further disappointment in store, however, for us as we controversially lost out on a UEFA Cup place on a technicality.

ALTHOUGH THE 1974/75 SEASON ended in ultimate disappointment for the club, it proved to be my Indian Summer… aged 34 to 35. It earned me one final year of a contract which had now lasted 16 years.

So, personally it was great.

I was so fortunate to be part of that era when we had success and a lot of fun. Also, when we were top of the league in 1974/75, I was earning over £100 a week, what with my appearance money and the bonus money we got for each place up the league above sixth we sat after each week's games – a fiver per position. So, for me, it really was a halcyon period.

I think Waddo created a brilliant team which should have won more. Really, we could, and probably should, have won the First Division that season. That was the closest we ever came to winning the league.

The club has never come so close to glory since. The following season the magic had gone and before long so had the money which had fuelled our rise.

In fact, the 1975/76 season saw Stoke finish back down in mid-table in 12th position and as the campaign wore on, I realised my time was now most definitely up.

Towards the end of my career I would be 12th man quite a lot, being used by Waddo to come on and close a game down if we were winning, but, by 1976, I was barely featuring in the first team picture at all. My thoughts were naturally turning to what would happen next. I felt I could still play on, just not at this highest level, so I thought I could get a contract somewhere. But I also knew that would be for another year or so at most.

Despite my fitness, I knew my game of tackling and interceptions was not one that could be sustained much longer. I was certainly not going to be like Stan Matthews and play until I was 50.

As I mentioned earlier, during my entire career my contract was only ever one season long. There were times when you'd get called into the manager's office at the end of the campaign and you didn't really know if you were being released or given a pay-rise. I remember when I got past 30, I was always so relieved to get offered my next contract.

I never negotiated wages at all, I just accepted what they offered. Nowadays, it is all negotiation, including length of contact and asking for more money, and there are, of course, agents who handle all of that for players.

Back then they just didn't exist.

All the more reason to get some funds in if my career was coming to a close then. I had got to know Kevin Donavan, the owner of the Jollees night club in Longton and The Place in Hanley, which me and my teammates frequented most Saturday and Monday nights.

Jollees at that time was nationally famous institution, having opened in October 1973 as the largest capacity cabaret venue in the UK, holding around 1,800 guests. Not that you would know it from the exterior of the building as it looked like a fairly drab place over the bus station in Longton, but that hid the plush wonderland you discovered once you were inside, with a huge auditorium containing hundreds of tables illuminated with fetching purple fabric lamps.

We had all attended its glamorous opening, hosted by comedians Little and Large, and the club played host to every variety act you can think of over the next couple of decades... we saw the likes of Cliff Richard, Petula Clark, Roy Orbison, Johnny Mathis, Norman Wisdom, Tommy Cooper, Ken Dodd... and even Pete Conway, father of the world's most famous Port Vale fan, Robbie Williams.

As well as the cream of show business, Jollees also hosted the World Professional Darts Championship from 1979 to '85. Even the Duke of Edinburgh and Princess Margaret visited, so we were in good company!

So why am I telling you all this?

Well, I'm trying to put into context the fact that I once headlined Jollees!

OKAY, SO IT was a benefit night for me which Kevin agreed to put on, but it was my name on the top of the billboard... well, the only name on the billboard actually, but we'll skim over that.

Kevin had become good friends with me and my wife and, when he knew I was thinking of calling it a day, he asked me if I would like him to set up a fundraiser, which was a very kind gesture. He was a cracking feller. Initially, he booked Ken Dodd to front the evening, but it turned out that Doddy had double-booked himself, so instead Kevin somehow persuaded Brian Clough, who had just been sacked at Leeds after an infamous and turbulent 44 days in charge at Elland Road and was between jobs.

I didn't really know Cloughie particularly well, but had said hello to him quite a few times in the players' lounges after various games against his teams and obviously I knew his reputation, not only in terms of the football he played, but also as a raconteur. I was delighted he was happy to help me out.

It turned out he knew Tony Waddington really well and he had actually come with us on the trip to Amsterdam when we played the UEFA Cup first round away leg against Ajax in October 1974, as well. So, Cloughie took the stage at Jollees in front of a packed house and told all these stories from his time as a player and manager, referring to me throughout.

He was great value and I'm delighted that there is a photograph that we've been able to dig out of that evening, showing me, on stage, but wrapt in his storytelling as he engages the audience. It was a really great night and Cloughie had the audience in the palm of his hands. Far better than me waffling on!

THERE WAS ONE other very notable event which occurred in January 1976, when a freak high wind blew the roof off the Butler Street stand at the Victoria Ground. I remember seeing it caved in onto the side of the pitch. I had no idea of the implications at all at the time, but they soon became apparent. In a way that storm killed that entire team as it led to the fire sale of talent such as Jimmy Greenhoff, Alan Hudson, Mike Pejic and, eventually, Geoff Salmons and Peter Shilton, to try and pay for the stand's rebuilding as it turned out there was a huge problem with the insurance.

The club had no money, having bought stars like Hudson and Shilton, and the directors were not made of money like Stoke's owners the Coates family are these days. They were just good local folk who were doctors or solicitors and owned construction companies back then. So, the prized assets just had to be sold.

I remember Jimmy Greenhoff crying the day he signed for Manchester United as he never wanted to leave Stoke. It was heartbreaking.

I suppose that disaster played a part in me not being retained as I would have been on a relatively high salary at that point, but my top-flight career was over, I knew that. I wasn't one of the ones who could be sold to generate funds, though. Me not being given another contract was merely a cost-saving measure.

I had made just four appearances in 1975/76, playing three of the first six games, then an isolated appearance in a 1-2 home defeat by Tottenham in February, filling in for John Mahoney when he was injured, which ended up being my 606th and final Stoke City appearance of my 17-season first-team career.

At the end of that campaign I knew my time was up.

There was still a tinge of disappointment though when my name simply appeared on the dreaded 'not retained' list, rather than having a fuss made of me for my long service. That's just the way things were back then for me.

I'd had 18 seasons since joining Stoke City as a triallist and, aged 36, it was time for me to open up a new chapter in my life away from the club.

Brian Clough holds court in front of a spellbound audience at Jollees night club in Longton during my testimonial night. Cloughie was simply breathtaking with an audience in the palm of his hand. Not sure I contributed that much to be honest!

Celebrating a goal for Seattle with Geoff Hurst (No 11) and Jimmy Robertson (No 19). And trotting out for Port Vale with full-back John Brodie when I was very much winding my career down in 1976/77 (note the Charles Bronson moustache!)

CHAPTER 11

After the Ball is Over

THERE WAS A great unity in those last few years I was at Stoke City and for that period we were a wonderful side… but also nearly men, aside from the 1972 League Cup triumph. The Victoria Ground was a special place to call home and an intimidating place for any visitor. The fans were so close and were as vociferous then as they famously were in the Tony Pulis era 30 or so years later.

But now I was no longer a Stoke City player, for the first time in almost two decades.

What would I do?

As I'd turned 30, I had begun to think about what I would do next after football, not that I was feeling like I'd be finishing any time soon at that point and it turned out I was right, as I had another six years left in me at the top level, thanks to my adaptability, fitness, work ethic and the belief in my abilities shown by Tony Waddington as manager. But I had to be realistic, especially if I was taking on the mortgage on that dream house.

So, having had a go at opening my shop with Willie Stevenson, I'd already decided because of that experience that being an entrepreneur was far too risky for me. I'd begun to talk with various people about what I might do next. There was no possibility of retiring and simply counting my pots of cash as players who retire do these days, unless they have real drive to stay in the game in coaching or management.

Instead, I needed to earn to pay my mortgage.

I had settled on the idea of becoming a publican, but before I could do anything about that, and just as I was getting used to the idea of not having anyone to play football for, I received a phone call from my former teammate Geoff Hurst, who had just signed for Seattle Sounders in America.

Opportunity had come knocking to continue my career in football, so I put thoughts of running a pub to one side and agreed to jet off to the northwest coast of the United States with my wife and family in tow.

I KNEW A bit about the North American Soccer League because Willie Stevenson had ended up out there playing for the Vancouver Whitecaps a couple of years before I did, while another former teammate Stewart Jump was at Tampa Bay Rowdies, along with maverick star Rodney Marsh. And, of course, we had played over there as the Cleveland Stokers back in 1967.

After putting the phone down to Geoff and thinking that I fancied taking the opportunity, I went and asked the wife, who spoke with the headteacher of the kids' school, and before we knew it we were all off to America for the summer. It was such a great opportunity as everything was being paid for and it turned out to be an amazing experience. Even the journey over was amazing as we stayed overnight, all expenses paid, in a swish hotel in London before catching the plane to Seattle.

When we arrived, we were taken to our new apartment, which was part of a complex in which Geoff Hurst and his family were living. It was really marvellous. The kids loved it over there. They did the homework their headteacher had set them as quickly as they could, then would go out playing and making friends.

Just after I pitched up, another new arrival joined the ex-pat crew when Harry Redknapp and his family arrived. Harry was a superb bloke. I'd got to know him when he was playing for West Ham and he would stay in Stoke after a Hammers game and come to The Place and enjoy our company. We liked each other and had got on famously.

That only increased with our time in Seattle together. Harry used to come round a lot and we got very friendly, as did our families. He rings me now and again these days to keep in touch as he lives on the south coast.

He's such a character.

Then another former teammate Jimmy Robertson came out to join the club. Jimmy was a typical Scot and loved playing golf. He still does these days, so is always on the course. Another teammate was Mike England, the player who I had nearly replaced at Blackburn all those years before, or so the papers had it. Mike was a very straightforward chap, not one for laughing and joking, unlike Harry who was all about the fun. Hursty could be a good laugh too, but he would also be very serious when it came to playing.

The Seattle manager at the time was a chap called John Best, who had started his career at Liverpool as a youngster and played a few times for Tranmere, before migrating out to the USA and becoming a citizen and earning one cap for the national team. He made sure we felt welcome and did a decent job managing all us old pros as we finished in second position in our section, qualifying for the play-offs.

I enjoyed America, as we had a huge car and a lovely house. We'd all go out for a meal together at least once a week. It was like going on holiday to a holiday camp. But the travelling was also a lot of fun and we did travel all over the country, playing in Los Angeles, Miami, Chicago, Boston and Dallas, amongst others. We used to come home from the long trips away and have to play down what we'd been up to as we were having such a good time. We were mostly playing in baseball stadiums, which was odd as the stands were in the wrong place, really, with one side, or end being completely open.

America was completely different to the Potteries, you won't be surprised to hear. Unlike in Stoke where I was completely welcome, in certain places you had to be careful where you went at night time when on away trips. I remember going down south to play in one of the big cities down there and for something to do, me, Hursty and Harry went to find a bar for a quiet drink.

We told the manager this and he informed us that when we left the hotel we had to turn left, not right... as doing that would take us into an area which was essentially not safe for white folk, unofficially, like. So, we did as we were told and turned left, but then we went left down the next street... and without realising at some point turned left again and carried on walking... right into this area we'd been told to avoid at all costs.

My geography paying off again, you see...

We ended up going to this cinema we came across and paid to go in. But the film had already started and the lights were down so we sat down and watched the first part of the film. When it came to the intermission (yes, there were breaks in films back then) the lights came up and we could immediately see that we were the only white people in the cinema. It was only then that the penny dropped and we decided we'd better hop it as the manager had warned us we could be in danger.

I must say though we didn't receive any funny looks or anything remotely approaching a threat at all. The folks were nice as pie.

I actually scored two goals and had two assists according to the official records, although I don't really remember much about the actual football out there. We got quite far in the league and into the play-offs, but I picked up a cracked rib and missed the last two games as we bowed out in the divisional championship game, losing 0-3 to Minnesota Kicks.

One thing I do remember when I was playing in America, was that the game would sometimes be stopped and the referee would head off to watch something on the TV at the side of the pitch. It was a kind of early VAR.

It was very strange not knowing what was being looked at or why, so I know a little bit about how modern players feel when they are waiting around for a VAR check.

BY THE TIME that 1976 summer season finished, I was nearly 37, so we headed home, having had an absolute blast, wondering what would happen next. When I got back, I found I had an offer from Port Vale, so I had a season there under Roy Sproson, playing in Division Three past my 37th birthday.

I got on well with the Vale players as they knew me from playing for Stoke and the annual friendlies we used to play against them. As I was winding down, I played just the five games and scored one goal, against Walsall at Fellows Park, the last goal of my not-so-prolific career. Even though it was the most recent goal, I don't remember it at all. We lost 1-3, so maybe I wiped the whole day from my memory because of that.

I left Vale in May 1977 after the team finished in 19th place, three points above the relegation zone. At that point I had had almost 20 years playing professional football, but for me the game was well and truly up.

The main thing that final season at Vale gave me the opportunity to do was get everything sorted out for my longer term ambition of going into the pub game, something I'd settled on, as I knew I didn't have any particular skill of any description to fall back on, as so many footballers of that era can attest to.

I'd been talking with my friend Dean Bibbey, who was the landlord at my local, the Red Cow at Werrington. Dean had been a professional wrestler who used 'Dean Stockton' as his wrestling name and made something of a name for himself on TV in the early 60s. He had originally been a florist in Hanley, but graduated to owning his own pub, which is where I got to know him when we lived nearby.

He acted as an advisor to me and told me all about the ins and outs of being a landlord, and I became convinced over a period of time that it would be a good option for me. It is a bit of a classic thing for a 60s and 70s footballer to do, but there's a reason for that. I knew that pubs that are run well will always be full.

And, of course, if I could persuade some of my footballer friends to pop over occasionally then it would encourage punters to come in as well.

Dean introduced me to people at the brewery, getting me invites to various functions to get me into the trade. One of the directors of the brewery told me to give him a call when I was ready, which I did as I was winding down my football career at Vale Park.

Eventually, we were offered a nice country pub in Glossop, Derbyshire called The Hare and Hounds. We agreed this was the best move for us and sold up in the Potteries, moving across to take it on, buying a house lower down the hill at the bottom of the garden for my in-laws to spend their final days in.

I had actually wanted a pub in Stoke, not out in the sticks, but when we got out there we found that it was a lovely country pub and we were there for around 10 years.

While in Glossop, I played a bit for Leek Town as we didn't open the pub until about 5pm on a Saturday, as these were the days before all-day opening was allowed, and I'd be back home by 7pm after a game. It really helped to keep me fit, although I missed Stoke-on-Trent as I couldn't get back to watch games much.

After a decade or so in Glossop, we moved back to the Potteries to take up the Noah's Ark at Hartshill, which was an old pub... a proper drinking pub. It was being revamped and redecorated as it had been flat as a pancake for the brewery and I went in to manage it for them as it reopened. I got the pool and darts teams going really well and started up some catering. It was full every night; a huge success. We had lots of lock-ins initially, but the police station was nearby, so we had to calm that down.

Because I was so busy working, running the teams and ensuring the bar was working well, while I went out or was working the missus started going out and enjoying herself what I thought was far too much, and we ended up finishing. My wife eventually left me for one of the punters who came into the pub in the late 80s, but by then we were living separate lives anyway.

I had met a lovely lady called Pauline, a local lass from Newcastle-under-Lyme, just before I left the Noah's Ark and we started dating after my wife had left. We married in 1991, living in Clayton and then moved to our bungalow we're in now a few years ago. We have a great view over the valley towards the Bet365 Stadium, looking across the site of the old Victoria Ground. I've included a photograph of a typically sunlit Potteries day for you so you can see the view!

Pauline and I had both been married before and each had two fairly grown up children, although hers are slightly younger than mine. We have now been married over 30 years and together for longer.

AFTER I LEFT the Noah's Ark, I got a job working at Staffordshire University. The way that happened was, I met one of the university directors in a pub I used to drink in and he asked me to work in the estates department at the university campus in Stoke. It was a great job.

I was managing caretakers and estates workers, being in charge of planning what they would be doing and ensuring their work was done to a high standard; it might be painting, maintenance, moving things around the buildings, fitting lights or anything else that had broken. The older fellers in the team were good, but the younger ones were often more interested in chasing after some of the students, so needed keeping in line.

The university was expanding and the bigger it got, the more we had to do, so I ended up jumping in and doing things myself. It kept me active and fit. I ended up doing shift work from 6am to 2pm, or 2pm to 10pm. I was also often security on the gate to the car park as well.

I did that job for 10 years or so and enjoyed it so much I kept at it until I retired at 65.

At the same time, I kept active by helping out a friend of mine with some work on building sites he was running, which took me back to what I might have been doing all my life if I hadn't been lucky enough to be spotted in that park in Eccles by Reg Savage all those years ago.

Reg's vision and determination to get me a trial had led to me living in the Potteries area for over 60 years, bar that decade in Derbyshire. I hope that has now earned me the title of honorary Potter.

All my brothers have passed on now, so I have not had ties in Manchester for a very long time. I am very much a Stokie, married to a Potteries lass.

I still go to the matches at the Bet365, but I don't really go for the football these days. I go to talk to people. Mostly my ex-teammates, but also the friends I've made within the supporter base over the years. I will say hello to anyone who is walking past me and most of the time in the Potteries they will reply with a cheery 'Hello' back. I like that. I don't like the kind of head down mentality. That's just me.

I find that Stokies are easy to talk to and to get on with.

I love it here, I really do. I've always been happy in Stoke-on-Trent. Even so, it still surprises me that even now, walking in town, supporters still recognise me all these years later. In the butcher's, bakery or fishmonger's, there's always people stopping me, asking me what I think of the Stoke team or the latest match.

These blokes are often around my age or slightly younger and they commonly look older than me, as they're using a stick or limping, and here's me well over 80 still feeling fairly sprightly, so it does me good to feel relatively fit and healthy.

My missus complains all the time how it takes us twice as long to do the shopping as it should do as I'm constantly getting stopped.

Well, I can't just ignore the fans, now, can I? Mind you, I say to her she can be on the phone for half an hour without actually saying anything from what I can tell, but that's the difference between men and women of our era.

Occasionally, when I go down into Newcastle nowadays, I will bump into Terry Conroy and his missus and we'll have a chat. Terry is the prime mover in the Stoke City Old Boys Association, or SCOBA for short. He's still got the same energy he had back when we played together and he is constantly getting the lads together for walks, coffee of occasional big events.

It's odd, actually, because after living and working so closely together as players over a decent length of time, once you've finished football, you go your separate ways. For example, our League Cup-winning captain Peter Dobing became something of a recluse, while Alan Bloor seemed to disappear from view as well.

I mean, I've also got my own life to lead, but when we get together at the match, as SCOBA get us tickets, there'll be a few of my former teammates there and we'll have a good chat. SCOBA is great because if I have a problem I want to know something about, I can ring SCOBA and ask questions about, say, cancer. Or SCOBA might be able to get you in private instead of having to wait for an NHS appointment. Thankfully, I've never had to do that at all.

Every Tuesday a group of us will go to Trentham for a walk round the lake. TC will always be there, rattling away.

We pay a small fee monthly to SCOBA, just a fiver or something like that, and get invited to do supporters' evenings and so forth. We've also just sponsored an allotment on the other side of Fenton. SCOBA have had a cabin built and got sponsors to donate things like spades, a heater… you know, things like that. There are also volunteers who do little jobs, like a bit of weeding, cutting or planting a few veggies.

It's lovely.

I DO FIND myself forgetting things now and again. My wife will ask me to do three jobs and if I get distracted by the phone ringing or something like that, then one of them will go completely out of my mind.

I also forget names quite a lot, or other little things such as being in the pub talking with you and a few minutes later I might tell you the same story again, or forget your name if I've only just met you. They tend to be short term memory things.

I don't think, thankfully, that is related to any brain injury caused by heading a football relentlessly throughout my career, although I've never been examined at all.

In fact, Pauline is always complaining that I am forgetful about things she just told me 15 minutes ago. What she doesn't realise is that's because she was asking me for some money and I didn't want to listen!

I also think lockdown didn't help, as us former players didn't get to meet up and talk with each other about old times, like we would usually do. So many of those memories have started to fade, which is one reason why I'm so happy to be writing this book now, so I can get everything down while I can still remember.

I was always heading the ball, but I don't believe that has affected me. My forgetfulness is just down to old age because I'm now 82, rather than from me heading the ball time after time. Despite me playing at centre-half quite a lot, I'd often be trying to bring the ball down on my chest or lay it off first time, rather than heading it anyway, so maybe that has helped me, unwittingly.

Of course, I'm lucky, because I could have ended up like Jeff Astle, the Notts County, West Brom and England centre-forward whom I made my first Stoke appearance on trial against back in 1958. Jeff had a brain injury which was shown to have been caused by heading the ball. Now others such as Denis Law have revealed they have a similar condition.

My former teammate Maurice Setters was in later years diagnosed with Alzheimer's disease, and he died as a result in November 2020. In fact, in 2019 it was reported that football players were three and a half times more likely to die from dementia.

As I've been writing this book, there have been restrictions placed on the amount of heading in training, thanks to the campaigning of Jeff Astle's wife and children.

My main health issue in later life was that I found I had a nerve wrapped around my spinal chord at vertebrae three and four, plus a bit of a leak of fluid. I had to go in for an operation as my consultant felt it could get worse and might end up crippling me; forcing me to walk with a stick or zimmer frame at best or confining me to a wheelchair at worst.

I remember, as I sat in front of him, the consultant told me, 'If you were my father I would tell you that you must have this operation'.

So, I went and had the operation.

Amazingly, despite it being full and significant spinal surgery, I was only in the hospital for two days. It is astonishing what can be achieved with modern surgical techniques. I then had to undergo therapy to recover and that has seen me walk without pain for the first time in years.

Modern medicine is a wonderful thing.

Being fit and healthy in later life has allowed me to enjoy my family to the full. My son Jeremy went into the Royal Navy, then became my helper in the pub in Newcastle when he left, before going into the fire service. He got promotion and became the person in charge across our area. He has just retired from the fire service aged 55 and lives in Cheadle, having had two children, Cainnan and Archie.

My daughter Sally-Ann lives near us at the top of Hartshill. She has three adult children, Daniel, Amy and Matthew, and my wife Pauline's daughter Paula also lives close by with her son James and daughter Millie. They often look after our dog, while Pauline's son Robert lives and works in Brighton, where he owns and runs a small chain of restaurants. He has three children, Ruby, Annabelle and Dexter.

We are very happy with our lot and enjoy our grandchildren when we can see them, which wasn't as often as we'd like during the Covid-19 pandemic. So, we're hoping to make up for that now.

I STARTED PLAYING professional football when boots were like clogs, the pitches were dreadful and the ball was like a bullet when wet. Players' careers could be cut short by dreadful tackles, which are now banned by law changes.

But I loved every second of it.

Things just happened.

There was no grand plan.

I didn't plan a career out. It just sort of happened and I made the most of it. I made my debut with the club 12th in Division Two and left after we finished 12th in Division One, so over the course of 17 seasons in the first team I helped move the club up exactly one division, if you like!

Given that at one point in my time we were actually bottom of Division Two and in 1974/75 we went top of Division One for several weeks, I'll actually claim two whole divisions.

Players now make enough money to wonder what to do with for the rest of their lives, and don't need a job after finishing. I may have never had that luxury, but when people ask me 'would you rather have played now?' I can honestly turn round to them and say that the only things that are better now are the pitches and the money.

Apart from that, our era was far better in my opinion.

But, of course, I would say that. We had a lot of fun, forged incredible bonds which last to today and I played against some amazing players and lived to tell the tale.

But that was then and my career finished over 45 years ago, so I thought the idea of writing a book about my life was something of a joke at first when I was contacted about it and I was a bit shell-shocked. *Why would anyone be interested in me?*

I thought people might be surprised I was actually still alive! But I've really enjoyed the process of reliving all those magic moments and tales throughout my career. I hope you have too.

When you think about it, what a way to make a living that was. Not bad for a lad from the backstreets of Eccles.

Taking a break from working hard on the book in Spring 2022, and the view from my front door across the valley towards the Bet365 Stadium on a misty winter's morning.

Epilogue

BACK IN 2013, Stoke City Football Club celebrated its 150th anniversary.

Having played in the centenary celebration game against Real Madrid, Puskás, Di Stéfano and all their stars, 50 years earlier, I was delighted to be invited to spend the day, along with around 60 former players, including many from my time at Stoke.

We started the day taking a tour of the state-of-the-art training facilities down at Clayton Woods, which are incredible, with pitches like snooker tables, and changing rooms so, *so different* to that old dressing-room at the Victoria Ground with the coal heater and the big bath with the boards over the top that Don Ratcliffe used to trap us beneath.

We enjoyed a champagne breakfast before moving on to the then Britannia Stadium to parade in front of a sell-out crowd ahead of the final home game of the 2012/13 campaign against Spurs.

It was a memorable occasion and we had a wonderful welcome from the fans.

Then, in 2022, we celebrated the 50th anniversary of winning the League Cup, although that was obviously slightly bittersweet for me as I was invited along, which was lovely, but as I wasn't in the 12-man squad for the final, I was slightly on the periphery of the celebrations. However, I did play a part in that cup run, including two of the semi-final games, so I felt I deserved my invitation and it closed a circle for me 50 years on.

The celebrations comprised three nights of events; two meals, one at the Bet365 Stadium, then one the following evening at the Town Hall… and then, finally, an event at the stadium before the game against Blackpool on March 5, 2022. It was great to see all the lads, although we all missed Gordon Banks, who died in 2019 and George Eastham, who wasn't well enough to attend, but thankfully recovered afterwards.

I did wonder if I'd have the energy for all three events, but, much like in my career, I had such a buzz and loved every minute of them.

Sometimes, when I'm down at Trentham on a Tuesday to walk with all my old teammates, like Terry Conroy, Denis Smith, Jimmy Greenhoff, Terry Lees or John Ruggiero, I look at them and think, *how you lot were ever footballers is beyond me?!*

We rarely talk that much about the good old days, actually.

It's usually about our current ailments! They've got about three cartilages and one original ankle between them. Some of them are, quite frankly, completely knackered.

Denis in particular really struggles even walking. Nowadays, his knees and ankles barely work. I, on the other hand, am fighting fit, despite being in my early eighties.

My upbringing in Eccles and all that dog walking has stood me in good stead. It's meant I haven't put any weight on at all. I also eat sensibly, taking a lot of fruit, rarely eating bread… a completely different diet to what I grew up on.

Though, like the old days of my childhood, I still have my dear four-legged friend… and religiously walk the dog twice a day.

I also keep myself fit by occasionally jogging up and down outside my house.

On the hill overlooking the site of the Victoria Ground… the place where I lived out all my boyhood dreams.

◊